From Teams to Knots

Teams are commonly celebrated as efficient and humane ways of organizing work and learning. By means of a series of in-depth case studies of teams in the United States and Finland over a time span of more than 10 years, this book shows that teams are not a universal and ahistorical form of collaboration. Teams are best understood in their specific activity contexts and embedded in historical development of work. Today, static teams are increasingly replaced by forms of fluid knotworking around runaway objects that require and generate new forms of expansive learning and distributed agency. This book develops a set of conceptual tools for analysis and design of transformations in collaborative work and learning.

Yrjö Engeström earned his Ph.D. from the University of Helsinki in 1987. He is a professor of adult education and Director of the Center for Research on Activity, Development and Learning (CRADLE) at the University of Helsinki. He is Professor Emeritus of Communication at the University of California, San Diego, where he also served as Director of the Laboratory of Comparative Human Cognition from 1990 to 1995. Engeström applies and develops cultural-historical activity theory as a framework for the study of transformations and learning processes in work activities and organizations. He is widely known for his theory of expansive learning and for the methodology of developmental work research.

Learning in Doing: Social, Cognitive, and Computational Perspectives

SERIES EDITOR EMERITUS

John Seely Brown, *Xerox Palo Alto Research Center*

GENERAL EDITORS

Roy Pea, *Professor of Education and the Learning Sciences and Director, Stanford Center for Innovations in Learning, Stanford University*

Christian Heath, *The Management Centre, King's College, London*

Lucy A. Suchman, *Centre for Science Studies and Department of Sociology, Lancaster University, UK*

Continued after the Index

From Teams to Knots

Activity-Theoretical Studies of Collaboration and Learning at Work

YRJÖ ENGESTRÖM
University of Helsinki

CAMBRIDGE
UNIVERSITY PRESS

CAMBRIDGE UNIVERSITY PRESS
Cambridge, New York, Melbourne, Madrid, Cape Town, Singapore,
São Paulo, Delhi, Dubai, Tokyo

Cambridge University Press
32 Avenue of the Americas, New York, NY 10013-2473, USA

www.cambridge.org
Information on this title: www.cambridge.org/9780521148498

First published 2008
Reprinted 2009
First paperback edition 2010

A catalog record for this publication is available from the British Library.

Library of Congress Cataloging in Publication Data

Engeström, Yrjö, 1948–
From teams to knots : activity-theroetical studies of collaboration and learning at
work / Yrjö Engeström.
    p.   cm. – (Learning in doing : social, cognitive & computational perspectives)
Includes bibliographical references and index.
ISBN 978-0-521-86567-8 (hbk.)
1. Teams in the workplace.   2. Organizational learning.   I. Title.   II. Series.
HD66.E54   2007
658.4'022–dc22   2007028833

ISBN   978-0-521-86567-8 Hardback
ISBN   978-0-521-14849-8 Paperback

Contents

Series Foreword

This series for Cambridge University Press is widely known as an international forum for studies of situated learning and cognition.

Innovative contributions are being made by anthropology; by cognitive, developmental, and cultural psychology; by computer science; by education; and by social theory. These contributions are providing the basis for new ways of understanding the social, historical, and contextual nature of learning, thinking, and practice that emerge from human activity. The empirical settings of these research inquiries range from the classroom to the workplace, to the high-technology office, and to learning in the streets and in other communities of practice. The situated nature of learning and remembering through activity is a central fact. It may appear obvious that human minds develop in social situations and extend their sphere of activity and communicative competencies. But cognitive theories of knowledge representation and learning alone have not provided sufficient insight into these relationships.

This series was born of the conviction that new and exciting interdisciplinary syntheses are underway as scholars and practitioners from diverse fields seek to develop theory and empirical investigations adequate for characterizing the complex relations of social and mental life and for understanding successful learning wherever it occurs. The series invites contributions that advance our understanding of these seminal issues.

Roy Pea
Christian Heath
Lucy A. Suchman

Preface

In the social sciences, we study phenomena that change while we are studying them. Being ourselves part of the phenomena we study, we researchers also change as our research objects change.

I began studying work teams in the early 1990s. The endeavor lasted approximately 15 years. This book is structured to reflect that journey. Instead of trying to construct a universal definition of "a good team," I follow and analyze the historical transformation of work teams in their organizational and cultural contexts. At the same time, I document the transformation of my own understanding. Toward the end of the book, the notion of team fades into the background and a new notion, knotworking, steps into the center.

The research journey of this book takes the reader to visit teams in a variety of workplaces in Finland and the United States. It also crosses boundaries among disciplines, notably among education, communication, and organization studies.

Cultural-historical activity theory is the unifying thread of the book. This is a general framework that requires creation and employment of context-specific intermediate concepts and methods every time it is applied to a specific empirical case. These intermediate theoretical concepts and methods are in themselves important outcomes of the research.

The empirical chapters of this book have collaborative histories of their own. The first version of Chapter 2 was written with Dennis Mazzocco and presented as a paper at the conference of the International Communication Association in 1995. The first version of Chapter 3 was written with Katherine Brown, Carol Christopher, and Judith Gregory and published in 1991 in the *Quarterly Newsletter of the Laboratory of Comparative Human Cognition* (Vol. 13, pp. 88–97). The first version of Chapter 6 was published in 1999 as a chapter in the *Perspectives on Activity Theory*, edited by

Yrjö Engeström, Reijo Miettinen, and Raija-Leena Punamäki (Cambridge: Cambridge University Press). The first version of Chapter 7 was written with Heli Ahonen and published in 2001 as a chapter in *Information Systems and Activity Theory, Volume 2: Theory and Practice*, edited by Helen Hasan, Edward Gould, Peter Larkin, and Lejla Vrazalic (Wollongong: Wollongong University Press). The first version of Chapter 8 was published in 1999 in the journal *Lifelong Learning in Europe* (Vol. 4, pp. 101–110). And the first version of Chapter 9 was published in 2005 as a chapter in the *Collaborative Capital: Creating Intangible Value*, edited by Michael M. Beyerlein, Susan T. Beyerlein, and Frances A. Kennedy (Amsterdam: Elsevier).

In the early phase of my research on teams, the Academy of Finland funded the work. In 2004–2005, the Academy of Finland again funded my sabbatical, during which I wrote the manuscript of this book. Throughout the journey, the communities of the Center for Activity Theory and Developmental Work Research at the University of Helsinki and of the Laboratory of Comparative Human Cognition at the University of California, San Diego, have been the intellectual and social homesteads for my research.

The drawings in Chapter 6 were made by Georg Engeström. I thank him for his lifelong support.

The love and collaboration of Annalisa Sannino and our son, Jurij Enzo, made it possible for me to complete this journey.

1   Teams and the Transformation of Work

Teams as a Puzzle

In 1995, my research group began to follow and videotape three adjacent work teams in a large manufacturing plant in California specializing in high-precision machining. The company was well underway in its efforts to organize its entire workforce into self-directed teams. The transition was a carefully planned strategy that was to take place over a period of several years. It was supported by some of the most prominent consultants in the field. The company gave its teams a great deal of training, and it had produced an impressive guidebook for the teams. The guidebook gave the following definition of work teams:

> A work team is an ongoing team which uses the talents and skills of various employees in the accomplishment of work (such as product, sub-assemblies, or service) on a routine basis to achieve common goals and shared vision.

The guidebook defined 12 responsibilities of work teams, ranging from "solve quality problems to achieve and maintain customer satisfaction" to "manage their own budget" and "give and receive on-going performance feedback."

As we started observing the teams, the largest one was meeting on a weekly basis and making important production-related decisions. The meetings were lively, tensions between perspectives were displayed and resolved, and innovative ideas were produced (an analysis of these early meetings is presented in Chapter 6).

Within 6 months, this most dynamic team stopped having meetings. Its last meetings were marked by an atmosphere of resignation and disappointment. The best management efforts did not lead to success.

At around the same time, my research group also observed a manufacturing plant in Finland specializing in production of prefabricated cabins for large ships. Following the bankruptcy of its parent shipyard company, the plant had gone through a major reorganization a few years earlier. The CEO proudly declared that they had all but eliminated meetings and paperwork. The employees were working hands-on, with minimum administration. When we asked about work teams, the CEO stated that teams would not work in the plant; Finnish metal workers are individuals, not team players. The shop steward gave basically the same answer. When problems had to be solved, this was done on an ad hoc basis – teams would not be needed.

About a year later, the workers started a team on their own. In the final assembly department, work on an assembly line was typically divided into four or five phases. The workers responsible for each phase had different pay levels based on how demanding the particular phase was determined to be. Thus, if there was an overload and a slowdown in one phase, workers from the other phases would get annoyed but would not help. This created tensions that erupted in a crisis on one of the lines. The shop steward intervened, and in a condensed series of emergency sessions with the workers of that line he designed a proposal for a team arrangement. All the workers on the line would get the same pay level, and all would be responsible for eliminating breaks in the flow of assembly. The workers proposed that all would get the highest pay level, arguing that the arrangement would save money for the company. The CEO agreed on the condition that there would be a test period during which workers would have to show that the team would save enough money to cover the increased wages and bring a significant benefit to the company.

The team passed the test, and soon there were six teams functioning on the shop floor. Initially, management provided no help. There were no guidebooks and no consultants. Yet, the teams began to flourish.

Cases such as these are puzzling enough to create a host of questions. What is a good team and what is a bad team? What is the role of models and constraints originating from the outside and from above versus processes and patterns created from below and within the teams? What is successful collaboration, and what are its obstacles inside work teams? How can teams produce innovations and creative solutions to problems of production and work organization? What makes teams survive, thrive, and develop – or, alternatively, stagnate and die?

A New Wave of Research

In the past 20 years or so, teams have gained unprecedented popularity as forms of organizing and managing work. The success of Japanese manufacturing has often been associated with teams. There is an abundance of enthusiastic management literature describing the virtues of teams. However, teams are also problematic. Peter Senge (1990, p. 24) characterized the situation as follows:

> All too often, teams in business tend to spend their time fighting for turf, avoiding anything that will make them look bad personally, and pretending that everyone is behind the team's collective strategy – maintaining the *appearance* of a cohesive team. To keep up the image, they seek to squelch disagreement; people with serious reservations avoid stating them publicly, and joint decisions are watered-down compromises reflecting what everyone can live with, or else reflecting one person's view foisted on the group. If there is disagreement, it's usually expressed in a manner that lays blame, polarizes opinion, and fails to reveal the underlying differences in assumptions and experience in a way that the team as a whole could learn.

Michael Schrage (1995) provocatively renamed his book on "shared minds" *No More Teams!*

> The concept of teams obscures, rather than reveals, the real relationship challenges our organizations face. Teams are a fiction, a verbal convenience, rather than a useful description of how people in a firm cooperate and collaborate to create value. Even worse, teams make it too easy for organizations to lie, cheat, and kid themselves about the way they work. More often than not, a "team" is as much a political entity as a value-creating one. (Schrage, 1995, pp. xi–xii; see also Beyerlein, Freedman, McGee, & Moran, 2002)

While I appreciate the candor of Schrage's observation, I cannot avoid noticing an irony in his crusade. In abandoning the concept of teams as one managerial holy cow, he immediately reverts to an even older managerial holy cow, namely, the seemingly self-evident yet extremely problematic notion of value.[1] Rather than giving up problematic concepts for other equally problematic ones, I intend to dig into the historical, practical, and theoretical dynamics behind the notion of teams.

---

[1] As Womack and Roos (1996, p. 141) observed: "for any product..., value must flow across many companies and through many departments within each company. Although each entity along the route may or may not define value for the end customer, it certainly will define value for itself – to turn a profit, to advance the careers of those in each department, to utilize existing production assets fully, and so forth. When all those definitions of value are added up, they often conflict or cancel out one another." For a serious theoretical treatise on value, see Graeber (2001).

A closer look at the literature reveals that underneath the surface of general descriptions and recommendations concerning teams, there is indeed fairly little critical and original theorizing on the collaborative work and associated cognitive and communicative processes within and between teams in real organizational contexts. Traditional empirical literature consists mainly of decontextualized experimental studies on the psychological dynamics of small groups. These traditional studies were aimed at finding laws of group behavior that are independent of cultural and institutional specifics. While a number of serious studies conducted in more realistic settings have appeared (e.g., Ancona & Caldwell, 1992; Barker, 1999; Beyerlein, 2000; Beyerlein, Beyerlein, & Johnson, 2003; Beyerlein & Johnson, 1994; Beyerlein, Johnson, & Beyerlein, 1995, 2000a, 2000b, 2000c, 2001; Ciborra, 1993; Donellon, 1996; Gersick, 1988, 1989; Guzzo, Salas et al., 1995; Swezey & Salas, 1992; Yeatts & Hyten, 1998), the overwhelming bulk of newer team literature consists of uncritical management texts, ranging from how-to handbooks to success stories of the alleged blessings of implementing teams in organizations.

Only quite recently has a new, theoretically more ambitious wave of research on collaborative work begun to emerge. Cognitive scientists, anthropologists, and sociologists have started to develop and apply approaches to work and collaboration that take the organizational and cultural contexts as integral constitutive aspects of the phenomena to be explained. This book is a contribution to this new wave of research.

The new wave is inspired by a number of theoretical and methodological approaches to workplace studies. These include pragmatism and symbolic interactionism, distributed cognition, situated cognition, ethnomethodology, conversation and discourse analysis, actor-network theory, and the cultural-historical theory of activity (for reasonably representative collections, see Engeström & Middleton, 1996; Luff, Hindmarsh, & Heath, 2000; for comparative discussions, see Lave, 1993; Nardi, 1996; Star, 1996). Such different approaches find common ground in discussions of socially distributed and artifact-mediated action and cognition in "communities of practice." This emerging new wave is also partly inspired by the new information technologies that are dramatically altering the technical possibilities of intellectual collaboration in work (e.g., Galegher, Kraut, & Egido, 1990; Greenbaum & Kyng, 1991; Heath & Luff, 2000; Nardi, 1996).

The research presented in this book is based on cultural-historical activity theory (sometimes called CHAT for short), initiated by Vygotsky (1978), Leont'ev (1978, 1981), and Luria (1978; see also Engeström, Miettinen, & Punamäki, 1999; Wertsch, 1981). During the past 20 years, a multidisciplinary group of Finnish researchers, now organized around the Center for Activity Theory and Developmental Work Research at the University of Helsinki, developed an activity-theoretical approach to studies of work and organizations called *developmental work research* (see Engeström, 1991b, 1993, 1996a, 2005a; Engeström, Lompscher, & Rückriem, 2005). Since the late 1980s, this approach has also been used and developed in the Laboratory of Comparative Human Cognition at the University of California, San Diego, and in a number of other research centers around the world.

In this book, I repeatedly use three theoretical constructs central to activity theory and developmental work research: *activity system, contradiction,* and *zone of proximal development.* Here I briefly characterize these key concepts. Their meaning and implications will be further elaborated upon in the following chapters as they are used in concrete analyses (see also Engeström, 1987, for theoretical groundwork).

An activity system is a collective formation that has a complex mediational structure. It is the foundational unit of analysis that I employ throughout this book. I will give a more precise definition of this concept in Chapter 2. Contradictions within and between activity systems are a key to understanding the sources of trouble as well as the innovative and developmental potentials and transformations of activity. The concept of contradiction will also be discussed in more detail in Chapter 2. The zone of proximal development is a concept originally developed by Vygotsky (1978, p. 86), who proposed that we can understand the potential for human development dynamically if we examine what a person can do with the help of another, more experienced person, rather than examining the person alone, without support and interaction. I use this concept in an expanded sense to characterize the developmental potential of collective activity systems interacting with other activity systems, both supportive and adversarial (Engeström, 1987, p. 174). The concept of a zone of proximal development will be used and made more concrete in Chapters 2, 3, 4, and 5.

Teams without Context and History

Teams are typically defined in a formal and self-sufficient way, without reference to the way the overall production and work are organized:

> A team is a small number of people with complementary skills who are committed to a common purpose, performance goals, and approach for which they hold themselves mutually accountable. (Katzenbach & Smith, 1993, p. 45)

Even overviews of broad transformations in work systems fall into this trap:

> By self-directed teams we mean groups of workers who have substantial discretion over the work process, make changes in production methods as needed, and take on many of the tasks traditionally carried out by front-line supervisors, such as allocating and coordinating work between different employees and scheduling. (Appelbaum & Batt, 1994, p. 253)

The first definition implies that the relevant parameters along which teams should be examined are such universal features as size, skill complementarity, purposefulness, mutual accountability, and commitment. The second definition implies the equally universal parameters of discretion and autonomy. These definitions ignore qualitative differences between historical types of teams. In what follows, I will try to change this ahistorical way of dealing with teams (for previous attempts in that direction, see Beyerlein, 2000; Tubbs, 1994).

The Sociotechnical Concept

The first major wave of writings about teams came from the sociotechnical systems approach initiated by the Tavistock Institute of Human Relations in England. Trist, Emery, and other Tavistock researchers were influenced by at least three important theoretical sources: Bion's (1961) group psychotherapy, Lewin's (1947, 1951) field theory, and von Bertalanffy's (1950) general theory of open systems (for historical overviews and a comprehensive collection of publications, see Trist & Murray, 1993).

The semiautonomous, self-managing, or self-regulating work group was the central idea of the sociotechnical approach: "it seemed that the small self-regulating group held the clue to a very great deal that might be improved in work organizations" (Trist, 1993, p. 43). The first major studies were undertaken in coal mining in England (Trist & Bamforth, 1951/1993) and in textiles weaving in India (Rice, 1958). The former study concluded by recommending "restoring responsible autonomy to primary groups throughout the system and ensuring that each of these groups has a satisfying sub-whole as its work task and some scope for flexibility in work pace" (Trist & Bamforth, 1951/1993, p. 83).

In 1953–1954, Rice successfully implemented an experimental work organization based on semiautonomous work groups, each responsible for production and routine maintenance on a group of looms. In 1970, Miller undertook a unique follow-up study in the textile company. He showed that the work organization and levels of performance at one of the original sites had remained virtually unchanged over the years:

The type of cloth woven was still the same and, as we have seen, norms of performance seemed to have persisted for 14 years. It was as though the shed had been held within a kind of stasis – a monument to the original experiment. (Miller, 1975/1993, p. 149)

However, in a newer automatic loom shed, group work had largely disappeared. This shed "was weaving the finest and most expensive sorts with a high fashion component (thus implying the need for cyclical adjustment), and these were also cloths most influenced by the company's search for new and profitable markets" (p. 152).

These findings suggest that a sociotechnical system of semiautonomous work groups may function well and survive in a stable, almost static environment but not necessarily in a more turbulent and innovative environment. As Miller (1975/1993, pp. 153–154) approvingly points out, Rice wanted to achieve "a quasi-stationary equilibrium" aimed at "minimizing the chances of disaster." There seems to be a built-in conservatism in the very design of this system. What exactly is the nature and source of this conservatism?

To examine the issue further, I will consider the experiences gained in Sweden at the Kalmar and Uddevalla plants of the auto maker Volvo. Already in 1976, Emery had discussed the design of Volvo's plant in Kalmar as a pathbreaker in creating a viable alternative to the assembly line:

The most striking outcome was the discovery that, in an appropriately skilled and sized work group, all the key parameters of mass flow production could come together and be controlled vis-à-vis each other at that level. Picturesquely, this was labeled "a lot of little factories within a factory." (Emery, 1976/1993, p. 209)

Sociotechnical versus Lean Production Teams

Volvo's plants in Kalmar and Uddevalla became, in a sense, the culmination of four decades of sociotechnical experiments. They were idolized for their human-centeredness and criticized for their inefficiency. Volvo's 1992 decision to close the two plants was echoed by an international debate on the merits and limitations of these experiments. The debate goes to the heart of the different conceptions of teams.

In Uddevalla, the more advanced and radical of the two plants, the assembly line with its 1-min repetitive work cycles was eliminated. Instead, 48 parallel stationary teams consisting of eight members each assembled whole cars with a work cycle of around 2 hours (see Sandberg, 1995). Instead of the traditional model, where about 700 workers put together a car, this was done by 8 workers in Uddevalla. This meant that the workers had to master a very broad range of tasks and skills. As Ellegård (1995, p. 54) proudly declared, one Uddevalla worker's "basic competence equals the competence of at least 60 workers taken together in a plant with an assembly line."

In their influential comparative analysis of auto manufacturing, Womack, Jones, and Roos (1990) coined the term *lean production*. The authors called Volvo's experiments *neocraftsmanship*, whose aim is to go "back toward an era of handcrafting as an end in itself" (p. 102):

> Simply bolting and screwing together a large number of parts in a long cycle rather than a small number in a short cycle is a very limited vision of job enrichment. The real satisfaction presumably comes in reworking and adjusting every little part so that it fits properly. In the properly organized lean-production system, this activity is totally unnecessary. (p. 102)

In 1993, Adler and Cole critically compared Volvo's Uddevalla plant and the Toyota–General Motors joint venture NUMMI plant in California. NUMMI also had teams, but the whole operation was based on the model of lean production. According to the authors, Uddevalla was not within striking difference of NUMMI's productivity and quality:

> Uddevalla workers ... had detailed information on their work cycle performance, but as this cycle was some two hours long, they had no way to track their task performance at a more detailed level. This problem was exacerbated by the craft model of work organization that encouraged Uddevalla workers to believe that they should have considerable latitude in how they performed each cycle.... Moreover, as the variety of models produced in a given plant increases, it becomes increasingly difficult for workers to recall the right procedure for each job, and shorter cycle times with well-defined methods help assure quality. (Adler & Cole, 1993, p. 89)

Adler and Cole continue:

> Although Uddevalla had a bonus system that encouraged work teams to improve performance continually, the teams had neither the focus on the kinds of microscopic *kaizen* opportunities that drive NUMMI performance (because of Uddevalla's long work cycle) nor the tools to capture these opportunities (because they lacked standardized work processes). To the contrary, in fall 1991, we were informed that there were [sic] no detailed documentation available to workers describing how to perform each work task and specifying how long it should take ... without a well-documented, standardized process, it is hard to imagine how these people could have spotted improvement opportunities or shared them across the teams. You

cannot sustain continual improvement in the production of products as standardized as automobiles without clear and detailed methods and standards. (p. 89)

We can summarize the key criticisms of lean production proponents against the sociotechnical or *neocraft* concept in three points:

1. Sociotechnical teams such as those in Uddevalla were based on autonomy in performing long work cycles. This autonomy tends to lead to *isolation*: "the teams were left to their own devices" (Adler & Cole, 1993, p. 90).

2. The long cycles and the associated philosophy of holistic learning led to a *neglect of standardization* of detailed procedures. This neglect prevented learning and continuous improvement based on deeper knowledge of the process: "you cannot identify the sources of problems in a process you have not standardized." This is also connected to isolation: "you cannot diffuse what you have not standardized" (Adler & Cole, 1993, p. 92).

3. Finally, the long cycles and lack of standardization led to an emphasis on *individual learning at the cost of organizational learning*: "little thought was given to how work groups might learn from one another to facilitate continuous improvement" (Adler & Cole, 1993, p. 92; see also Adler, 1993; Wilms, Hardcastle, & Zell, 1994).

Berggren (1994) responded to Adler and Cole by pointing out that during the last year of the plant's operation, the management of Uddevalla took important steps to overcome these problems. He did not, however, deny that the fundamental concept of whole-car assembly behind Uddevalla was modeled on the ideal of craft work and thus was dramatically different from that of lean production (see also Adler & Cole, 1994).

If the three points previously listed are limitations of the sociotechnical team concept, what is the alternative offered by the model of lean production? The first key is elimination of buffers and breaks in the production. In a just-in-time production and delivery system, there is no room to store inventories, and the need for rework at the end of production is eliminated by installing continuous quality control in every step of the line. Womack et al. (1990, p. 99) define the idea further as follows:

> The truly lean plant has two key organizational features: *It transfers the maximum number of tasks and responsibilities to those workers actually adding value to the car on the line, and it has in place a system for detecting defects that quickly traces every problem once discovered to its ultimate cause.*

This, in turn means teamwork among line workers and a simple but comprehensive information display system that makes it possible for everyone in the plant to respond quickly to problems and to understand the plant's overall situation.

A recent Scandinavian attempt in the sociotechnical tradition goes under the rubric of *democratic dialogue* (Gustavsen, 1992; see also van Eijnatten, 1993, pp. 68–75). Robert Cole (1993) compared the Japanese quality improvement movement and the Swedish notion of democratic dialogue. This comparison is helpful in pointing out some of the crucial differences between teams in lean production and teams in a sociotechnical scheme.

> We have seen that to create communicative competence the [democratic dialogue] approach envisions a gradual joint shaping of vision and development among all participants through a democratic dialogue.... Unlike the production of visible quality improvement in Japan, however, it is more difficult for management to directly see such efforts as leading to bottom-line results in quality and productivity improvement. There is also no guidance per se provided by democratic dialogue on the substance of the proposed development. The use of quality as a common language cutting across organizational levels and functions does not directly challenge managerial control as does democratic dialogue. But it does have a very specific and concrete content in terms of tools, approaches, and objectives.
>   ...the improvement programs of the Japanese have a concrete substance: they rest on the tools, methods, and objectives of the quality movement involving all employees and using quality as common language. There is in short an engine here that is totally lacking in the use of democratic dialogue as a generative force for change. (Cole, 1993, p. 124)

Cole depicted grave consequences for teams:

> The work team is typically portrayed as "context-less." That is, it is not embedded in the work flow and not tied to a customer. Given the lack of linkage to the work process, management support for participation fades because participation is seen as a peripheral activity. (p. 126)

Autonomy versus Quality as Object

At the general ethical and political levels, I am sympathetic to the democratic ideals of our Scandinavian colleagues working within the sociotechnical tradition. Yet, my own approach requires that we put the arguments of the two schools just discussed in a critical historical perspective.

Expressed in the conceptual framework of activity theory, sociotechnical teams and lean production teams have very different *objects* and object-related *motives*. Therefore, their entire activity systems are qualitatively different. For sociotechnical teams, the object and motive are centered inward, around the team's own *autonomy* and its derivative, participation. For lean production teams, the object and motive are directed outward, around *quality*.

Autonomy, as an object and a motive, stems from the historical context of small, independent craft workshops making products from the beginning to the end. The idealization of this mode of production overlooks the fact that at least the European and North American craft workshop was typically hierarchically organized around one all-powerful master, that the rules of the craft deliberately restricted and prolonged learning on the part of the apprentices so that they wouldn't become competitors to the master, and that innovation in work procedures and products was stifled by secrecy and strict adherence to the tradition (see Rorabaugh, 1986). Given these conditions, the autonomy of a craft shop becomes a very specific historical setup, not an ideal condition to be sought after universally. And like any historical mode of activity, it is not something that can be reinstated or reinvigorated regardless of the existing societal conditions.

In sociotechnical teams, it is difficult to combine the archaic object and motive of autonomy with the turbulent context of market-driven business. This tension contrasts with what Womack et al. (1990, p. 102) call the "creative tension" in lean production:

> This creative tension involved in solving complex problems is precisely what has separated manual factory work from professional "think" work in the age of mass production.

Beyond Lean Production: Variety, Innovation, and Knowledge

So, is lean production the answer? This would mean that quality is historically an adequate and sufficient object and motive in the present and foreseeable future contexts of work. I do not think that this is the case. Quality in itself is a relatively conservative notion. It implies that there is a known product and a known production process; what is needed is improvements and eradication of faults, not radically new products and processes. Innovation and production of new knowledge are not directly implied.

In some ways, the auto industry is a very restrictive example to be used as the sole paradigmatic case illuminating the development of work. Almost by definition, this industry is an ecologically wasteful mass producer of consumer goods based on relatively traditional technology. The auto industry has an extremely poor track record in adopting such radical innovations as electric and hybrid cars. I suspect that this historical legacy may have prevented some proponents of lean production from seeing more advanced aspects in the current development of work organizations.

To extend the horizon beyond lean production, the historical field of the transformation of work organization needs to be theorized. A first step in this endeavor is to specify key dimensions in the development of mass production. In this, Williamson's (1975) pioneering work on transaction cost theory is helpful. Williamson distinguished between two basic forms of organization within capitalist firms: hierarchy and market. In a nutshell, the two are alternative solutions to the question: Make or buy?

The vertically integrated, centralized functional organization is the classic form of hierarchy. Ouchi (1984) paints a picture of this ideal type:

> No subportion of the organization can exist on its own. Research and development by itself would have no product to sell; manufacturing alone would have no designs to work from; sales alone would be empty. More importantly, none of the subunits...can measure its performance in a clear or simple manner. No subunit has its own "bottom line"; it cannot be treated as a profit center. Because each subunit is wholly dependent on the others, the organization tends to be highly centralized. (p. 19)

Market organization implies a move from vertical integration to semiautonomous subunits and contracting inside the corporation. Again, I use Ouchi's description:

> Here, each unit stands alone; it can be evaluated as a profit center or an investment center; its management can be directed simply to maximize profits and can then be left on its own. (p. 21)

For my present purposes, it is not necessary to go into the details of and debates evoked by Williamson's theory (see Francis, Turk, & Willman, 1983). Organizations are seldom pure examples of the ideal types. Yet, it seems more than likely that the introduction of teams is a very different matter in predominantly hierarchical and predominantly market-based organizations.

Hierarchy and market as the two opposite ways of organizing mass production seem to be indifferent to the nature of the products demanded by customers and put out by the firm. The historical transformation of products and production processes seems to happen relatively independently of these two organizational forms of mass production. A key to this transformation is the concept of *mass customization*.

Mass customization, as discussed and defined by Pine (1993), is a theoretically more ambitious attempt to conceptualize many of the same phenomena that Womack et al. (1990) call lean production. Moving beyond the general notion of quality as the object, Pine (1993, p. 47) characterizes mass customization as "developing, producing, marketing, and delivering affordable goods and services with enough variety and customization that nearly everyone finds exactly what they want."

The driving force behind mass customization is the market. Demand for individual products has become unstable. What used to be large demand for standard mass-market products has fragmented into demand for different "flavors" of similar products. The heterogeneous niches are becoming the market, shifting power to buyers who demand higher-quality goods that more closely match their individual desires.

Since profits cannot be maintained the old way, the production system must be changed. It must produce a number of different high-quality products via short production runs, short changeover times, and low work-in-process. This requires general-purpose machinery and highly skilled workers (Pine, 1993).

> Mass Customization . . . contains elements of both Craft and Mass Production. As with Craft Production, Mass Customization commonly has a high degree of flexibility in its processes; it uses general-purpose tools and machines as well as the skills of its workers; it builds to order rather than to plan; and it results in high levels of variety and customization in its products and services. Moreover, like Mass Production, Mass Customization generally produces in high volume, has low unit costs, and often (but not always) relies on high degrees of automation. (Pine, 1993, pp. 51–52)

This depiction of mass customization as a combination of craft and mass production defines it as a transitional form. The dominant object and motive are centered on the notion of *variation*. Gilmore and Pine (1997) identify four basic approaches to mass customization: collaborative, adaptive, cosmetic, and transparent. None of them implies the generation of radically new products and processes (see also Kotha, 1995; Lampel & Mintzberg, 1996).

Symptomatically, much of the recent literature on new organizational forms goes beyond variation and focuses on the production of *innovations* and *knowledge* as strategic factors – objects and motives in our terminology.

In this literature, teams are still important, but they are even more embedded in the broader texture of the organization's activity than in the lean production literature. A case in point is Nonaka and Takeuchi's (1995) theory of knowledge-creation in companies. The authors argue that knowledge-creation begins with "building a team whose members share their experiences and mental models" (p. 225). Similarly, in her book on organizations as producers of innovations, Leonard-Barton (1995, p. 75) states that product development teams "comprising [sic] of individuals who operate from a base of deeply specialized knowledge need mechanisms to translate across the different 'languages' and encourage the depersonalization of conflicting perspectives."

Kenney and Florida (1993) developed the concept of *innovation-mediated production*. Their model rests on five principles:

> (1) a transition from physical skill and manual labor to intellectual capabilities or mental labor, (2) the increasing importance of social or collective intelligence as opposed to individual knowledge and skill, (3) an acceleration of the pace of technological innovation, (4) the increasing importance of continuous process improvement on the factory floor and constant revolutions in production, and (5) the blurring of the lines between the R&D lab and the factory. (Kenney & Florida, 1993, p. 14)

This model connects continuous incremental improvement with radical new product innovations and "constant revolutions in the production process itself" (p. 16):

> The underlying organizational feature is the self-managing work team that enhances the *functional integration* of tasks. The new shop floor thus integrates formerly distinct types of work – for example, R&D and factory production, thus making the production process ever more social. (p. 16)

Looking more closely at the organization of knowledge- and innovation-driven production, two dimensions are crucial for my analysis. These are (1) the extent to which product development and production are integrated and (2) the extent to which customers are involved in production and product development. I expect that the nature of teamwork in innovation-driven production – particularly the degree of cross-functionality and the degree of outward-orientedness of teams – will be radically influenced by the location of the organization along these two dimensions.

Much of the literature on new organizational forms and work teams focuses on industrial work. The integration of product development and production may indeed be most vividly observable in advanced manufacturing. But the other dimension of knowledge- and innovation-driven production, the involvement of customers in production and product development, is probably more salient in other areas. By their very definition, human services such as health care and education are leaders in customers' direct involvement in production. In product development and innovation, customer or user involvement seems most advanced in areas that cut across services and manufacturing, such as software development and the production of complex customized systems of equipment (see von Hippel, 1988). All this calls attention to teams in environments ranging from manufacturing to human services.

Literature on the organization of work in the digital economy is still mainly programmatic and visionary (e.g., Leadbeater, 2000; Lipnack & Stamps, 1997; Malone, 2004; Tapscott, 1996; Wallace, 2004). Interestingly enough, at least in name, teams seem to keep their position as one of the key features of the envisioned cellular, networked, knowledge-creating company. But now the emphasis is on *project teams, internetworked teams, virtual teams,* and *global teams* that use information and communication technologies that enable integrated work group computing networks linking design and problem-solving teams across the globe. Complex product development efforts are used as prime examples of such teams. According to Tapscott (1996), the Boeing 777 airplane was designed by teams including customers and suppliers:

> About 230 cross-functional teams, with up to forty members, were organized around parts of the aircraft rather than according to function, as they had been in the past. The teams brought together engineering, procurement, manufacturing, operations, customer services, and marketing. (p. 146)

This implies that teams are becoming increasingly distributed in space. Such global distribution entails new challenges related to communication delays and breakdowns. Teasley, Covi, Krishnan, and Olson (2000, p. 339) observe that "to overcome some of these, companies are beginning to experiment with putting an entire project team in one room for the duration of the project" – a strategy the authors call *radical collocation*. In other words, both distribution and compression are enhanced: There is no single linear form in which team arrangements are shaped in the new economy. It actually seems that the term *team* is being used as a placeholder for an increasing variety of forms of collaborative work. A new, more adequate terminology is yet to be developed.

The Field of Transformation

I will now sum up my argument thus far. As a basis for my analysis of teams, I suggest a preliminary general map of the field of transformation in the organization of work (Figure 1.1). On the one hand, the map depicts a progression from craft production to mass production to mass customization

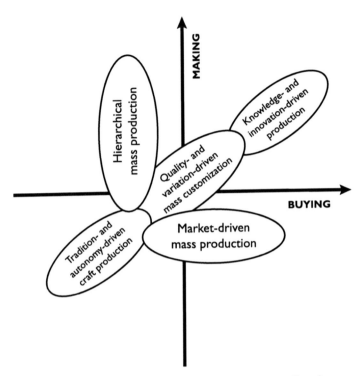

Figure 1.1. Field of transformation in the organization of work.

to knowledge- and innovation-driven production. On the other hand, the map integrates the two basic forms of the organization of mass production put forward by Williamson, depicted here as alternative directions called simply *MAKING* and *BUYING*.

These alternative directions remain relevant even in conditions of mass customization and innovation-driven production. While it seems obvious that truly knowledge- and innovation-driven organizations, such as the biotechnology firms analyzed by Powell, Koput, and Smith-Doerr (1996), typically operate through interorganizational learning networks, the alternative directions of hierarchy and market, or making and buying, will still loom large when organizational decisions are made.

The Historical Place of Teams

In light of the preceding analysis, teams appear as transitional forms. They are like vehicles moving in the gray gateway squeezed between the

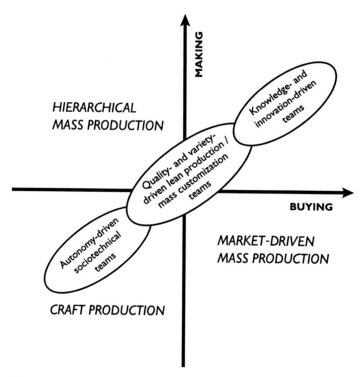

Figure 1.2. The historical place of teams as forms of organizing work.

traditionally dominant hierarchical and market-based types of work organization in mass production. The gateway leads to an uncertain field of historically new organizational patterns.

Sociotechnical, autonomy-driven teams started it. Quality- and variety-driven lean production and mass customization teams still occupy much of the center stage today. Innovation- and knowledge-driven teams are rapidly taking shape and gaining in importance. This general historical hypothesis is schematically depicted in Figure 1.2. The figure represents the historical movement from craft to three other ideal-typical organizational modes along the lines of increasing vertical integration and centralization on the one hand and increasing decentralization and contracting on the other hand.

The lower left field of Figure 1.2 represents the historically oldest currently observable layer of work organization: craft, driven by tradition and autonomy, typically guarded by occupational and professional guilds and secrecy. The upper right field represents attempts to overcome the limitations of mass production by combining standardization and customization, collaboration and competition, collectivity and flexibility. This field is "neither market nor hierarchy," as Powell (1990) put it.

Within organization studies, Adler and Hecksher's (2006) recent work describes one historically grounded way to conceptualize this emerging field. Building on the classic sociological distinction between the traditional hierarchical gemeinschaft community and the modern market-oriented gesellschaft community, the authors argue that a third historical form is currently emerging, particularly in knowledge-intensive firms. This third historical type of community is called the *collaborative community* or *collaborative interdependence*.

> Collaborative community in modern industry needs to coordinate interactions that span a wide range of competencies and knowledge bases, and that shift constantly to accommodate the evolving nature of knowledge projects. The challenges it faces cannot be met through 'teamwork' in the usual sense of small, homogeneous, and informal groups. (Adler & Heckscher, 2006, p. 44)

Adler and Heckscher list four challenges that this emerging third type of community must meet (p. 44):

1. The boundaries of solidary groups must be far less fixed than those in traditional communities, far more capable of being bridged and merged.
2. It must accommodate a very high level of technical division of labor and diversity of knowledge and skills.
3. It must allow for authority based not on status but on knowledge and expertise – that is, *value-rationality* – meaning that people must in many cases be accountable to peers or those below them in the hierarchy rather than to their formal superiors.
4. It must bring values into the realm of public discussion so that they can become common orienting and motivating elements for all the members of the community.

Interestingly enough, the authors suggest that *process management* in corporations is a key ingredient and enabler of collaborative community. Process management is seen as the avenue to transparent coordination of large, diverse communities and high levels of complexity. Process management has two aspects, namely, developing a shared purpose across organizational units and divisions, and coordinating work among various skills and competencies along the value chain.

> These new formalisms are sometimes experienced as oppressive, and indeed the language of process management can become a cover for coercive bureaucratic control; but when it is successful, people experience the rules of process management as enabling rather than constraining, as helping to structure new relations rather than limiting them. (Adler & Heckscher, 2006, p. 44)

Process management has progressive potential in many cases. But it is not the core coordinating mechanism of historically new forms of community at work. Process management is foundationally a linear view of work and production. In its linearity, it follows, albeit in expanded and more sophisticated forms, the same basic logic that was the core of standardized industrial mass production. Mastering and updating this logic may be a necessary precondition for successful introduction of more interactive and flexible forms of production, such as *process enhancement, mass customization*, and *co-configuration* (to use the terms of Victor & Boynton, 1998). But particularly in conditions of innovation- and knowledge-driven production that involves customers as coproducers and co-innovators, the linear logic of process management is simply not enough.

At present, highly interesting developments are associated with the emergence of what Victor and Boynton (1998, p. 195) call *co-configuration work*. A critical prerequisite of co-configuration is the creation of customer-intelligent products and services that adapt to the changing needs of the user and evolve in use over long periods of time. We may provisionally define co-configuration as an emerging, historically new type of work that relies on adaptive "customer-intelligent" product–service combinations; continuous relationships of mutual exchange between customers, producers, and the product–service combinations; ongoing configuration and customization of the product–service combinations over lengthy periods of time; and active customer involvement and input into the configuration. These characteristics have commonalities with von Hippel's (2005) notion of *user innovations*, as well as with Prahalad and Ramaswamy's (2004) notion of *co-creation of value*. In their different ways, both emphasize the growing role of users in the creation of innovations and in the shaping of products and services.

My research groups have been particularly interested in what we call *negotiated knotworking* as an emerging way of organizing work in settings that strive toward co-configuration (Engeström, 2005b, 2007; Engeström, Engeström, & Vähäaho, 1999). In knotworking, collaboration between the partners is of vital importance, yet it takes shape without rigid, prederminded rules or a fixed central authority.

The notions of co-configuration and knotworking are but initial attempts to sketch the contours of knowledge- and innovation-driven production. Organizations break through into this poorly charted gray zone where they face constant disturbances, ruptures, and unanticipated learning imperatives. There is an ongoing struggle between competing organizational options. If innovation and knowledge are the emerging new objects and motives for work, what does this imply for teams? What are the emerging characteristics of innovation- and knowledge-driven teams? Can they be called teams anymore? How do they differ from autonomy-driven and quality-driven teams? These are questions that motivate the research reported in this book.

Table 1.1. *Settings, questions, and concepts of case studies*

Chapter	Setting	Question	Concepts
2	Television broadcast team	Why does a team stagnate?	Disturbance Contradiction Masking
3	Court trial team	How do innovation possibilities emerge in a team?	Expansive transition Coordination, cooperation, and communication
4	Primary care teams	How does a new team construct its mode of operation?	Two layers of history in teams Fixation and flow
5	Elementary school teacher teams	How can teams cross built-in boundaries of work practice?	Motivational sphere Boundary crossing
6	Industrial machining team	How do teams create knowledge?	Expansive cycle Learning actions What, how, why, and where-to artifacts Perspectives
7	Telecom call center team	What could social capital mean in teams?	Infrastructures Cycles of social capital formation

The Structure of the Book

This book is built on six case studies of teams operating in diverse organizational settings located in the United States and in Finland. Each case study focuses on a set of specific theoretical questions and employs a set of specific conceptual tools. The settings, questions, and key concepts are summarized in Table 1.1.

The data analyzed in the different chapters stem from several successive field projects, starting in the early 1990s and ending in 2003. Thus, the chapters tell a story of the changing shapes and fates of teams over a period of more than 10 years. They also reflect my personal lengthy journey through the changing world of teams and collaboration at work.

In Chapter 8, I draw an intermediate balance of my analysis of teams and learning at work by means of three central theses. At that point, it will be clear that the case studies point to forms of work organization and workplace learning that go beyond teams.

Finally, Chapter 9 opens up the study of fluid and distributed collaborative organizational patterns, focusing on the crucial issue of agency. If the center does not hold anymore, if work is in constant flux, where is the locus of intentionality and how is agency constructed? Chapter 9 delineates theoretical and methodological principles for analyzing such knotworking forms of organizing and learning. A fictional case and an empirical case from medical work are used to ground the principles in workplace realities. I propose the notion of *mycorrhizae*, the invisible undergrowth of fungi, to capture some crucial aspects of the new forms of social production that are gaining momentum with the help of the Internet. The chapter ends with a condensed agenda for future research in collaborative work and learning.

2 Disturbance Management and Masking in a Television Production Team

Teams are not always dynamic and innovative. To the contrary, they are often breeding grounds of defensive routines and protective encapsulation. These phenomena have not often been studied in detail in real organizational settings. In this chapter, I will ask why a seemingly very successful team did not learn, why it stagnated and resisted change and innovation.

The pervasive influence of information technologies on work is turning communication into a key component of an increasing number of work processes that have traditionally been considered as predominantly instrumental constellations of jobs or *man-machine systems*. Zuboff (1988) characterized this change as proliferation of *informated* work. The transition is reflected in the birth and rapid growth of new fields of research, such as computer-supported cooperative work (CSCW) (e.g., Bowers & Benford, 1991; Greenberg, 1991; Schmidt & Bannon, 1992) and distributed cognition (e.g., Galegher et al., 1990; Hutchins, 1995; Rasmussen, Brehmer, & Leplat, 1991; Resnick, Levine, & Teasley, 1991; Salomon, 1993). Prominent organizational theorists have begun to incorporate these issues and ideas in their work (e.g., Weick, 1993; Weick & Roberts, 1993).

These changes make the Habermasian separation of communicative and instrumental action (Habermas, 1984) all but useless for concrete analysis. Communication is increasingly intertwined with core productive processes. Thus, it is increasingly difficult to understand or change organizational communication without understanding and changing those core productive processes.

In this chapter, I will analyze one process of production, namely, the production of a live TV sports broadcast. Analyzing in detail the communicative texture of such a relatively well-bounded work process will yield new insights into the broader communicative culture of the organization under scrutiny. This type of investigation can also lead to new conceptual tools and theoretical constructs, hopefully useful in the ongoing redefinition of the discipline of organizational communication.

To analyze a reasonably complete process of work, one typically needs to cover a lengthy chain of actions, a trajectory from the initial "raw material" to the finished product (Strauss, Fagerhaugh, Suczek, & Wiener, 1985). This is attempted by various methods of business process reengineering (Hammer & Champy, 1993). The weakness of such attempts is that they typically miss much of the "invisible work" (Nardi & Engeström, 1999; Star, 1991) of small everyday contingencies, troubles, innovations, and sideways interactions, often giving an idealistically streamlined picture of what is going on (Engeström, 1999b).

To capture in detail the rich texture of communicative events and interactions, on the other hand, one typically needs to focus on small chunks of the process and to look at them as if through a magnifying glass. This approach is taken by various recent studies of conversation, discourse, and collaborative cognition in work (Button, 1993; Chaiklin & Lave, 1993; Drew & Heritage, 1992; Engeström & Middleton, 1996; Luff et al., 2000). A common weakness of these attempts is that they tend to focus on relatively arbitrary segments of work and communication, with no interest or ability to connect the analysis of local interactions to broader institutional, cultural, and historical forces.

Taylor (1995) calls for new types of empirical and theoretical studies in organizational communication based on an "autonomous worldview" of organizations:

> To accomplish this, field research in naturalistic circumstances, idiographic in its emphasis, will be even more salient than it now is, but, in addition, we will need to develop new instruments for the analysis of discourse if we are to show, rather than take for granted, how organization is constructed through conversation, how boundaries of conversation can be recognized, and how individually self-organized communities of discourse are coupled one to the other. This will lead to a new emphasis on the phenomena of stability and change. Organizational research will find it imperative to integrate into its modes of analysis the models and methods of discourse and conversation analysis – fields that have previously evolved in their own fashion. This will require a broadening of the objectives of those latter fields, as they are now constituted, to take account of the institutional moorings of talk – a sensitivity to the macro as well as the micro dimensions of talk that I do not find in them as they stand. (p. 29)

This chapter should be read as an attempt to do what Taylor called for. I will try to combine and integrate the two levels of analysis. I will analyze the entire process of preparing for and executing a live TV broadcast on location. The process consisted of five preparatory meetings of the production crew and the final airing of the broadcast, all within a period of 2 days. My detailed analysis will focus on a few key discursive interactions selected from the process. To select those key interactions in a theoretically justifiable manner, I will develop and use a conceptual framework centered on the notion of disturbance management. And to interpret the findings, I will employ conceptual tools of cultural-historical activity theory (Cole & Engeström, 1993; Engeström, 1987, 1993a; Leont'ev, 1978).

Discursive Disturbances and Their Management

By *disturbances* I mean deviations from the normal scripted course of events in the work process, normal being defined by plans, explicit rules and instructions, or tacitly assumed traditions. A disturbance may occur between people and their instruments or between two or more people. Disturbances appear in the form of an obstacle, difficulty, failure, disagreement, or conflict. In her analysis of disturbances in aircraft cockpits, Rogalski (1994, p. 190) points out that "disturbances may be caused by technical or environmental incidents, by unexpected interventions of other operators, or by the requirements of a secondary task."

In studies of discourse and conversation, disturbances have been analyzed as "troubles of talk," "troublesome moves," misunderstandings, complications, and conflicts of interpersonal interaction, especially between professionals or bureaucrats and their lay clients (e.g., Conley & O'Barr, 1990; Coupland, Giles, & Wiemann, 1991; Grimshaw, 1990; Lynch, 1984; West, 1984; Whalen, Zimmerman, & Whalen, 1988). These studies have tended to limit their focus on relatively short sequences of talk itself, rather than seeing talk as a constitutive but by no means the sole medium of longer-lasting, institutionally organized, and historically changing work activities. Such conversation analysts as Christian Heath (Heath & Luff, 1996), Charles Goodwin (1994, 1995), Elinor Ochs (Ochs, Gonzales, & Jacoby, 1996), and Lucy Suchman (1987, 2006) have, however, expanded their repertoires to include the uses of material artifacts and spaces, gestures and bodily positions, and visual representations as integral aspects in the analysis of discourse. Correspondingly, Ed Hutchins (1995; Hutchins & Klausen, 1996) has included detailed analyses of talk in studies of distributed cognition in technologically complex collaborative work settings, or *functional systems*.

While knowledge of the mediating technological artifacts, material surroundings, visual representations, and bodily positions is important for understanding team interactions, I will emphasize them more in later chapters and restrict my focus in this chapter on recorded talk as data. I call disturbances that appear in the talk *discursive disturbances*. A detailed analysis of discursive disturbances is warranted in a work activity such as broadcasting, in which spoken discourse is a predominant medium.

In many complex work activities, it is not feasible to distinguish between an actual disturbance and a public anticipation of one. Many work activities require constant anticipation as an integral part of the work itself. Thus, when a potential problem is anticipated and made manifest, it typically leads to a break in the normal flow of work, including some sort of diagnosis and repair – in a very similar fashion to the case in which the anticipated disturbance actually takes place.

The following is an example from my data involving an incident that occurred in the final rehearsal, about 16 min before the broadcast. A new set was built for the TV announcers of the sports event. A design problem with the set prompted the director to request that the announcers stand during their opening presentations. The principal announcer was quite upset with the decision and demanded that it be changed the following week.

> *Announcer:* This is very awkward, Larry. I can only tell you . . . because the lights are so bright – I can't see the monitor!
>
> *Director:* Chris, Chris – as soon as you introduce Bo, and as soon as I zoom in on Bo, you can sit down.
>
> *Announcer:* Okay – but next week, please do it differently.
>
> *Director:* Chris, what did I tell you an hour ago? This show only. This show only.
>
> *Announcer:* Well, I just want to be sure.
>
> *Director:* This show.
>
> *Announcer:* Because I couldn't see.
>
> *Director:* I understand. As soon as I zoom in on Bo, you sit down. Bo, as soon as I get off "five – four – three – two – one," you sit, it's as simple as that. That's why we work these problems out.

Anticipation of a disturbance by the announcer (being unable to see the monitor in the actual broadcast) became a discursive disturbance in itself. It had to be dealt with by the director because, had the announcer remained upset, that might have led to unanticipated further problems. Cases like this are frequent in the data. Anticipatory talk is a key ingredient of the productive work itself. Thus, explicit anticipations of disturbances become discursive disturbances in themselves.

Disturbances may be managed in a variety of ways, ranging from tacit withdrawal to innovative and collaborative efforts to develop the work activity in a preventive manner (Norros, 1996). Identification of types of disturbances and ways of managing or containing them opens up a new layer of work for analysis – a layer of constant negotiation and problem solving "from below."

Activity Theory as a Framework of Interpretation

Disturbances are important because, when traced and analyzed over time, they indicate persistent "resident pathogens" (Reason, 1990) or "weak points" (Rogalski, 1994) in work. A singular local disturbance may point to broader structural tensions in the organization (Perrow, 1984). In other words, disturbances offer a potentially powerful lens for understanding the interconnection between micro-level events and macro-level structures. Although this link has been demonstrated in concrete cases, theoretical tools have been largely missing for its systematic conceptual elaboration.

Activity theory offers a three-pronged analytical distinction between molar collective activity, modular individual actions, and their component automatic operations (Leont'ev, 1978). Activity is here seen as a collective, systemic formation that has a complex mediational structure. Activities are not short-lived events or actions that have a temporally clear-cut beginning and end. They are systems that *produce* events and actions and evolve over lengthy periods of sociohistorical time. I use the diagram of Figure 2.1 to represent the mediational structure of an activity system.

The model reveals the decisive feature of *multiple mediations* in activity. The interplay between the subject and the object, or the actor and the task domain, is mediated by instruments, including symbols and representations

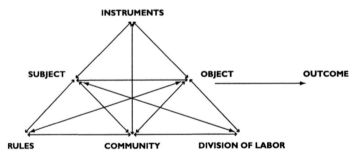

Figure 2.1. The mediational structure of an activity system (Engeström, 1987, p. 78).

of various kinds. This uppermost subtriangle, however, is but the tip of an iceberg. The less visible social mediators of activity – rules, community, and division of labor – are depicted at the bottom of the model. Between the components of the system, there are continuous transformations. The activity system incessantly reconstructs itself.

An activity system contains and generates a variety of different viewpoints or "voices," as well as layers of historically accumulated artifacts, rules, and patterns of division of labor. This multivoiced and multilayered nature of activity systems is both a resource for collective achievement and a source of compartmentalization and conflict. A conceptual model of the activity system is particularly useful when one wants to make sense of systemic factors behind seemingly individual and accidental disturbances, deviations, and innovations occurring in the daily practice of workplaces.

On this view, artifact-mediated, collective activity system is the primary unit of analysis. Situated actions can be understood and changed as manifestations of the activity system. Disturbances are essentially actions that deviate from the expected course of normal procedure. They can be interpreted as symptoms or manifestations of historically evolving *inner contradictions* in the given activity system. Such systemic contradictions are a key to understanding the sources of trouble as well as the innovative and developmental potentials of the activity (Engeström, 1995a, 1995c; see also Putnam, 1985).

Figure 2.1 calls attention to both the personal perspective of the subject – any given member of the community involved in the collaborative activity may take the subject position in an action – and its relationship to the systems perspective that views the activity from the outside. Entire organizations as well as their relatively autonomous departments, units, or teams may be analyzed as activity systems.

Contradictions can typically be identified as tensions between two or more components of the system. Such inner contradictions emerge when one component changes or develops beyond the operational logic of the other components, originally due to interaction with and influence from other activity systems.

Inner contradictions may be understood when data on current disturbances are interpreted against a historical analysis of the evolution of the activity system. Such a historical analysis helps the researcher to trace the formation of current tensions through earlier cycles of development. The identification of inner contradictions of the activity system provides pointers toward remapping the seemingly chaotic realm of local disturbances and innovations as an emerging zone of proximal development of the collaborative activity system (Engeström, 1987; Vygotsky, 1978).

Activity theory has its roots in the cultural-historical psychology developed by Vygotsky, Leont'ev, and Luria in the postrevolutionary Russia of the 1920s and 1930s (see Luria, 1978; Wertsch, 1981). Activity theory has only recently been expanded and brought to bear on analyses of organizations and organizational communication (Ahonen, Engeström, & Virkkunen, 2000; Blackler, 1993; Engeström, 1999a, 2000a; Engeström, Puonti, & Seppänen, 2003; Holt & Morris, 1993). Instead of providing a detailed conceptual introduction to the theory, I will now illuminate some of its potentials by applying it to the case at hand. At the end of the chapter, I will return to the broader theoretical implications of the analysis.

The Setting

The focus of my analysis is the workplace of one of the most popular sports television productions in U.S. television history, the ABC television network's Professional Bowlers Tour (PBT). Our data collection took place in 1994. With consistently high audience ratings over the years, PBT had become the longest-running (33 years in 1994) live sports special on U.S. network television.

The production control room is the principal command center on every live or videotaped telecast, where various centers of production and technical staff activity are coordinated and monitored during the production of a program. It is also a central disturbance management center for several different subsystems of crew activity. The control room personnel working there serve as supervisors of different, but always quite tightly coupled, program production operations that must be coordinated and managed during the program.

The production work in the PBT control room revolved around the following six principal crew positions:

Producer – first in command; had overall editorial responsibility for all production staff members and technicians. Reported to the executive producer and vice presidents of production at the New York production headquarters.

Director – second in command; had complete production responsibility (under the supervision of the producer) for the technical crew as they fulfilled the editorial objectives established by the producer and her superiors. Supervised all production and technical crew members in conjunction with, and certainly in the absence of, the producer.

Associate Director (AD) – third highest production member in command; had responsibility for the timing and coordination of the program under the supervision of the producer. The AD also often worked without the producer and director (but always with their approval) on preproduction and postproduction editing or video-gathering in the field. During a live broadcast, the AD's most important function was to compute the length of the remaining program so that the producer would be able to end the program on time and broadcast all scheduled commercials.

Assistant to the Producer (PA) – fourth in command. This production staff person was not located within the production control facility but instead worked from the graphics area of videotape control truck during the broadcast. The PA's primary responsibility was to coordinate and arrange the on-screen graphics that were used to identify and locate sports participants for the audience. The PA also had to hire and maintain a cadre of one to three per-diem production assistants (in network television jargon "runners") who helped out wherever an extra hand was needed on a production.

Technical Director (TD) – fifth in command. The TD was the most senior technician (in salary and job complexity), who often served as liaison between production and the technical crew on a given program. During the course of the telecast, the TD operated the video switcher and was responsible for creating the video special effects with the director and videotape, graphics, camera persons, lighting director and crew, and other crew members. On live remote programs, the TD was also responsible (with the senior video operator, who monitored and adjusted the proper technical levels of the video signal) for technical coordination between the production truck and the studio from which the program was being broadcast to the viewers.

Senior audio technician – sixth in command. This was the second most complex technical position on the program. The audio technician operated the audio control board and supervised the placement of audio equipment with several other audio associates in the bowling lanes.

Figure 2.2 shows the locations of the personnel working in the production control room each week as the PBT series traveled across the United States during the 14 weeks or so that the series ran, beginning in January of each year.

The spatial distribution of work among the various technological centers of coordination becomes a key factor in explaining how work may be coordinated and how disturbances are (or are not) managed. There were seven spatially separated subsystems of activity operating on PBT: (1) main control room (video switching/special effects, audio, and the production

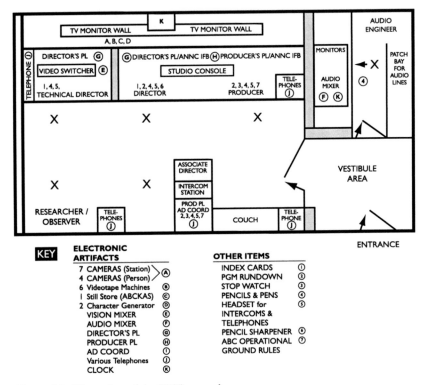

Figure 2.2. Floor plan of the PBT control room.

command center, which were all located in the principal production control van outside of the bowling lanes); (2) videotape playback and editing
(including slow-motion replays), located in a subsidiary control truck that
was parked beside the principal control room truck outside the bowling
lanes; (3) electronic graphics (located in the videotape control truck); (4)
cameras and lighting (inside the bowling lanes); (5) announcers and stage
manager; (6) liaison to the PBT sanctioning organization (inside the bowling lanes); and (7) the New York City commercial coordination studios
where the program was transmitted to the more than 200 U.S. television
stations that, in turn, transmitted the program to audiences watching at
home.

    While separated spatially, these smaller systems of activity, or subcen-
ters of coordination, had to be closely aligned during the production of
a live telecast for a program to become a reality. The coordination and
alignment required constant communication, largely through the complex
set of intercom and telephone links shown in Figure 2.3.

LOCATION KEY:

T-1	Main Control Truck	C	NY Commercial Integration Studio
T-2	Support Truck / Graphics & Videotape	H	NY "Host" Studio Principal Sports Control Studio
A	Announcer's Position (Inside Bowling Lanes)		& Coordinating Producer, Wide World of Sports
F	Competition Area (Inside Bowling Lanes)	M	NY Technical and Operational Support Systems
P	Bowling Warm-Up Area (Inside Bowling Lanes)		

```
┌──────────────────┐      ┌──────────────────┐          ┌──────────────────┐
│ PRODUCER (T-1)   │      │ DIRECTOR (T-1)   │          │ ASSOCIATE        │
│    "PL"          │      │    "PL"          │          │ DIRECTOR "COORD"**│
└──────────────────┘      └──────────────────┘          └──────────────────┘
```

• ASSOCIATE DIRECTOR	(T-1)
• STAGE MANAGER	(A)
• ASSISTANT TO PRODUCER	(T-2)
• PBT LIAISON	(F)
• VIDEOTAPE	(T-2)
• GRAPHICS	(T-2)
• AUDIO	(T-1)

• TECHNICAL DIRECTOR	(T-1)
• ASSISTANT TO PRODUCER	(T-2)
• VIDEOTAPE	(T-2)
• GRAPHICS	(A&F)
• CAMERAS	(T-1)
• AUDIO	(T-2)
• VIDEO CONTROL	(F)
• LIGHTING DIRECTOR	

• Commercial Integration Associate Director	(C)
• Host Studio Associate Director	(H)
• Host Executive Producer and Other	(H)
Supervisory Production Staff	
• NY Technical and Operation Studios	(M)

Regular Telephone	Announcer's IFB
Circuits (3)	(**)

Emergency Back-up
Telephone Circuits
In Case of Coord Technical Failure

• NY Production Staff	
• Any Other Contact	
Required	

• Announcer	(H,F,P)
• Expert Analyst	(A,F,P)
• Guest Interviewer	(A,P)

Figure 2.3. Intercom and telephone links of the PBT activity systems.

Narrative of the Production Process

The crew preparation plan for the PBT was generally the same each week. For most of the shows, the crew would arrive on Thursday in anticipation of the Saturday show. If the program was headed for a city or bowling lanes that had not served as a host for a previous program, an advance team, made up of the director, producer, and unit manager, would generally scout the location. They would look for any unforeseen difficulties and confirm that suitable electricity and power facilities would be available. The advance team would determine where the production vans should be parked during the weekend of the broadcast and handle other final logistical details. Generally, the producer, director, AD, and PA would meet on Wednesday in New York before leaving for the site to prepare videotape and graphics presentations for that week's program.

If the crew was arriving from the New York area on Thursday, most members would generally appear at the bowling lanes to double-check and prepare for any work that had to be done in order to transform the bowling lanes into a remote television studio by Saturday morning. On Friday morning, the technical and production crew would begin its day at approximately 9 a.m. and finish at 5 p.m. Some of Friday's duties included the preparation of feature material for Saturday's broadcast, as well as any technical set-up details possible for Saturday's broadcast.

The actual bowling competition began each week on Tuesday and culminated in the televised matches between the top five finishers on Saturday's program. This means that, for most of the day on Friday, there was competition on the lanes that prevented full-scale preparations for Saturday's broadcast (e.g., rigging lights, constructing the set for the announcers, installing fixed cameras and microphones, and handling other set-up details). The technical crew did as much as it could until 5 p.m., took a few hours off, and then returned at midnight on Friday. At that time, intensive preparations began and continued through the early morning hours of Saturday.

At approximately 5 p.m., there was a weekly Friday evening production meeting for the key members of the production staff and representatives from the Pro Bowler's Tour Association (PBA) – the sanctioning body for the broadcast. At this meeting, the producer, director, AD, stage manager, PA, announcers, PBT liaison, and PBT public relations representative discussed the program format that the producer had assembled for that week's show, any up-to-date news that might affect the Saturday broadcast, and news about future programs that needed to be discussed. Because not everyone in attendance at the meeting lived in New York during the week, the Friday meeting was generally the first opportunity the group had to see each other since the preceding week's program. While there may have been telephone contact, this was the first person-to-person meeting of the week.

After those assembled at the Friday night meeting discussed the program format for Saturday, generally they viewed tapes of their previous shows that had been prepared in New York. This helped to build team morale and maintain a shared purpose as the crew began the Saturday program. On the particular program analyzed here, the first show of the 1994 PBT season (sent on January 22, 1994, from Long Beach), most members of the group had not seen each other since the series ended the previous April. At the conclusion of the meeting, most of the group returned to the bowling lanes in order to see who would be the top five bowlers appearing the next day.

By 7 a.m., on Saturday, the majority of preparations had been made for the broadcast, which in the case of West Coast broadcasts hit the air at 12 noon Pacific time (3 p.m. Eastern time). The production crew arrived between 7 and 8 a.m. Videotape editing and graphics preparations began at 7 a.m. and continued throughout the broadcast. When the program was telecast in the East or Midwest (3 p.m. or 2 p.m., respectively), the broadcast day generally began at 9 or 10 a.m.

On the Saturday being observed, because it was the premiere program of the 1994–1995 season, the director held a short camera meeting commencing at 8 a.m. for the camerapersons, some of whom were new to the show.

At 9 a.m., there was another production meeting for key production staffers and PBA representatives in which any last-minute details concerning the field of bowlers for that day's program were discussed and contingency plans were reviewed for ending the program. At 10 a.m., there was a preproduction session in which small portions of the program were prerecorded for the broadcast. At 11 a.m. there was Telco check, a 30-minute period in which the production crew established video, audio, and other communication links with the New York studio complex that would receive the program and, in turn, send it out to the approximately 200 ABC stations. Following the Telco break, the crew had about 20 to 25 min to rehearse the opening and any pieces that would run during the broadcast. This rehearsal could extend up to 5 min before the broadcast. At 12 p.m., the program began broadcasting; it left the air at exactly 1:28:39 p.m.

Data Collection

The field data were collected by Dennis Mazzocco, a doctoral student who worked as a participant observer throughout the 2 days of intensive preparation and airing of the program. He had occasionally worked on PBT as an AD and stage manager since 1984, as well as a producer, director, writer, and AD on a large number of other live and taped programs for all of the U.S. television networks (subsequently, Mazzocco took a faculty position at Hofstra University).

We obtained permission for Mazzocco to videotape and observe the interactions in the control room (the location of the researcher is shown in Figure 2.2) and in all the preparatory meetings in Long Beach. We recorded six successive steps of the production process in their entirety: the Friday production meeting, the Saturday morning camera meeting, the Saturday production meeting, the Saturday preproduction session, the Saturday rehearsal, and the Saturday broadcast. Moreover, the crew recorded for us the conversations on the three production intercoms shown in Figure 2.3.

In addition to these parallel recordings, we conducted interviews and had supplementary discussions with several of the crew members.

Three Types of Disturbances

Producing a TV program is an ongoing process of crisis negotiation, resolution, and avoidance by the crew that starts well before the program ever
reaches the viewer's screen at home. More precisely, producing any kind
of television program, not only one that is live, involves hundreds of unexpected contingencies, disturbances, and disturbance-related decisions by
the program's work team as it goes about the business of preparing and
broadcasting a program.

I identified three analytically distinct types of disturbances in the work
interactions of the crew in the data. Type I may be called *local disturbances*.
These were manifest problems, or the crew's manifest anticipations of a
potential problem, that involve only, or may be limited to, the production control room crew. None of the other six subsystems of activity (see
Figure 2.3) was involved in a Type I disturbance. These could be minor
problems of a clerical nature, such as the PA forgetting to include an information sheet for the director at the Friday night production meeting. Or
they could be something more serious, such as a disagreement between
the producer and AD that led to an on-air mistake that was noticeable to
viewers at home.

Type II incidents were *intermediate disturbances*. This category included
any disturbance, or anticipation of a disturbance, that involved the control
room crew and one or more other activity systems of the seven identified
earlier in this chapter. In other words, this type of situation could involve
three or four activity systems such as videotape, announcers, cameras, and,
of course, the control room crew. The upper limit of "no more than six" was
selected to distinguish between intermediate disturbances (Type II) and full-
blown crisis situations that involved all seven activity systems contributing
to the production of the PBT broadcast.

Type III was a *global disturbance* or anticipation of a global disturbance
in which all seven activity systems were involved. This type would call for
the most expeditious and coordinated response.

Table 2.1 shows the frequency and temporal distribution of Type I, II,
and III disturbances in the production of the PBT program observed on
January 21–22, 1994.

As the table shows, 330 disturbances were identified in the data. This
translates into approximately one disturbance every 90 sec. Although the
highest number of global disturbances did occur early, in the Friday evening
production meeting, the total number of disturbances did not decrease in
the final airing. In all phases of the production process there was a constant
stream of disturbances, especially intermediate ones.

Table 2.1. *Distribution of disturbances by type and time of occurrence*

Type	I (local) $f(\%)$	II (interm.) $f(\%)$	III (global) $f(\%)$	Total $f(\%)$
Fri. night	5 (6.9)	26 (36.2)	41 (56.9)	72 (100.0)
Sat. camera	–	14 (100.0)	–	14 (100.0)
Sat. prod	–	41 (83.7)	8 (16.3)	49 (100.0)
Sat. preprod.	2 (2.6)	74 (97.4)	–	76 (100.0)
Sat. rehearsal	4 (7.8)	38 (74.5)	9 (17.7)	51 (100.0)
Sat. air	5 (7.4)	46 (67.6)	17 (25.0)	68 (100.0)
TOTAL	16 (4.8)	239 (72.4)	75 (22.8)	330 (100.0)

Given the large number of continuous disturbances in the production process, it is particularly interesting to see how they were managed.

Modes of Disturbance Management

According to Argyris and Schön (1978), there are two qualitatively different ways of reacting to disturbances in organizations. The authors call these two modes *single-loop learning* and *double-loop learning*. Single-loop learning leads to repair by adjusting organizational practices within a constant framework of norms for performance. Double-loop learning leads to questioning and changing the norms of organizational performance. Various other theories have subsequently elaborated the distinction between adaptive and innovative organizational learning, the latter being a process whereby "one rises above the day-to-day routines of managing the operational deviations from plans" (Garratt, 1990, pp. 80–81; see also Engeström, 1995a).

In preliminary analyses of the data, I identified five modes of managing disturbances, namely, *negotiating*, accepting *responsibility*, using *authority*, *complaining*, and *avoiding confrontation*. In addition, on the basis of previous studies, I expected to find, on closer analysis, examples of engaging in open *conflict* (e.g., Grimshaw, 1990) and attempting or completing an *innovation* (e.g., Engeström, 1995a) as modes of managing disturbances. Following is a brief description of these seven categories.

1. Negotiating: One or more crew members make adjustments or concessions, or agree to take joint action to correct or resolve a problem.
2. Accepting responsibility: One or more crew members accept personal responsibility for a problem.

3. Using authority: A crew member invokes his or her superior rank, experience, or expertise, demanding action or compliance from subordinate crew members in a problem situation.
4. Complaining: One or more crew members express discontent about some element of the production process or output; the complaint remains unanswered.
5. Avoiding confrontation: One or more crew members challenge some aspect of the production and/or someone above them in authority; the challenge is handled by damping down or changing the subject by means of joking, acknowledging the problem without taking further action, or indicating that action will be taken later.
6. Engaging in open conflict: Use of authority or a complaint leads to disagreement and open argument between persons with conflicting viewpoints.
7. Attempting or completing an innovation: One or more crew members suggest changes, improvements, or novel procedures and tools in response to a problem.

Table 2.2 displays the distribution of the modes of disturbance management found in the final analysis of the data. The table shows that negotiation and the use of authority were by far the most common modes of disturbance management. Interestingly enough, the relatively frequent use of authority did not increase but rather decreased in the final airing of the broadcast; negotiation was clearly the predominant mode at that point.

The most striking finding is, however, that I could not identify a single instance of either open conflict or innovation as modes of disturbance management in the data. This is indeed surprising, given the large number and great density of disturbances in this production process.

The first five modes of disturbance management are manifestations of containment, of repair without intervention in the given norms of the practice. Open conflict and innovation would indicate that there is at least a possibility of questioning and perhaps changing or improving the practice – characteristics of double-loop or innovative organizational learning, as discussed previously. How might one explain the absence of these features?

Perfection or Masking?

It seems that the PBT had developed an intricate and quite robust set of mechanisms for dealing with continuous disturbances without creating conflicts or questioning and changing the norms of the practice. We have

Table 2.2. *Frequencies of modes of disturbance management by time of occurrence*

	Neg	Resp	Auth	Comp	Avoid	Confl	Innov	Total
Fri. prod. (100)	23 (29.1)	3 (3.8)	33 (41.9)	3 (3.8)	17 (21.5)	–	–	79
Sat. cam. (100)	1 (7.1)	1 (7.1)	7 (50.0)	2 (14.3)	3 (21.4)	–	–	14
Sat. prod. (100)	25 (46.3)	7 (13.0)	18 (33.3)	1 (1.9)	3 (5.6)	–	–	54
Sat. pre. (100)	32 (41.6)	4 (5.2)	29 (37.7)	12 (15.6)	–	–	–	77
Sat. reh. (100)	13 (27.7)	4 (8.5)	18 (38.3)	7 (14.9)	5 (10.6)	–	–	47
Sat. air (100)	28 (40.6)	8 (11.6)	19 (27.5)	8 (11.6)	6 (8.7)	–	–	69
TOTAL (100)*	122 (35.9)	27 (7.9)	124 (36.5)	33 (9.7)	34 (10.0)	–	–	340

* The total number of modes is slightly higher than the total number of disturbances displayed in Table 2.1. This is due to the fact that in some disturbances we observed more than one distinct mode of disturbance management emanating from the different crew members present.

37

here an activity system almost obsessively preoccupied with upholding and perpetuating the status quo of its familiar and trusted procedures.

Such a preoccupation with keeping the practice as it is might be interpreted as *perfection*, as attainment of a degree of smooth fluency that makes conflicts and innovations simply irrelevant and unnecessary. Many theories of skilled performance (e.g., Dreyfus & Dreyfus, 1986) regard such perfection as the highest stage of expertise.

On the other hand, this predominance of containment and single-loop learning may be interpreted as *masking*, as a forced attempt to repress and hide any signs of conflict and any attempts to step over the boundaries of normal procedure. This would indicate that there were serious contradictions and tensions within the activity system. This would be closer to what Argyris (1986) calls *skilled incompetence*.

To examine these alternatives more closely, I will return to the disturbances and their management. If we are in fact dealing with a case of forced masking, there should be instances where the tensions partially spill over the edges of the mask of containment. In other words, there should be *critical disturbances* that are not technical in nature. Such critical disturbances should at least momentarily reveal substantive disagreements, fears, or other strong indications of systemic contradictions in the PBT activity. These instances are most likely to be found in the "using authority," "complaining," and "avoiding confrontation" modes of disturbance management. A variant of discursive asymmetry (e.g., Linell, 1990) and potential conflict is embedded in each one of these categories.

Among the incidents classified under these three categories of disturbance management, I found four clear instances of critical disturbances. In what follows, I will briefly analyze each one of the four incidents.

Incident 1

Saturday Rehearsal (4 min before the broadcast)
Key: C = Control AD
     AD = Associate Director
     P = Producer
     D = Director

C: Barbara's controlling?

AD: Yes.

C: Why?

AD: I don't know.

P: She's never done it, and it is supposed to be Russell Brooks.

D: I thought it was Ben Harvey.

AD: It was supposed to be Ben today, but he had to go shoot something...

P: Well, why is Barbara doing it? She's never done it before.

AD: I have no idea. I had no idea until this morning when I called.

P: Bullshit. You should have told me. Who's the person on duty today?

AD: I think it's Marilyn. She [Barbara] can do it.

P: That's not the point. That's not the point. The point is...I'm the producer and I would like to know. Do you understand that? I would like to know. That's the point of that...

Here the producer objected to the selection of the New York AD who was controlling the New York commercial integration studio because she had never done it before and might make a mistake. The AD on site in Long Beach tried to defend the New York AD. Although the exchange was brief and ambiguous, the unusual intensity with which authority was emphasized seems to indicate serious tension in the relationship between the local production team and the New York headquarters.

Incident 2

Friday Production Meeting (approximately 17 hours before the broadcast)
Key: P = Producer
 D = Director
 A = Announcer
 EA = Expert Analyst
 PBL = Pro Bowler's Liaison

EA: That was great.

PBL: That's excellent.

A: I like that...I like that.

P: Good. I have a few things I have a problem with. I don't like those words going on the screen...when he is talking.

D: That's the whole way we do things now.

P: [inaudible] As a piece on the side, it is fine.

Here the crew had just finished screening a pretaped produced feature that would air during Saturday's broadcast. The feature was not produced by anyone from the PBT crew. Rather, the central feature group within ABC produced the report, in part as a result of cost containment strategies put into effect by ABC Sports. Another reason the piece was produced by the ABC feature group was to achieve a highly stylized look (and uniformity) for all features being produced. Initially, there seemed to be consensus among the PBT crew assembled at the meeting in favor of endorsing the finished piece. However, the producer raised some objections to the stylistic presentation of the feature. The director, seeking to contain objections, seemed to affirm the company's position ("That's the whole way we do things now"). The producer responded by also reaffirming company goals. Again, in spite of its brevity, the incident points to tension between the PBT production crew and the central management of ABC.

Incident 3
Saturday camera meeting (less than 4 hours before the broadcast)
Key: D = Director
      C/1 = Camera One

D: To their credit, they're working really hard and are trying very, very hard to get some commitments to sell the show, so we can be here next year.

C/1: Can I ask you a question, Larry? Is this feasible? When they, like, owe, you know, the buybacks to the commercial people . . . If they put them on this show and they don't sell the time – then write it off as a loss on this show . . . that they lose all this money?

D: I don't know how that works. I really . . . I wish I could answer your question. But I would misspeak if I answered you.

C/1: No, that's. . . .

D: I honestly do not know. . . . The only thing we can hope is that something, something will happen to keep the show on the air. . . . The way I look at the show. It has a solid audience. What it's rating, three and change? It creates a build-in for Wide World?

In this case, the most senior cameraperson on the crew queried the director on reports that the PBT would be canceled. The cameraperson was essentially questioning the conventional wisdom of ABC's management that the bowling program was losing money. The director avoided confrontation by claiming ignorance.

This incident was already quite substantive. There seemed to be a fear among the crew concerning the continuation of the PBT based on information or rumors implying that the show was losing money. Interestingly enough, the fear was voiced by a cameraman instead of anyone in the control room. This is understandable, as camerapersons were unionized and outside the circle of corporate loyalty. They had less pressure to maintain the mask of containment.

Incident 4

Friday Evening Production Meeting (about 17 hours before the broadcast)
Key: P = Producer
   D = Director
   PA = Production Assistant
   A = Announcer
   Expert Analyst

D: Carol, did you bring the hard copy for Chris and Bo?

PA: I got a copy in the road box.

P: I think you did.

D: I was very impressed and I'm not easily impressed. They put together a slide show as part of their sales presentation, and came down and presented it to us at our production meeting. I mean I can't think ... from a sales perspective ... of any better way to approach our sales department. And I really think it is very good.

A: The one we used with Dodge?

D: I don't know if it was the one with Dodge or not. It was excellent.

A: Was it good?

P: It wasn't that one.

EA: For network buys on our show?

D: For network buys.

P: Something like that ...

D: The salespeople do it ...

EA: You want me to tell you?

D: And they tailor it. So, if you are selling bubble gum, they will tailor the demographics to show people eighteen to thirty-five that chew bubble gum. It's really well done.

EA: I was doing a local commercial.

D: We'll show it to you.

EA: I want to show you something interesting. My cousin owns a brokerage firm in St. Louis. I was sitting in his office.... The ABC sales ladies come in. He does commercials. And I already talked

him into doing the Pro Bowler's Tour. He's looking for fifty and
over. I say that's our show. Mike, we'll do it. You'll save a lot of
money. It's a ten thousand dollar buy. But she came in and do you
know that. . . . Even though it is a fifty-year-old audience and an ABC
affiliate . . . had nothing to do with the Pro Bowler's Tour. She wanted
to sell news and I'd let her give her whole spiel. And then he introduced me. . . . This is my cousin, Bo Burton. He is an announcer in the
Pro Bowler's Tour. And we would like to do a commercial together.
What is the demographics? She says, I don't know. You wonder, even
at . . . I know . . . our network level. . . . But what about at the affiliate
level? They don't even pitch us. Not a single pitch, Frank.

D: The sales department, if they do, let perception versus reality type of
presentation. . . . And the perception is that the show skews old, and
the reality is that it doesn't and they put the numbers down. . . .

EA: Even if it skews old, why aren't they pitching to people who buy
fifty years and over? That's my point.

D: This thing is really done. I was very impressed. But unfortunately
it isn't generating the kinds of revenue that we need to generate.
Although we are in a better position than we look like. Schenk, what
time do you want to get picked up at the airport tomorrow?

Here the director and the expert analyst were disagreeing over whether
or not the ABC sales department was working hard to sell the PBT to
advertisers. ABC Sports executives seemed to have used the "hard-to-sell"
argument in their appeals to the PBA to lower telecast rights fees. At this
point, rumors were circulating among the show's crew that the PBT would
not be renewed for the next season. Over the past several years, ABC executives had maintained that the program had not been able to generate the
revenues that it had in past years. EA was openly challenging this point with
the director, whereas the director appeared to be accepting the company's
premise that the PBT was a hard sell. In the end, the director avoided
confrontation by switching the topic to the practical matter of picking up
someone at the airport.

The discursive contents of these four critical disturbances strongly suggest that the masking explanation is in fact valid.

Inner Contradictions of PBT as an Activity System

The incidents just presented generate a picture very different from that of a
system so close to perfection that it does not need conflicts and innovations.

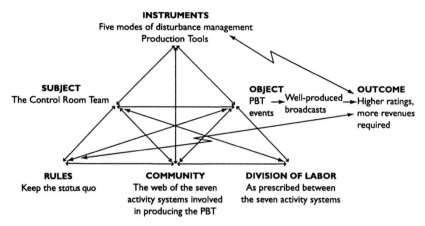

Figure 2.4. The PBT activity system and its inner contradictions.

They indicate that PBT, taken as whole, was an activity system torn by contradictions but desperately trying to deny them so as to maintain the appearance of a smooth, well-controlled operation.

To pursue this line of inquiry further, I have constructed a model of those inner contradictions of the activity system, which is presented in Figure 2.4. The contradictions are depicted by two-headed lightning-shaped arrows.

Taking the control room team as the subject of this activity, the most obvious object appears to be the sporting events of the PBT that must be turned into quality broadcasts. However, behind that obvious object, there is the object of viewer ratings and revenues as the perceived final outcomes. Both were mentioned by participants in the critical disturbances analyzed previously (ratings in Incident 3; revenues or money in Incidents 3 and 4). From the four incidents it seems that this component of the activity system, *the relationship between required and achieved outcome*, had changed: "unfortunately it isn't generating the kinds of revenue that we need to generate" (incident 4).

My hypothesis is that the contradictions emerged in the form depicted in Figure 2.4 when the control room team responded to the new pressure from the demanded outcome by sticking to the rule of the status quo and, correspondingly, by cultivating and employing the one-sidedly defensive tools exemplified by the five modes of disturbance management found in the data. The new demanded outcome required change; the activity system responded by trying to do things exactly as they had been done before, only more smoothly. In one instance (Saturday camera meeting), the director told the cameramen: "There is only one way to cover bowling, and what we do is right." This is almost a textbook example of a double bind that seems to offer no way out (Bateson, 1972).

Historical Perspective on PBT

To elaborate further on the hypothesis presented in Figure 2.4, I turn to a brief historical examination of the activity system of the PBT. Here I rely largely on the autobiography of Jim Spence, a longtime ABC Sports senior vice president who joined the company as a PA in 1960 and who also served as the first PA on PBT in 1961 (Spence, 1988).

The most obvious changes from 1961 to 1985 in the PBT consisted of technological advances involving satellite transmission, graphics, videotape, robotic cameras, and digital electronic video and audio devices. During this period, the PBT developed into one of the most frequently watched and profitable programs on the ABC television network schedule. According to Spence (1988, p. 282), the PBT "was one of the greatest success stories in the history of television sports."

According to Spence, the built-in system ABC instituted in the early years of the telecast helped to maintain coordination and minimize disturbances, regardless of whether an experienced or inexperienced crew was assigned:

> Through the years, the bowling show is one we've been able to use for the baptism of our young producers and directors, in that the program is well established, with a rigid format that limits both innovation and opportunities to make mistakes. The action is concentrated on two lanes that we used to call the "the TV pair," but which are now called "the championship pair." That came about in part because of my feeling that the first term suggested the sport was being subjugated to television. Young producers can get their feet here before graduating to more difficult shows – or they can flop under the pressure of being on live network television for ninety minutes. Helpful to them is the feeling of "family" on the tour, embracing not only the bowlers but the television crew as well. (Spence, 1988, p. 281)

This is corroborated by PBT producer Don Ohlymeyer's account (cited in Spence, 1988, pp. 281–282) of starting out on PBT telecasts in the early years of his career:

> I was scared shitless when I first went out there. The technical director on the series then was a wonderful guy named Walt Kubilus, who had been doing the show for years and years. The way he treated me showed the spirit that existed at ABC in those days – and I'm not talking just about inside the

sports division but in engineering and everywhere else, you name it. I'd say, "Take three," but Walt knew better, so he'd punch up camera two, which was the show we should have had on the air. I mean the man would just not *allow* [author's emphasis] me to make a mistake. This went on for the first few weeks. I'd be calling for one camera, and he'd just punch up another one, and invariably the one he chose was the right one. Finally, when he figured out I was ready to do it on my own, he let me go and I was calling the shots and really being the director on the show.... It was unbelievable, the spirit and the sense of family that existed. It was real fellowship. You know, crews can kill you if they want to, and Walt Kubilus could have killed me. It's staggering to think of the number of young producers and directors who have come up through that bowling series and won their spurs.

These observations indicate that the emphasis on a rigid format and deemphasis on innovation had long historical roots in the PBT activity system. However, in the data I saw little evidence of the kind of apprenticeship and family atmosphere described by Ohlymeyer. My analysis indicates that the ethos of pedagogy had been replaced by an assembly line ethos coupled with forced, anxious self-preservation.

In 1985, Capital Cities Communications (CCC) bought out the assets of American Broadcasting Companies, Inc. (ABC), which had formerly produced the PBT with the PBA. A new corporate culture was enforced by Capital Cities' managers after the takeover of ABC. Capital Cities Communications was well known as a "lean and mean" corporate broadcasting organization that had always placed a high value on cutting costs and employees. As Thomas Murphy, Capital Cities' second chair and CEO since 1965, was fond of saying, "what I learned [over the years] was how few people you really needed to keep things running" (Williams, 1989, p. 215).

After the takeover, Capital Cities instituted a series of layoffs and firings throughout ABC that forced all premerger employees to assess their future. By April 1987 about 1,850 employees had been laid off, many in the twilight of their careers and with many years of service to the old ABC. These staff cuts and payroll reductions, amounting to some $100 million, were justified by the Capital Cities mandate to make ABC more cost conscious. During the first few years following the merger, the areas mostly exempt from the company's massive personnel reductions were the sales departments (Fabrikant, 1987; Mazzocco, 1994; Williams, 1989).

In 1994, Capital Cities/ABC forced the PBA to accept a major reduction in broadcast rights, from $200,000 per show to about $50,000, or risk losing the series altogether, allegedly due to dramatically increasing program costs. However, industry trade magazines reported that total programming costs at ABC had not risen significantly between 1986 and 1991. Although Capital Cities' corporate officials portrayed the network as being squeezed by production costs, the cost increases (adjusted for inflation) amounted to just 1% per year (Baldo, 1990; *Broadcasting*, 1991).

The issue of whether the PBT was now making money or not was a constant source of worry for members of the crew. "I honestly do not know.... The only thing we can hope is that something, something will happen to keep the show on the air" (Incident 3). On the basis of my data, it is hard to avoid the impression that the lack of clear feedback on how well the show was doing and the resulting uncertainty concerning its fate were systemic features of the corporate culture in this case. This would mean that the outcome component of the PBT activity system, depicted in Figure 2.4, was chronically and possibly deliberately vague and ambiguous, and thus was very difficult to analyze and influence by the crew.

By the early 1990s, new media technologies, such as satellite-delivered cable sports television, pay-per-view sporting programs, and other new sports home viewing possibilities, had begun to offer the audience new, largely unregulated competition for network sports programs such as the PBT. In this dramatically changed environment, it was hard to see how any program, no matter how impressive a history it might have, could survive without constant innovation that would draw upon the collective expertise and flexibility of its crew.

This points to an inner contradiction in the activity system of the management of ABC Sports. While the activity of management was not the object of our study, the present findings may be projected so as to raise important questions and lead to tentative assumptions about that activity. Presumably the management wanted higher ratings and revenues from the PBT activity. It seems that the management had chosen, deliberately or inadvertently, not to make the criteria, the measures, and the actually achieved outcomes explicitly available and accessible to the PBT crew. This choice, or exclusion, of instruments may have functioned as an incentive for the crew to maintain a predominantly defensive posture in its work – a posture that all but excluded innovation and thus jeopardized ratings and revenues in the long run.

Conclusion

The stagnation I observed in the PBT team resembles the observations Miller (1975/1993) made about the textile weaving teams initially implemented by Rice (1958). As I pointed out in Chapter 1, Miller (1975/1993, pp. 153–154) characterized those teams as being in "a quasi-stationary equilibrium" aimed at "minimizing the chances of disaster."

What kind of team was the PBT team? It started out as an autonomous craft team, built on tight and durable ties between its members and on the concept of a unique product as its object. As the program format matured and became standardized, the work of the team began to look increasingly like hierarchical mass production. With the acquisition of ABC by Capital Cities Communications, an abrupt shift from hierarchy to market took place, manifested by increasing profit pressure. One might say that the PBT team was *internally* a combination of tradition-driven craft and standard-driven hierarchical mass production, whereas the *external* demands were those of market-driven mass production.

The contradictions I identified previously centered on access to information – and thus possibilities for explicit negotiation – about the demanded and actually achieved outcomes of the work activity of the production team. I also projected our findings onto the management of ABC Sports, hypothetically formulating a corresponding contradiction in that activity system. These contradictions within and between the two activity systems explain the stagnation of the team.

The contradictions also point to a zone of proximal development for the PBT production team. In order to move to a new developmental phase, the team would have needed to take up, discuss, and resolve the issue of the expected and actually achieved outcomes of its work. To step into such a zone of proximal development would have meant opening up a discussion on criteria and indicators of quality and productivity. This reconceptualization would necessarily include a transition from smooth status quo to risky variation. In the historical terms summarized in Figure 1.2, this would imply that the team would break into a new developmental phase, namely, some form of quality- and variety-driven lean production or mass customization.

Would such a breaking away from tradition have been possible? It is, of course, impossible to predict what might have happened had the team initiated an expansive transformation of its way of working. However, as the following chapters will show, such attempts are indeed made by teams. Transformation attempts have their own contradictory dynamics, and they are seldom linear success stories. But teams do break out of their traditional molds and open up expanded possibilities of productive work.

3   Teamwork between Adversaries

Coordination, Cooperation, and Communication in a Court Trial

In Chapter 2, I showed how stagnation and defensive encapsulation took hold of a team even though the team was ostensibly successfully engaged in creative work. In this chapter, I will analyze an almost opposite phenomenon: How do new possibilities for expanded dialogue and innovation emerge in a highly rule-based team engaged in what is commonly not regarded as particularly creative work?

Work in courts of law is historically heavily anchored in the individual craft skills and idiosyncratic personalities of the judge and the attorneys. On the other hand, work in courts of law is also among the most formal and rule-based processes in industrialized societies. In this sense, court work is a peculiar blend of autonomous, tacit craft and highly codified and standardized bureaucratic mass production.

However, the intricate division of labor in court organizations and the increasing complexity of cases give rise to various kinds of disturbances and unexpected contingencies in interactions inside and outside the courtroom. In the United States, as in many other countries, courts face rapidly growing caseloads with much less impressive growth in the number of judges and other personnel. As Heydebrand and Seron (1990) show, the way to cope with this dilemma has been increasing rationalization. Such rationalization includes novel scheduling techniques as well as increasing reliance on magistrates, probation officers, and law clerks instead of judges alone. Most importantly, it includes new mechanisms for resolving and settling cases before they reach the stage of a full-scale jury trial.

Rationalization is often regarded as synonymous with either bureaucratization in the Weberian sense or assembly-line Fordism. On the basis of a careful historical and statistical analysis, Heydebrand and Seron (1990) demonstrate that rationalization in courts is a much more open-ended endeavor:

The growth and complexity of the organizational structure of courts is an undeniable development. But there are few signs that such growth is bureaucratic in the sense of Weber's model. Judicial case management has clearly played an important role in the rise of no-action and pretrial dispositions. Yet, the mandatory settlement conference or other pretrial mechanisms of dispute resolution are not necessarily "bureaucratic" since they involve a host of informal procedures that deviate from the formal adversary-adjudicatory model alike. What is perhaps more crucial (...) is how these conferences are conducted, what mix of formal rational and informal-social elements they use, and what innovative alternatives they admit into their arsenal of conflict resolution techniques. (p. 157)

Heydebrand and Seron (1990, pp. 156–157) further observe that developments in court organizations, particularly in metropolitan areas, "point to the emergence of a highly elaborated network of organized activities," whereas many judges' orientation and policies may be changing "from that of formal adjudicators of cases to that of informal processors of disputes." Seron (1990, p. 461) crystallizes the argument by pointing out that the new organizational model in American courts relies increasingly on teamwork that will eventually transcend bureaucratization and deprofessionalization.

In this light, I hypothesize that the currently emerging zone of proximal development for work activity in courts is a terrain of constant ambivalence and struggle between autonomous craft, hierarchical mass production, market-oriented rationalization programs, and emergent experiments aimed at more negotiated, dialogical, and innovative forms of work. The struggle is manifested in ruptures, disturbances, top-down reform programs, and local bottom-up innovation attempts that disturb the routine flow of work. In any case, the emergence of partly improvised, partly institutionalized forms of *teamwork between adversaries* is expected to be a spearhead of the development

I will look at one complex case of civil litigation that took place in the spring of 1991 in the superior court of a large city in southern California. The case involved a dispute over construction defects found in a 240-unit condominium complex. The homeowners demanded approximately $6 million from the developer for repair of the defects. After a year and a half of pretrial procedures and settlement attempts, the case went to a jury trial. The trial lasted for 2 weeks, 1 week less than estimated by the judge and the attorneys. Forty-three witnesses testified, and more than 200 exhibits were introduced (the two parties had originally prepared more than 700 exhibits).

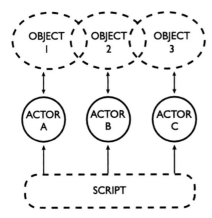

Figure 3.1. The general structure of coordination.

This case exemplified the increasing complexity of many cases of civil litigation. It also represented a test case for the independent calendar and the delay reduction program, a case management strategy for dealing with the growing volume of litigation in which the judge handling this case was an active practitioner.

Theorizing Expansive Transitions

In analyses of work, a crucial question is how to combine the subject–object and the subject–subject, or the instrumental and the communicative, aspects of activity. Arne Raeithel (1983) and Bernd Fichtner (1984) suggest three developmental types of epistemological subject–object–subject relations: *coordination, cooperation,* and *communication.* I shall briefly sketch my interpretation of these types and of the possible mechanisms of transition between them.

I will call the normal scripted flow of interaction coordination. The various actors are following their scripted roles, each concentrating on the successful performance of the assigned actions, or, to paraphrase Goffman (1959), on "the presentation of the self." The script, coded in written rules, plans, and instructions or engraved in tacitly assumed traditions, coordinates their actions as if from behind their backs, without being questioned or discussed (Figure 3.1). In this and the following two diagrams, the unbroken boundaries indicate that the entities are the focus of the subjects' critical attention. The broken boundaries indicate that the corresponding entities are not the focus of their critical attention.

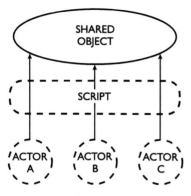

Figure 3.2. The general structure of cooperation.

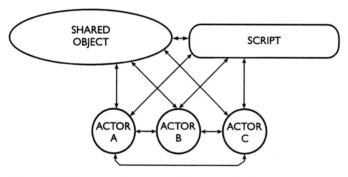

Figure 3.3. The general structure of communication.

By cooperation I mean modes of interaction in which the actors, instead of focusing on performing their assigned roles or presenting themselves, focus on a shared problem, trying to find mutually acceptable ways to conceptualize and solve it. The participants go beyond the confines of the given script, yet they do this without explicitly questioning or reconceptualizing the script. The general structure of cooperation is depicted in Figure 3.2.

By reflective communication I mean interactions in which the actors focus on reconceptualizing their own organization and interaction in relation to their shared objects. Both the object and the script are reconceptualized, as is the interaction between the participants. Transitions to communication are rare in the ongoing flow of daily work actions. The general structure of reflective communication is depicted in Figure 3.3.

I suggest that the mechanisms of transition between the levels include *disturbances, ruptures,* and *expansions*. Disturbances are unintentional deviations from the script. They cause discoordinations in interaction, which in turn may lead to disintegration (e.g., confusion and withdrawal), contraction (e.g., by authoritative silencing of some actors or by softer evasion), or expansion, that is, collaborative reframing of the object by moving to cooperation or communication. Expansions may also occur without being triggered by immediately preceding disturbances.

Whereas disturbances are deviations in the observable flow of interaction in the ongoing activity, ruptures are blocks, breaks, or gaps in the intersubjective understanding and flow of information between two or more participants of the activity. Ruptures do not disturb the flow of the work process, although they may often lead to actual disturbances. Ruptures are thus found by interviewing and observing the participants outside of or after the performance of work actions.

Disturbances, ruptures, and expansive transitions are important manifestations of the zone of proximal development of the activity system. But what facilitates expansive transitions? In particular, what kinds of linguistic and other tools are used and invented to initiate and complete them?

Disturbances and Expansions in Court: The Question of Data

Since court proceedings are excessively scripted and well rehearsed, it is often not easy to observe deviations from the normal in court. This is particularly true of trials where the parties are represented by skillful lawyers but is much less so in cases where laypersons are directly involved (for examples of the latter, see Conley & O'Barr, 1990; Engeström, 1996b; Haavisto, 2002; Merry, 1990). In the case analyzed here, the absence of visible deviations became an important problem. The litigating parties were very smooth, polite, and flexible in their interactions. Toward the end of the 2-week trial, I was increasingly worried because no data on disturbances were appearing on videotape.

During the trial, procedural disagreements between the parties are commonly handled by means of so-called sidebars. When one party objects to a move by the other party, either one or the judge will usually call a sidebar conference. These conferences are short breaks in the procedure in which the judge hears the procedural arguments of both parties and makes a ruling on that basis. Sidebars often take place in the courtroom in front of the bench. In our case, they were held in the judge's chambers adjacent to the courtroom. Usually an observer has no chance of hearing or recording the contents of the sidebars.

In the present case, the judge habitually asked the official court reporter to join in the sidebars. This gave me the idea of analyzing the official sidebar transcripts as data on disturbances. Sidebars are indeed disturbances by definition. They break the normal flow of interaction in the courtroom, and the judge is often quite conscious of the fact that they annoy the jurors, who cannot hear or understand what is going on. In this case, sidebars were more than just a necessary evil; the judge used them as a means to maintain and enforce what he saw as teamwork between the attorneys and himself.

To my knowledge, sidebar transcripts have previously not been systematically used as data in studies on court interaction. During this trial, 19 sidebars were held in the presence of the official court reporter. The transcripts of these sidebars are the data analyzed for this chapter. Courtroom transcripts prepared by researchers from videotapes representing phases immediately before and after sidebars differed from the corresponding transcripts prepared by the court reporter only in very minor ways. This indicates a high verbatim accuracy on the part of the court reporter (see, however, the discussion of Walker, 1986, on the myth of the verbatim record). In the excerpts to be presented, I reproduce the official court reporter's transcripts, deleting only names and other identifiable terms and adding necessary contextual information in brackets [ ].

Returning to Coordination by Contraction

The most typical way of dealing with a sidebar in the data consisted of returning to business as usual by means of a quick unilateral decision from the judge. This is exemplified in excerpt 1.

Excerpt 1 from the court records

> [*Direct examination of the plaintiff's witness, Mr. W, by the plaintiff's counsel, Mr. G. Mr. V is one of the two defense counsels*]
>
> *Mr. G:* Mr. W., in – are you personally aware, given your special knowledge, skill, and expertise, of how much it actually costs to move people from their homes and then to move them back into their homes?
>
> *Mr. W:* I am aware of some of the costs, based on what we have done in the past.
>
> *Mr. G:* All right. And based upon your special knowledge and expertise, what has it cost homeowners in the past in condominiums such as D [the name of the complex under litigation]?
>
> *Mr. V:* Same objection, your honor.

Mr. G: It is facts.

Mr. V: The objection wasn't on foundation.

[The judge leads the parties into a sidebar. The following takes place in the judge's chambers without the presence of the jury.]

The judge: Maybe I am not tracking. Now, what is it that you say? There was actual discovery on this?

Mr. G: Oh, yes, your honor. It was in the deposition.

The judge: So, let's go back, then. What was the basis for the objection?

Mr. V: Beyond the scope of the expert designation in the case. There was a motion in limine granted to limit the experts to the scope of the expert witness declaration filed by counsel. Nowhere is Mr. W. designated as an expert on moving costs. He is an expert on costs to repair. He is a general contractor. And this testimony goes beyond the scope of his designation, even if it was disclosed in deposition.

The judge: All right. It is overruled. I will consider the cost of repair. You can proceed.

[The parties return to the courtroom.]

The judge quickly eliminated this disturbance by means of one type of authoritative silencing. He heard the arguments of both parties and then decided in favor of the plaintiff without further discussion.

In spite of the rather straightforward nature of this interaction, certain hesitation and ambivalence may be observed even here. First, the judge seemed to regard the very sidebar as unnecessary: "Maybe I am not tracking." He seemed to be ready to make a unilateral decision right away: "So, let's go back, then." But then he backed up and heard the defense argument. Only afterward did he reconfirm his initial decision.

This pattern of contraction by authoritative silencing was followed in 12 of the 19 sidebars. In every single one of those there were interesting minor ambivalences, implying an emerging fundamental instability in this pattern.

Transitions to Cooperation

There were six sidebars in which an expansive transition from coordination to cooperation (Figure 3.2) took place. Instead of sticking to their assigned roles as adversaries and as an objective authority figure, the parties and the judge embarked upon joint construction of a novel problem and a novel solution. The production of the new in these occasions resembles what

Weick (1979) calls *enactment* and Rittenberg (1985) characterizes as *objectification of situated meaning*. Excerpt 2 gives an example of such an expansive transition.

Excerpt 2 from the court records

[Direct examination of plaintiff's witness, Ms. P, by plaintif's counsel, Mr. G]

Mr. G: Other than the water stain beneath that window on the wall and the water stain in the living room ceiling, are there any other concerns or complaints about the condition of your condominium?

Ms. P: Yes, there are. I also have – Shall I go on?

Mr. G: Yes.

Ms. P: I didn't realize it was a problem, because the fire investigator –

Mr. V: Objection, your honor.

The judge: Sustained. What we are interested is things that you know about rather than what somebody has told you.

Ms. P: I know about it now, though, because –

The judge: I mean, that you observed, you know, yourself, other than something that somebody said. Go ahead, Mr. G. You take over the questioning. [Laughter]

Mr. G: Thank you, your honor.

Ms. P: I don't understand. I am sorry.

Mr. G: What are you talking about? What condition have you seen that you are now concerned about?

Mr. V: Could I have a sidebar for a minute, please?

[The following held in chambers between the judge and counsel.]

Mr. G: I am doing the best I can.

Mr. V: I understand. I think the danger that we are running into now is the area where she is going to testify that a fire investigator – meaning Mr. H, in his volunteer fire department uniform – came into her house and took out her light fixture. That's the testimony that was the subject of a motion in limine –

The judge: All right.

Mr. V: – whether a fireman or a fire investigator determined that her light fixtures were a fire hazard. And that's the testimony that I wanted to avoid before we tried to unring the bell.

The judge: That makes sense. We've already talked about it. Can you – will she avoid that? Will you talk to her about that?

Mr. G: I will whisper in her ear and say, "Don't mention anything about what somebody else said, and don't mention what he was wearing."

Mr. V: If she is talking about Mr. W and the fire investigator in the chimney, I don't have a problem with that. But if we are talking about Mr. H in his fireman's uniform, that's where we have the problem.

The judge: Just spend a minute and lay out to her the fact that she should just avoid referencing Mr. H and what he was dressed in or what he represented himself to be. He already testified. The jury knows. And go from there.

Mr. V: I have no objection if Mr. G leads Ms. P through the testimony.

The judge: Okay. That's thoughtful. She is nervous, so that might help.

Here the counsel and the judge were facing an unexpected problem. Essentially, the witness did not understand a crucial part of the script, namely, the so-called hearsay rule, which prohibits using what others have told as evidence. The sidebar was turned into shared problem solving. This was triggered by the initial disarming utterance of Mr. G: "I am doing the best I can." This unusually personal statement received a sympathetic response from Mr. G's adversary: "I understand." Here the problem was redefined as no longer an issue of contest. It became an issue of finding a mutually acceptable way of coaching or guiding the witness.

The rather striking innovation produced in this episode was that the defense counsel actually suggested that Mr. G should "lead Ms. P through the testimony." In the legal script, "leading a witness" is prohibited just as strictly as using hearsay evidence. Here, however, the parties and the judge all agreed that leading the witness was exactly what had to be done. In other words, to avoid breaking the hearsay rule, another rule had to be broken by joint decision.

Mr. G and the judge, in particular, used the linguistic tools of personalization and familiarization – recourse to everyday language – to achieve this expansive transition. The judge concluded the sidebar using the nonlegal words *thoughtful, nervous,* and *help.*

On the other hand, Mr. V used the metalinguistic tool of reflecting on the preceding discourse: "And that's the testimony that I wanted to avoid before we tried to unring the bell." The judge joined in, reflecting on a longer history of previous discussions: "That makes sense. We've already talked about it."

Perhaps the most sophisticated tool was used by Mr. G when he employed reported speech (Goffman, 1974; Goodwin, 1990; Volosinov, 1971) in a proactive, anticipatory fashion: "I will whisper in her ear and say,

'Don't mention anything about what somebody else said, and don't mention what he was wearing.'"

In the other five sidebars displaying a transition to cooperation, similar tools were used. Excerpt 3 is another example of the effective use of personalization.

Excerpt 3 from the court records

Mr. S: (...) I could be wrong, Bob [addressing Mr. G], and if you have something.

The judge: All right. I am going to allow you to cross on this and if you are correct you'll look fine. If you are not correct...

Mr. S: I'll look silly.

The judge: Then you wouldn't look fine.

In a similar vein, excerpt 4 demonstrates the use of familiarization.

Excerpt 4 from the court records

Mr. G: My thinking is that, in the first five, ten, fifteen minutes that they [the jury] are in there, we can quickly consider those items and get them into them

The judge: Sure.

Mr. G: – while they are still talking about the C's [name of the local baseball team].

Attempts at Reflective Communication

In one of the sidebars, there was a piece of discourse that differed qualitatively from both authoritative silencing and cooperation.

Excerpt 5 from the court records

[Held in the judge's chambers without the presence of the jury.]

The judge: All right. I am going to allow him. But this is the other side of a problem that Mr. S experienced. And you can now – both of you can – so that – the problems it causes, when new figures come in, and by making somebody available the night before at five fifteen really doesn't comply with what I have in mind in terms of the "spirit of cooperation." It might have been the only time that he was available or the time that you were available, but, really, when I – if I make this kind of ruling in the future – what I mean by that, to both counsel, is that you set up a time that's convenient for the other person and really break your backs to get that information.

In this excerpt, the judge was teaching or reminding the attorneys to follow the rules of cooperation. In that sense, the script itself as well as the interaction of the participants became the foci of attention. These are hallmarks of reflective communication (recall Figure 3.3). Yet, there was something peculiarly noncommunicative in the discourse. The judge was, in effect, presenting a monologue to which the attorneys did not respond in any noticeable way. The content was reflective communication; the form was noncommunication.

When the judge referred to the "spirit of cooperation," he was not just talking about a general principle. He was referring to the contents of an issues conference, a special meeting he had with the attorneys immediately before the trial. This meeting was actually a tool with which the judge attempted to achieve reflective communication between himself and the parties of the trial.

The delay reduction program officially adopted by the court introduced a mandatory disposition conference to be held in good time before the trial. The issues conference, however, was the judge's own invention. In his interview, he characterized these two conferences as follows:

> *The judge:* The delay reduction program really is generated by the control of the case from the very first time that it's filed and answered, with mandatory deadlines for certain things to happen. And about two months before trial, the final thing before trial is the disposition conference. And they have to prepare a joint document, both sides or all sides, listing all their witnesses, all the issues they say are still unresolved, instructions, things that were unheard of to do ahead of time. Back when I still was practicing, you never knew who the other side's witnesses even were, and now you know two months ahead of time.
>
> *Interviewer:* Did you have a disposition conference in this case?
>
> *The judge:* No, because I had the case managed so that I told them to file their witness list and things, they did it on an informal basis.
>
> *Interviewer:* So you didn't have to have it all at once in writing?
>
> *The judge:* Exactly. And they were working well enough together so I didn't require them to file this formal disposition conference document that requires both their signatures. But that funnel-shaped item is a reduction with dates and fines, money fines, sanctions, if you don't live up to them. Very negative.
>
> *Interviewer:* Now the issues conference, that is really your own tool. How is that related to the disposition conference?

The judge: That disposition conference, that's a formal document. And I take the disposition conference report, and I say, okay, this is what you've said, but now we're right down to trial, and what is the reality of this?

Interviewer: So the issues conference is really about the trial in actual practice?

The judge: Right, exactly. And we are going to trial on this. They've been sent out – Every case, two months ahead of time, files a disposition report, conference report. But not every case goes down to trial. And these people actually are, they show up at my doorstep, supposedly ready for trial. Now, because I'm usually in trial, I'm not ready for 'em that day. So I'll have an issues conference for them, which says, now you've said you're ready for trial, but let's make sure we are.

(...)

The judge: I mean, we talked over some potential things. It gets timelines set up and gets when people expect things to happen, and gets 'em in the frame of mind that I want them in when they try a case here.

(...)

Interviewer: Did you invent that or did you learn it from somebody else?

The judge: No, I invented it because I found that I was talking about the same things with these people in front of me, the same time, so I just started keeping a list and then I'd add something. Then I made the list, then I typed it out. Then I put, y'know, it just grew, just one of those things that grew. But it's helpful.

The list to which the judge was referring was an artifact created by him to sustain and consolidate the innovation. It was his standard agenda for an issues conference. It contained 17 items. The last item was simply "Work together." According to the judge, one of the aims of the issues conference was to make sure that the parties would focus on the essential questions in the case, not confusing the jury by digressing to insignificant details. Another aim was to reduce the anxiety of the parties, to get them to collaborate and interact. These aims emphasize the judge's intention to achieve reflective communication between adversaries in the process of complex litigation.

I tape-recorded the 2-hour issues conference preceding the case. A couple of examples will make it clear that the contents of the conference corresponded to the agenda.

On the quality of interaction:

The judge: Ah, so, I just want you to understand that I don't, I don't want me, er, to sound like I'm lecturing you but that is a real important thing, as I sit here, that I wasn't as sensitive to, ah, when I was sitting where you are. So I am now, and that will be a lot of my, my feeling as to keep the jury, ah, respectful of the process. It's real important. Now, with that in mind, it's the philosophy I want between you two, and I say two because of the size, I don't know who will be trying the case, is that I want you to assist each other in putting your cases on. The time for gamesmanship, or trial by ambush or, ah, tactics that make the other attorney look bad, ah, are over, as far as I'm concerned. So, when – when Mr. G, when your witnesses are going on, on Monday afternoon, or Tuesday, ah, I want you to tell Mr. S who they are going to be, and about how long they'll take. I'll direct, Mr. S I want you to do exactly the same thing. Everything in this courtroom applies both ways, so, eh, when your case is on I want you to cooperate with each other.

On the mutual definition of the object:

The judge: (...) Ah, take a look at his verdict form. The only reason that I want, and I want you, if there's something dreadfully wrong with it or if it doesn't, or if it isn't this case that we're trying, then I want you to prepare a verdict form that you think reflects the case. The reason is simple. PM [name of another judge] was talking about this early, about a year and a half ago when I first started. And I thought it was ludicrous until I had about twenty trials where at the last day of trial nobody could agree on the verdict form because they had been trying, essentially, a different case. They said, "Well, gee, we, we didn't present any evidence on these elements here, you know, because we thought we were trying this case over here." And this is the last day of trial. Then what will I do? Well I've learned if, if you at least show each other the verdict form early in the case, ah, if there's a great deal of difference then, ah, let me know. I mean, I'll look at them both and it will give me an idea anyway. At least I know that you agree on what elements of each, ah, cause of action. (...) Ah, I don't care if you agree at this point. I just want you to have exchanged one. Or if you're satisfied with the one that's produced, fine. We're trying the same lawsuit. You don't have to agree to individual language. But you know what I'm talking about.

Mr. G: Yes, sir.

The judge effectively used reported speech, among other means, as a tool to convince the attorneys. Yet, there was no interaction except the mandatory "yes, sir" from one of the attorneys. In the issues conference, the attorneys took the initiative and talked actively only about matters requiring technical coordination for the trial. In other words, the communicative contents were all but nullified by the noncommunicative form of the discussion.

What may have been the reason for this? Obviously, it may have been the judge's habitual dominating or lecturing style that precluded interaction. But the attorneys were experienced and not at all timid. They could have responded more actively if they wanted to do so.

A more plausible explanation is found in the posttrial interviews of the attorneys. First, the plaintiff's side:

> *Interviewer:* He [the judge] also uses what he calls the issues conference just before the trial. We were actually present when that took place on Friday just before the trial. And, I was wondering, did you find it useful? First of all, is that a common procedure?

> *Mr. G:* Oh, it's usually that it's a month before the trial. Three weeks to a month. And it is important to do that three weeks to a month, from both parties' point of view. And I was critical of the judge for having and holding that issues conference so soon before trial. Things occurred in trial. Now, it was a very efficiently run trial and it went fast. But there were several sidebars there that occurred that wouldn't have occurred had they been talked about in the issues conference. We also call it a "disposition conference," the terms are used interchangeably. And, you talk about the law. Like, what's the law here? [laughs] What are you going to tell the jury the law is? And, let's rule on the admissibility of some of these exhibits before we go and prepare them or blow them up.

Then the defense's side:

> *Interviewer:* There is a particular situation where we were actually present. And that was what he [the judge] calls the issues conference, which was just the last Friday before the actual trial. And it seemed to be somewhat of an invention of the judge. He has this list of things that he went through. What did you think about it, was that useful or sensible?

> *Mr. S:* Actually it's very useful and that's one of the new things that our court system has, it's called "the fast track." And this is part of the fast track procedures. The idea is that we're gonna have this issues conference, usually that occurs about a month before trial, to

sit down and make the attorneys have this case ready for trial a month beforehand. So that when the trial comes, we can get it done a lot more quickly and efficiently. They tell you, you determine what evidence is gonna come in, what witnesses are gonna be there, work out all your problems, come with a list of what the exhibits are, and basically you're ready to go with trial and it's gonna go smoothly on this game plan.

Interviewer: This time you had it just before the trial.

Mr. V: Because the subs [the subcontractors] were still in.

Mr. S: It was all because the subs were still in and he didn't want to have it until he made a decision as to whether or not the subs were gonna get out. Because if the subs were involved, it would have been much more complicated.

Interviewer: Did you feel it was problematic so close to the actual trial date?

Mr. S: We didn't. The plaintiff did.

So, both attorneys confused the issues conference with the disposition conference. This is something the judge explicitly rejected in his interview cited previously, emphatically pointing out the crucial difference between the two conferences. Somehow the judge's entire innovation was misunderstood by the litigating attorneys. This is a prime example of a rupture that effectively prevents an expansive transition from being realized. One wonders what would have happened had the judge prepared the attorneys by simply telling them the same things about the issues conference that he told the researcher in the interview.

The Invisible Battleground

The data just presented describe the zone of proximal development as an invisible battleground. In the ongoing work activity, disturbances occurred continuously. They were dealt with both regressively and expansively. Innovative solutions appeared. But innovations were occasionally blocked by lack of appropriate communicative tools, causing ruptures in the intersubjective understanding between the participants of the activity system.

What kind of team was formed by the attorneys and the judge? In light of the historical types of teamwork summarized in Figure 1.2, this was a hybrid, or transitional, team.

The basic institutional framework of the trial was hierarchical, standardized mass production. But the judge was a strong proponent of the delay reduction program and the so-called independent calendar adopted as reform programs by the court. Both reforms were aimed at achieving streamlined, cost-effective case management or movement toward market-oriented mass production. However, the judge's attempt to achieve reflective communication by means of the issues conference went beyond those top-down programs. It was an example of a bottom-up innovation aimed at informal and dialogical teamwork, ready and willing to modify the rules and standards situationally in the interest of reaching mutually acceptable solutions (for another example of this, see Engeström, 1996b). The persistent lecturing style in the judge's approach to the attorneys represents the strong tradition of autonomous craft, dominated by the personal characteristics and authority of the individual master practitioner.

The fact that all four models, or developmental options, of court work were relatively openly displayed and allowed to clash may explain why interesting expansive transitions and attempts to innovate took place. On the other hand, the fact that there were no conceptual and communicative tools to articulate these models and to bring them into dialogue at a meta level may account for the activity system's failure to achieve reflective communication in any sustained sense.

Yet, it is important to note that the expansive transitions found in the sidebars could not have been achieved by the judge alone. To the contrary, excerpt 2 is a good example of a transition in which the innovation emerged through an effort fairly equally distributed between the two attorneys and the judge. What was missing was conscious and articulated input from the lay clients. While such active client participation may represent the far end of the current zone of proximal development in court work, it is entirely possible, as shown by Haavisto (2002).

4 Displacement and Innovation in Primary Care Medical Teams

The television production team and the court trial team, analyzed in Chapters 2 and 3, respectively, are examples of teams that were not specifically designed as teams, based on some explicit theory or form of team organization. In the court case, the judge attempted to design the teamwork, but this attempt was not based on an articulated theory or framework. In both the television team and the court team, this absence of deliberate design also meant that the teams had created few if any tools to enhance collaboration and reflection. This instrumental poverty seemed to account for many of the difficulties in the work of those teams.

In this chapter, I analyze health care teams that were deliberately designed as new forms of organizing work. Will such teams develop and use specific tools to facilitate their collaboration and collective reflection? How do such tools interact with the objects of work that the teams try to formulate and accomplish? And what is the role of scripts in the work of such teams? In sum, how does a new team construct its own practices, its *modus operandi*?

Complex clinical procedures such as demanding surgeries have always required collaborative teamwork. However, in such operative medical teams there is usually a very clear vertical command structure and a predetermined division of labor that make the team more like a commando task force dedicated to a single purpose than a general-purpose method of organizing cooperative work and enhancing horizontal exchange of information across potential boundaries. Ideas and solutions of the latter type are fairly recent in health care.

Multiprofessional health care teams have been increasingly used and written about since the late 1960s (e.g., Beloff & Willet, 1968; Horwitz, 1970; Lashof, 1968). One of the pioneering texts was Alberta Parker's (1972) monograph *The Team Approach to Primary Health Care*. Parker (p. 10) listed five characteristics of a functioning primary care team: (1) team members provide care to a common group of patients; (2) team members develop common goals for the patient outcome and work to reach these goals; (3) appropriate roles and functions are assigned to and accepted by each team member; (4) the team possesses a mechanism that enables all members to contribute and share information essential for effective patient care; (5) the team possesses a mechanism to ensure that patient care plans are implemented, services are coordinated, activities are administered, and the performance of the team is evaluated.

In practice, health care teams are commonly confronted with difficulties that stem from the strong traditions of craft professionalism and bureaucracy. As Tichy (1977, p. 7) noted, the health teams' "internal structure often has tended to replicate that of the hospital hierarchy." Similarly, Bruce (1980, p. 165) pointed out that "cooperation between professionals has not been found to result automatically either from physical proximity or from being involved with the same client."

Health care teams and their operating contexts are special in at least three respects. First, health care teams are often comprised of members of professions with very different training, ideology, and status and with a tradition of more or less open tensions between them. Second, health care institutions – at least the larger ones – have traditionally been very centralized and dominated by strong autocratic leaders, by physicians and increasingly by professional business managers. Third, frontline health care teams deal with clients who can decide whether they will or will not follow the recommendations of the professionals; thus, the success of the team is dependent on the involvement and cooperation of the patient, which makes the client something of a coproducer of the services.

In the following, I will present data from two examples of health care team interactions recorded in Finland. I will analyze the examples, using and developing further the conceptual framework of coordination, cooperation, and communication presented in Chapter 3. The first example is a meeting between an elderly client and two collaborating home-care professionals in the client's home; the meeting is subsequently discussed and evaluated by a newly created multiprofessional primary care team responsible for the patient. The second example is a meeting of a primary health care team discussing a source of tension between the clinic and the laboratory.

In order to understand the cases, the reader should know that since 1972, every Finnish municipality is required by law to organize a health center that offers comprehensive primary health care services to the inhabitants for a modest fixed fee or free of charge. Health center personnel work in clinics (called *health stations*) as well as in schools and preventive guidance clinics. In the late 1980s and early 1990s, many Finnish health centers launched multiprofessional teams responsible for assigned geographical areas and subpopulations as their emerging organizational mode of operation.

Refining the Conceptual Framework

Deborah Ancona's studies suggest how teams may formulate a new, expanded conception of the objects of their work. Ancona (1991) found three different strategies teams developed for their environment: *informing, parading,* and *probing.* The informing teams had a primary goal of creating an enthusiastic team with open communication among members – but with a low level of interaction with clients. The parading teams wanted to obtain visibility among clients or within the organization. Finally, the probing teams opted for high levels of two-way communication with the external environment. They emphasized diagnosis of the clients' needs and feedback on team ideas:

> They did not use existing member knowledge alone to map their external environment; members were encouraged to take on new perspectives and bring in new data. These teams had the highest level of external contact, were aggressive not only in testing potential interventions but also in actually implementing new programs, and convinced people in both the field and top management that they were doing a good job. (Ancona, 1991, pp. 7–8)

Permanent teams, with their meetings and internal dynamics, have a strong tendency to turn inward and encapsulate themselves. In this process they often substitute for their objects in the outside world *pseudo-objects*, or layers of talk, artifacts, and busywork that function as blankets covering and muffling the objects. The probing strategy counteracts this tendency. Such a strategy seems to be a crucial precondition if teams are to constitute active nodes in a network. In activity-theoretical terms, the probing strategy aims at constant reconceptualization and expansion of the object of activity. The object is not seen as consisting of separate fixed tasks or items to be acted upon in a one-way manner. The object is viewed as interconnected tasks embedded in their respective activity systems that have to be understood and interacted with.

Ancona points out that the three strategies imply different modes of learning:

> Informing is similar to learning about the outside world through contemplation; if you leave us alone to think and discuss, we will tell you what you need when we have figured it out. Parading is similar to learning through observation. The message here is that we want to watch you, to understand you, and to let you know that we are around to respond to your needs. Finally, probing (. . .) occurs through experimentation, trying out a new idea and seeing the reaction, making an intervention and evaluating the result. (Ancona, 1991, p. 9)

As pointed out in Chapter 3, disturbances are of central importance as potential triggers of qualitative transitions in team interaction. Disturbances in interaction are typically discoordinations or conflicts between participants' different voices that draw on different social languages (see Bakhtin, 1982; R. Engeström, 1995; Wertsch, 1991). The Bakhtinian concept of *voice* should be distinguished from the generic notion of *perspective* (e.g., Holland & Reeves, 1996). Perspectives typically refer to points of view defined by social position or ideological standpoint. Voice, on the other hand, refers to the speaking subject's action of addressing an utterance to an interlocutor. Voices draw on historically evolving social languages but are not reducible to them. A voice always contains the creative moment of constructing meaning in a unique situation.

Innovations are more or less intentional attempts by some or all of the participants to go beyond the given standard script in order to find a more meaningful way of interacting and conceptualizing the object of interaction. Innovations may or may not succeed and become objectified, that is, consolidated in the form of explicit new tools, symbols, or shared procedures (Rittenberg, 1985). An innovation may lead to an expansion, a qualitative transformation of the object of the activity. In Chapter 3, expansions were analyzed as transitions from coordination to cooperation and reflective communication. Both disturbances and innovations may be interpreted as indications of the zone of proximal development of the activity system (Engeström, 1987).

Within this conceptual framework, the notion of *script* deserves further attention. Scripts evolve historically to codify and regulate standard procedures in repeatedly occurring cultural situations. Although the script may be available in an explicit form (e.g., as a written formula, rule, or agenda), the participants in a scripted event are seldom fully aware of the script they are following. The script has an algorithmic, stepwise character, dictating the sequence of events from beginning to end. The script also has the function of distributing roles and defining more or less clearly the scope and character of input expected from each role. This social and artifactual notion of script should be distinguished from predominantly mental and individual notions, such as that of Schank and Abelson (1977).

Due to its rulelike character, the script is a peculiar cultural artifact. In the present context, I will distinguish between the script and other artifacts that play predominantly a toollike instrumental role. Artifacts used as tools are important mediators of organizational cognition (e.g., Gagliardi, 1990; Norman, 1993; Schrage, 1990). The form and contents of spoken interaction in group meetings may be strongly dependent on the external artifacts used by the participants before and during the meeting (Virkkunen, 1991). On the other hand, it must be emphasized that the role of an artifact in a living activity system is in constant flux; what is now a tool may soon be an object or a rule (Engeström, 1990 [chapter 8], 1996b). Especially complex tools often tend to take on a life of their own, becoming substitute objects and ends in themselves (Engeström & Escalante, 1996; Hasu & Engeström, 2000).

Case 1: The Old Woman and the Practitioners, or How the Tool Displaced the Object

Health centers and municipal social welfare agencies offer partially over-lapping services in Finland, typically to clients such as the elderly, families with small children, and alcoholics. To coordinate services and avoid excessive use of resources, the two institutions are trying out various forms of joint teamwork in many municipalities.

In Case 1, such a form of teamwork was being developed to provide home health care for the elderly (a function of the health center) and home services for the elderly (a function of the social welfare services). The former delivers medical services to old people living at home and suffering from chronic illnesses. The latter delivers services such as cooking, cleaning, shopping, and often making sure that the clients are taking their prescribed medications. The former services are typically delivered by home nurses or health visitors who visit the home usually once a week. The latter services are delivered by home service assistants who may visit the home on a daily basis. Home nurses or health visitors are trained nurses, medically supervised by physicians. Home service assistants don't necessarily have any special training for their job. They are supervised by a home service supervisor, usually trained as a social worker.

In this particular city, the health care and social welfare services were integrated administratively. But at the level of daily work, they remained relatively separate. The two branches decided to start ground-level team collaboration by sending home nurses and home service assistants together to their patients in order to create a shared care plan for each patient. The care plan was a structured document initially developed and used by nurses in the health sector.

In this case, the patient was an 80-year-old woman. Although mentally and verbally quite alert, she had difficulty moving around. The home service assistant visited her daily. The home nurse visited her approximately once a week. She was generally cosidered a difficult patient by the practitioners.

The conversations that occurred between the home nurse (called the *nurse* for short), the home service assistant (called the *assistant* for short), and the patient (called *Alma* in the conversation) during this visit were tape-recorded by another employee of the health center. She was otherwise not directly involved in the work of either practitioner. The following excerpts illustrate the structure of interaction during this visit.

In excerpt 1, the participants had been discussing the patient's various medications and related symptoms.

Excerpt 1

01 *Patient:* Dr. A gave me O [name of a tranquilizer], and I took two pills a night. One nurse almost got a stroke when she saw it. So one would be enough, not more in any case. Then it was reduced.

02 *Nurse:* Perhaps that, anyway. Are you writing these down for yousef? [to the assistant]

03 *Assistant:* Yes.

04 *Nurse:* And that tranquilizer thing. It could be her problem, using tranquilizers. Now it's not, if she wouldn't use those . . .

05 *Patient:* [speaking over the nurse] I had such a terrible pain on Saturday, such a hard pain.

06 *Nurse:* Should we write down that she likes to take extra pills of O, grown fond of O [name of the tranquilizer]?

07 *Assistant:* Hm. I'll make a clean copy of this, then.

[*Short pause; both professionals read their versions of the care plan.*]

In this excerpt, the patient initiated dicussion on tranquilizers and said that her prescribed dose had been reduced. The nurse picked up the topic and stated that the patient had a problem of excessive use of tranquilizers – an interpretation not at all in line with what the patient said. The practitioners then proceeded to formulate a statement about the patient's tendency toward excessive use in their care plan document, ignoring the patient's remark about a terrible pain (turn 05 in excerpt 1).

Excerpt 2

01 *Nurse:* Then there's the functioning of the stomach. It's one... probably the biggest one.

02 *Assistant:* Yes.

03 *Nurse:* And for that we have this trip notebook?

04 *Assistant:* Yes, there's again in it, I guess, yeah, I guess, from the weekend. [She is referring to a trip notebook in which all the home service staff who visit the patient are supposed to enter their notes concerning the visit; during the weekend, home service staff other than the regular assistant have visited the patient]

05 *Assistant:* On Friday I wrote down...

06 *Nurse:* Which Friday, this?

07 *Assistant:* Yes. I wrote down kind of... about the whole week.

08 *Nurse:* Yes.

09 *Nurse:* The stomach has been constipated again.

10 *Assistant:* I wonder if Saturday's visitor has even read this?

11 *Nurse:* Yes.

12 *Assistant:* Probably not... Hm, I was thinking [lowering her voice] if Alma has told...?

13 *Nurse:* Just so.

14 *Assistant:* Since this has been all week now.

15 *Nurse:* Yes, the last time I looked at the trip notebook it said the stomach has funcioned well.

16 *Patient:* Don't I have something to say about my own care?

17 *Nurse:* [raising her voice] Yes, of course.

18 *Patient:* It can't be dictated by others, can it? According to the existing law...

19 *Nurse:* We are just checking, checking out the functioning of the stomach.

20 *Patient:* According to the existing law.

21 *Nurse:* Yes, we are only looking into the functioning of that stomach, because...

22 *Patient:* All the time I feel like my bowels were moving, but nothing comes.

23 *Nurse:* Yes.

24 *Patient:* It is . . .

25 *Nurse:* Well, according to this trip notebook, however, the stomach is functioning.

26 *Patient:* It contracts and contracts, the muscle, but only very thin stuff comes out . . .

27 *Nurse:* [speaking over the patient] But according to this notebook, the stomach functions anyway . . . every day [lowering her voice toward the end].

In excerpt 2, the patient interrupted and confronted the practitioners, forcefully demanding their attention (turns 16, 18, and 20). The patient claimed that her stomach did not function. The nurse responded by referring to the trip notebook, a traditional informal record kept by the practitioners of their visits to the patient's home. According to the trip notebook, the patient's stomach had functioned every day during the week. An absurd situation emerged in which the professionals considered their notebook contents to be evidence against the patient's claim about her own bodily functions.

These excerpts are representative of a long series of confrontations during the visit. All followed the same basic pattern, with variations in contents and in degrees of aggravation.

The structure of this sequence of interaction may be interpreted as follows. The practitioners were interacting with each other quite intensively. Their script was engraved in the structure of the care plan document. They focused on the construction of a shared care plan for the patient. In this sense, their interaction appeared to be genuine cooperation. However, the care plan effectively muffled the voice of the patient. It was, in effect, a substitute object that displaced the patient as object and thus prevented the professionals from focusing on the patient as the subject of her own life activity. In other words, the interaction had the structure of pseudo-cooperation.

The practitioners used the trip notebook as a mediating artifact from which they gleaned information for the construction of the care plan. The trip notebook was used as an evidentiary or argumentative artifact to prove that the patient's stomach had actually been functioning, no matter what the patient said. The practitioners "owned" the trip notebook, whereas the

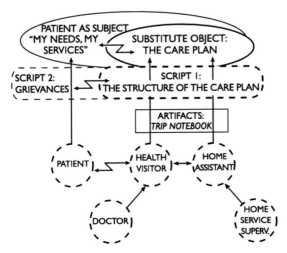

Figure 4.1. The structure of discoordinated pseudo-cooperation in Case 1.

patient was excluded from using it. The trip notebook could well have been used as a means of discussing the patient's needs; now it was restrictively subordinated to the peparation of the care plan. The text served another text. With regard to its epistemic function, the trip notebook was used as a "what" artifact, helping to identify and classify "facts" about the patient (Engeström, 1990).

The structure of the pseudo-cooperation in this episode was complicated by the active presence of the patient. She had her own object: her felt needs, her desire to be acknowledged as a subject of her own. She was following a grievance script, taking up a long string of problems and needs, one at a time – and thus disturbing time and again the professionals' agenda of constructing an appropriate care plan document. This tension took the form of repeated discoordinations, ranging from occasions where the practitioners ignored what the patient said to occasions of open confrontation.

This complex structure of pseudo-cooperation and simultaneously extremely discoordinated interaction is schematically depicted in Figure 4.1. Two-headed lightning-shaped arrows stand for tension and conflict in the interaction.

This case demonstrates how the care plan that originally was supposed to function as a shared tool was turned into a monstrous caricature, a pseudo-object that dictated the interaction of the professionals instead of helping them to interact with the patient. Such displacement is not uncommon (Engeström & Escalante, 1996; Hasu & Engeström, 2000). The case also demonstrates how helpless team members can be when faced with a demanding client – a live object from the outside world. The discoordinations did not lead to innovations and expansive transitions. They were met with various forms of evasion.

The health center where Alma's case was recorded was one of the participants in a large interventionist research project, and much of the collection of field data was organized by a local project group. After the recording and transcription of the encounter in Alma's home, members of the local project group interviewed the practitioners involved in Alma's care (including Alma's physician). The group conducted some preliminary analyses of the encounter and the interview transcripts, using the human activity system model as a conceptual framework (see Figure 2.1). A member of my research group analyzed the interview transcripts, using and developing a version of the explanatory models approach (Helman, 1985; Kleinman, 1980) as an intermediate instrument. Provisional outcomes and tools of this analysis were presented to the local project group.

The local project group organized a series of meetings at the health center where Alma's case was used to initiate discussion and analysis of problems and prospects in multiprofessional teamwork. The first of these meetings demonstrates well the problems of emerging team interaction.

The meeting was attended by three members of the local project group: a psychologist (P), a day-care supervisor (DS), and a social worker (SW). The other participants included two health center physicians (HP1 and HP2, neither one the doctor in charge of Alma's home care at the time of the recorded visit), the home service assistant (HSA) who participated in the original encounter with Alma, and the home care nurse (N) who also participated in that encounter. Members of the project group used a graphic triangle model (Figure 2.1) as a conceptual tool in the meeting. Transcripts of the original encounter with Alma and of the interviews had been given to the participants before the meeting, and they were at hand during the meeting.

The organizational identity and purpose of the meeting were not clear. At the time of the meeting, two multiprofessional teams, each responsible for providing services to the population of a given geographical area, were taking their first shaky steps toward functioning as semiautonomous work teams. The two physicians and the home care nurse were members of the same team. However, the team consisted of some 20 members, so the meeting was definitely not a regular team meeting.

The meeting lasted slightly more than 90 min. It was tape-recorded by the participants. The discussion may be divided into phases as follows:

1. Complaints and apologies about the appearance of practitioners' names in the transcripts
2. General review of the project and its key concepts: what kinds of analyses had been done, the importance of the concept of contradiction
3. Day care as an example of a setting where the concepts could be useful
4. General discussion of Alma's case, its components and its possible contradictions, without focusing on any particular aspect or the specific contents of transcripts
5. General discussion of changes in the work activity of the various practitioners
6. General discussion of Alma's case, its components and its possible contradictions, without focusing on any particular aspect or going into concrete contents of transcripts
7. *Discussion focused on the contradiction between the proclaimed desire to turn clients into subjects and the actual discomfort with active clients*
8. General discussion of professionalism, authority, and collaboration across professions
9. *Discussion focused on the use of the home service assistant as an instrument to cope with Alma's alleged psychic problems*
10. *Attempt to analyze Alma as a troublesome case*
11. *Discussion focused on the collaborative use of the care plan and on Alma's role in determining the goals of her care*
12. *Discussion focused on Alma's dependency on medications and her ways of fooling the practitioners*
13. *Discussion focused on the collaboration between practitioners dealing with Alma and the trip notebook as their instrument*
14. Assurances that this kind of analysis is not aimed at finding better solutions and that all participants have learned something

In the list of the phases, those focusing on specific contents of Alma's case are printed in italics. Notice that none of the first six phases, which took well over half of the meeting time, dealt with such concrete, particular issues. The participants at the meeting had a strong tendency to avoid or gloss over the issues considered crucial by the patient. Phases 1 to 6, and subsequently phases 8 and 14, may be interpreted as a multilayered muffler or blanket constructed to cover the core object.

There were three layers in this muffler or blanket. First, there were specific side issues or diversions, such as complaints about the appearance of real names in transcripts or examples from other fields (phases 1 and 3). Second, there were generalities that kept the discussion at an abstract level (phases 2, 4 to 6, and 8). Finally, there were meta-discussions of "what we are trying and/or not trying to do." Phase 14 is the prime example, but phase 2 also has this characteristic.

The phases where specific contents of Alma's case were actually discussed were relatively brief but very interesting. Excerpt 3 is from phase 6.

Excerpt 3
Phase 7

01 *HSA:* When I read this, I thought that we are not changing Alma much here. [participants laugh] Alma makes her own decisions and choices, passing over and under us.

02 *HP1:* Is that self-management of the client, then?

03 *SW:* Not yielding to become an object.

04 *HP2:* Alma is troublesome as a subject, so she should be kept as an object. [laughter]

05 *DS:* Yes, doesn't Alma become a bit troublesome when she changes into a subject? Isn't it quite an interesting contradiction? I mean, haven't we got actual documents, in social work for example, and in all person-to-person work, stating that the client is to be activated?

06 *HP2:* To be made self-reliant.

07 *DS:* Self-reliant, and this self-management of the client. I think there are countless examples from day care, from social work . . .

08 *HP1:* From anywhere . . .

09 *DS:* From anywhere, that when the client changes, starts to use active tools of her own, she becomes troublesome, because we don't have instruments with which to work. Our old tools don't necessarily function anymore.

Here the discussion reached a crucial question: the adequacy of the tools used by the practitioners. Instead of being pursued, the issue somehow evaporated.

Excerpt 4
[short pause]

10 *HP2:* Or if we think of different patients, a patient who is very active needs only information from the doctor so that he can make choices himself. Then the doctor is that kind of a tool.

11 *HP1:* Is that a troublesome patient?

12 *HP2:* No. One must only treat different patients in different ways. There are patients for whom one is like a shaman . . .

13 *N:* Yes, but in Alma's case Alma will change the doctor. [general laughter]

As phase 7 demonstrates, the participants used the concepts of subject, object, and tool as analytical devices. However, the actual transcripts were not quoted, not even discussed so that a specific phase or turn would have been referred to. This fluent use of general conceptual instruments and simultaneous neglect or avoidance of concrete transcripts as specific instruments became repeatedly manifest throughout the transcript.

Excerpt 5
Phase 10

01 *P:* We could think about what could be an analysis of such so-called trouble. We could go back to the first picture [triangle model of activity]. Perhaps we could approach the trouble by putting Alma where she now is, that is, into the subject's place. And the object could be Alma's life, from Alma's point of view.

02 *DS:* But just a while ago we said that if Alma is the subject, she is troublesome.

03 *HP2:* That's right.

04 *P:* Mm.

05 *DS:* Because Alma, didn't it come up . . .

06 *HP1:* . . . Or is it up to us, that when someone who we think should be an object becomes a subject, we experience her as trouble? Does Alma herself experience herself as trouble? [pause, then laughter]

07 *P:* Yes, that's something we should ask . . .

Again, the analysis evaporated without producing concrete results or conclusions. This lack of conclusions and solutions makes the discussion look somewhat like an end in itself. The discussion appeared as an instrument and an outcome of the project group rather than an effort to create an agentic subject of transformation. At the end of the meeting, members of the local project group expressed this attitude rather emphatically.

Excerpt 6
Phase 14

01 *DS:* Have you got an impression that this whole Alma case is done in order to find a better model for working with Alma? Because we haven't thought about it that way. The more we find out about Alma, the humbler

we become in relation to your work. Somehow I just want to say that we in the project group, we haven't found any new...

02 *SW:* No solutions, no...

03 *DS:* No solutions. The whole approach is such that we are not looking for solutions but just that we together begin to investigate what can be found in this kind of a complex work situation.

04 *HSA:* For my part, as a practitioner I don't expect anything but to get through the day. I will now go and have a weekend break... [laughter]... Somehow old and new things. I myself don't even expect more than to get from one day to another.

05 *DS:* I only thought that if you as practitioners feel that we in the project group presume that we can from the outside invent something better than you can. We don't presume anything like that...

06 *SW:* Yes.

07 *DS:* To the contrary, we've only found more new questions.

08 *SW:* Yes, no solution. And we didn't actually think that was needed, nor possible for us.

Interestingly enough, members of the local project group seemed so busy ensuring that no solutions were sought that they ignored the home service assistant's acknowledgment that she only wanted to get from one day to the next.

The participants were given the transcripts, which were to be used as a mirror for critical self-reflection. The transcripts were at hand, but the participants never quoted them or went into their detailed contents. In other words, they did not take a collective look at the mirror. No intermediate concepts were used in the discussion to analyze the transcripts. These factors, together with the vague organizational identity and responsibility of the group, probably explain the appearance of the multilayered muffler or blanket around the core issues as well as the lack of concrete outcomes from the meeting.

Case 2: The Team and the Hierarchy

My second example is taken from a joint meeting of two teams set up at a primary care health station. The teams had been functioning for 2 years. They consisted of the personnel responsible for treating ill patients in consultations at the station and in home care. Each team comprised four physicians, two assistant nurses, a nurse working at the station, and home care personnel who were mainly in the field and usually were represented by one or two home nurses in team meetings. Each team was responsible for a given subpopulation and the corresponding geographical area. The teams did not have fixed leaders. All team members, regardless of profession, took turns as coordinators. The teams met separately once a week. Once a month they had a joint meeting.

The teams were founded on the principle of population responsibility, meaning that each team had its designated population to care for. Initiated and designed by the local practitioners themselves, the teams demanded autonomy and self-initiative in decisions concerning their own work. But there were other entities in this health center that were not organized on the basis of population responsibility. At this fairly small station, the laboratory was one such entity. It was supervised by a head nurse in charge of the laboratory sector and located at the central board of health in the administrative center of this relatively large city. There was a history of tension between the teams and the laboratory, as well as between the teams and the traditional sectorally organized administration in general.

The meeting took place in September. The past summer, the central administration had closed the laboratory in order to save money. There was a strong possibility that the head nurse in charge of the laboratory sector would propose closing that laboratory permanently. The closings did not threaten the jobs of the lab personnel; they would be transfered to a bigger station with a bigger lab.

In the meeting, the teams discussed the closing. They had prepared a draft letter to the central administration demanding that the laboratory remain open. Fifteen team members, two representatives of the laboratory, and the chief physician of the district where the station was located participated in the meeting.

The following statement by a home nurse was typical of the turns taken by the team members in the discussion.

Excerpt 7

01 *Home nurse:* Well, for home care, at least, during the summer we had such a situation that we had summer substitutes, and they are usually students. And they don't necessarily even know how to take laboratory samples. Their skill with the needle is so meager that taking samples doesn't work. So the samples had to be taken by the few permanent home nurses. And the number of samples to be taken is the same as usual, even more in the past summer. Some of the patients refused to go to L [the next, bigger station that had a functioning laboratory]. They have the strength to come to our station, but to L they need to take a taxi, or it's otherwise such an unfamiliar, frightening, big place where they don't find their way

to the laboratory, particularly the elderly patients. So their opinion was that they cannot go to have lab samples taken in L. So we had to take them, so we nurses had a very busy summer, indeed. And we used quite a lot of our precious time for driving those samples to L for analysis. And there's one more point, namely, that particularly serum samples are so sensitive that they are easily spoiled in the car, being transported from one place to another. In the lab the sample can be immediately stored in an appropriate place. But when they are driven around in car in the hot summer weather...

After this statement, other related issues were discussed for about 5 min. During that time, the chief physician expressed her support for the teams in their effort to secure the continuing laboatory services at their station. However, she advised them to formulate their letter so that the central administration could not find any counterarguments in it. After this, the following exchange took place.

Excerpt 8

01 *Team physician:* I think it's noteworthy that samples are getting spoiled. They must be redone several times. It costs money. On the other hand, the patient has to come to tests several times. And she may come to consultation to ask for results, but the sample has been spoiled again.

02 *Lab nurse:* Well, lab samples do not get spoiled in car transportation. Our samples make a long tour in a taxi...

03 *Home nurse:* Ah, yes...

04 *Lab nurse:* ...and there are containers for cold transportation. Samples do not get spoiled in a car. If they are spoiled, it happens already when they are taken.

05 *Team physician:* Maybe they were spoiled because of these inexperienced summer substitutes. But that's the same...

06 *Chief physician:* ... Since there was no lab personnel to take those samples. It does require professional skill, doesn't it?

07 *Lab nurse:* Well, sure, professional skill. But in transport they won't get spoiled. That's what I wanted to point out.

This sequence was typical of the structure of interaction. The team members testified that the closing of the lab had disastrous effects on the patients as well as on the staff. The chief physician supported them, with administrative qualifications. A few times the laboratory nurse interrupted, pointing out that some of the arguments were not accurate, as if indicating that the participants lacked knowledge of the special operation of the laboratory. However, the lab representatives did not openly oppose the letter drafted for the administration. When asked directly for their opinion, they merely pointed out that it was not they who decided to close the lab. The discussion resulted in the acceptance of the letter.

This sequence was dominated by the team agenda of protesting the closing of the lab. The discussion proceeded mainly in coordination with the script that aimed at the acceptance of the letter. However, there was a latent competing script, or counterscript (see Gutierrez, Rymes, & Larson, 1995), represented by the laboratory staff. It manifested itself in occasional discoordinations, such as the one in excerpt 8.

The full objects of the team members and the laboratory staff were never explicitly spelled out. Inferring from the transcripts, I suggest that the object for the teams was the principle of population responsibility as the rationale for the work at the station. The object for the laboratory representatives was the legitimacy of sectoral specialization as the rationale for their work at the station. The chief physician's object seemed to be twofold: population responsibility and administrative rationality.

The exchange reported in excerpt 9 occurred almost at the end of this part of the meeting. It indirectly illuminates the objects of the teams and the laboratory staff.

Excerpt 9

01 *Team assistant nurse:* We could naturally invite the head nurse of the laboratory sector to come and get acquainted with our activity. I've worked here for six years but I've never met her at the station. I wonder how much she knows about our activity and about work based on population responsibility. She pretty seldom visits here.

02 *Laboratory nurse:* We do meet her quite often, but...

03 *Team assistant nurse:* ...yes, but to visit here. I mean how much does she know about our way of working? We could give her an orientation and tell her about our idea.

After the letter to the administration was accepted, the floor was given to the laboratory nurse so that she could describe the needs of the lab. She complained at length about the way laboratory work was constantly being disturbed by patients coming at the wrong time, and about their not being well informed and instructed by the team's staff.

Excerpt 10

01 *Laboratory nurse:* ...So that patients should not be sent in vain to our door. But maybe they come even on their own...

02 *Team assistant nurse:* I do think lots of them come on their own. After all, they have been waiting for two and half months.

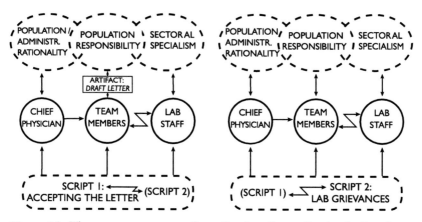

Figure 4.2. The two-step structure of coordination-discoordination in Case 2.

This little exchange exemplifies how this part of the meeting was a mirror image of the preceding part. This time the lab staff went through their own agenda, but they were disturbed by an occasional remark from the teams, such as the one in turn 02 of excerpt 10. The structures of interaction in these two steps of the discussion are presented in Figure 4.2.

It is noteworthy that the only artifact ostensibly used in these parts of the meeting was the text of the draft letter. It was not distributed to the participants, but only read to them by the team assistant nurse chairing the meeting. There was no discussion about the contents of the letter. Thus, the draft letter seemed to function as a symbol of the identity of the teams rather than as an instrument of discussion. On the other hand, the letter was used as a transmission and implementation artifact, that is, as a message to the administration.

The rather straightforward coordination character of the interaction in the meeting was altered at one point after the lengthy presentation of grievances by the laboratory nurse.

Excerpt 11

01 *Team physician:* Would it help if you put a big sign on the door of the laboratory, which would say "Only with appointment and acute samples" . . . ?

02 *Lab nurse:* . . . We can put there such a sign.

03 *Team physician:* And "If you don't have an appointment, you can go to L station lab without appointment." Not too much text, but so that patients will realize that there is such an arrangement in place . . .

04 *Lab nurse:* . . . Yes . . .

05 *Lab nurse 2:* As little text as possible.

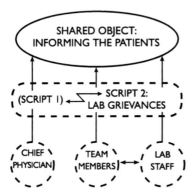

Figure 4.3. The structure of cooperation in Case 2.

During this exchange, a change in the atmosphere took place. The team physician and the laboratory nurse both leaned forward to look each other in the eyes. They were suddenly talking about the same "springboard" (Engeström, 1987) or "boundary object" (Star, 1989) out there in the "real-time" activity. This object nicely brought together the interests of the population responsibility and the interests of the laboratory specialists: Informing patients would enhance the patients' self-reliance, as well as help the lab staff get some peace and quiet.

The collision of the two scripts led to an opening of a fertile "third space" (Gutierrez et al., 1995). This did not happen automatically. A critical initiative was needed (turn 01 in excerpt 11). Significantly, this critical initiative was taken with the help of specific discursive tools. The suggestion was formulated as a question (Would it help if you put a big sign on the door of the laboratory . . . ?), and it was concretized using reported speech ("Only with appointment and acute samples"). These tools turned the suggestion into an open invitation for others to test and develop the proposed idea.

This is a small but important example of an innovation leading to an expansive transition from coordination to cooperation. It did not resolve or eliminate the tension between the team's principle of population responsibility and the laboratory's rationale of sectoral specialization permanently, but it demonstrated that the tension was not unsurmountable. It is also important that the innovation proposed by the team physician did actually materialize. The sign was placed on the laboratory door. The structure of the cooperation momentarily reached in this episode is depicted in Figure 4.3.

Two Layers of History in Teams

Both cases just analyzed deal with deliberately designed teams in their early, formative stages. In both cases, the dominant script had not yet been crystallized. There was an ongoing search for a script and competition between scripts represented by the voices of different participants.

Neither case exemplifies neatly any one of the three strategies found by Ancona (1991). In the first case, the professionals went to the object in what looks like an example of the probing strategy. Yet, they all but excluded their client, the patient, from the interaction. In the second example, the team seemed to focus entirely on its internal relations in a way that resembles Ancona's informing strategy. Yet, they generated an innovation that momentarily changed the nature of the interaction and led to a tangible artifactual product that had an impact on the daily practices of the activity systems of the teams and of the laboratory. In other words, at least in newly emerging teams, strategies are contradictory and fluid, not clean and predictable.

These findings point to the importance of *two layers of history* in the study of teams. Beginning teams differ from well-established or aging teams, such as the television production team analyzed in Chapter 2. Thus, it is not enough that we understand the macro history of teams, that is their nature and place in the scheme depicted in Figures 1.1 and 1.2. We also need to understand the micro history, in other words, the phases of local development in a particular team. This requires genuine local historical research, not shortcuts that reduce the micro history of a team to such universal "stages" as the "forming, storming, norming, and performing" suggested by Tuckman (1965), adopted as a handy but mindless formula by innumerable consultants, and still used today.

Being well aware that a separation between the micro and the macro is unwise (Alexander, 1987; Knorr-Cetina & Cicourel, 1981), I use these notions here as heuristic pointers only. From an activity-theoretical point of view, one may in fact distinguish between multiple layers or scales of history, not just two (Scribner, 1985). The history of a team is embedded in the history of the organization and often also in the history of the professions involved.

At the macro level, the health care teams analyzed in this chapter represent deliberate attempts to break out of the confines of standardized, hierarchical mass production to form autonomous groups responsible for substantial improvement of processes and enhancement of the quality of care. But in both cases, the identity and mission of the team were ambiguous with regard to the tension between sociotechnical and lean production models, discussed in Chapter 1. The emphasis on team autonomy and self-sufficiency resembles sociotechnical models, whereas attempts at networking beyond team boundaries resemble lean production models. One might argue that these teams were created with little conscious reflection of their macro-historical place and mission – or their object, in a general sense.

Fixation and Flow

At the micro level, both cases deal with teams in an early phase of their developmental cycle. In both cases, the teams were trying to identify, articulate, and stabilize their objects, tools, and scripts. This search for a mode of operation was a delicate balancing act between the flow of demands and possibilities emanating from the living object, on the one hand, and developing at least some workable tools, scripts, and rules to ensure reasonable stability and predictability in the work, on the other hand.

In the first case, the two team practitioners visiting Alma were fixated on their attempt to stabilize the care plan tool, following the script engraved in this tool, and they all but disregarding the live object – the patient with her vocal demands. In the second case, both the team members and the laboratory practitioners were initially so fixated on their respective objects that productive dialogue seemed impossible. The friction generated by this incommensurability led to an innovative opening, but only thanks to the employment of additional discursive tools, namely, a suggestion formulated as a question and reported speech. These phenomena of early team formation may be characterized as *tension between fixation and flow*. Smith talks about this tension in terms of *stabilization and destabilization*:

> Stabilization is not just a process of standing back in order to let the object quieten: it also involves reaching out and bashing the object into shape, so that it will be stable enough to register. (...) *You have to work in order for it to continue to be the kind of thing that it is.* Processes of intervention, maintenance, tilling, and stabilization of this sort are in general necessary in order to sediment any object as an object. In their inexorable in-the-primordial-world-ness, the stuff of objects is by nature unruly. It is a collaborative achievement for them to hold, or be held, still enough to be brought into focus. (Smith, 1996, p. 300; see also Cussins, 1992)

In a similar vein, Ciborra writes about the dialectics of *control and drift*, suggesting that our deep-seated obsession with control may need to be replaced by care, hospitality, and cultivation:

What if our power to bring to life sophisticated and evolving infrastructures must be associated with the acceptance of the idea that we are bound to lose control? And that any attempt to regain top-down control will backfire, lead to further centrifugal drifts, and eventually impede our making sense and learning about how to effectively take care of the infrastructure? (Ciborra, 2000, pp. 39–40)

The cases analyzed in this chapter also demonstrate the pain and power of going beyond team boundaries. Both cases involved encounters between teams and others, whether the other is a client, as in Case 1, or a neighboring work unit, as in Case 2. In Chapter 5, I will dig more deeply into the dynamics of boundary crossing in teamwork.

5   Crossing Boundaries in Teacher Teams

The culture of the classroom has been found to be an extraordinarily uniform and persistently stable formation (Cuban, 1984). Numerous attempts at school reform seem to have produced relatively few lasting effects (Sarason, 1990). Tharp and Gallimore (1988) suggest that this is because school reforms have remained at the level of systems and structures, not reaching the daily practices of teaching and learning in classrooms. On the other hand, attempts to change daily instructional practices, such as the program designed by Tharp and Gallimore themselves, have not been particularly successful in the long run either.

The dichotomy between systems and structures, on the one hand, and daily classroom practices, on the other hand, may itself be an important reason for the difficulties. These two levels are explicit: One is codified in laws, regulations, and budgets; the other is codified in curricula, textbooks, and study materials. There is, however, a middle layer between the formal structure of school systems and the contents and methods of teaching. This middle layer consists of relatively inconspicuous, recurrent, and taken-for-granted aspects of school life. These include grading and testing practices, patterning and punctuation of time, uses (not just contents) of textbooks, bounding and use of the physical space, grouping of students, patterns of discipline and control, connections to the world outside the school, and interaction between teachers as well as between teachers and parents. This middle level has been called the *hidden curriculum* (Snyder, 1971; see also Henry, 1963, and Holt, 1964; for a recent powerful account of one version of the hidden curriculum, see Høeg, 1994; see also Gatto, 1992; Gordon, Holland, & Lahelma, 1999; Nespor, 1997).

Much like going to work in any complex institution, going to school is an exercise in trying to make sense of what is going on. As Leont'ev (1978,

p. 171) pointed out, "sense expresses the relation of motive of activity to the immediate goal of action." The middle-level features and processes previously characterized are fundamental in that they largely determine the sense of schoolwork and thus the experience of what it means to be a student or a teacher. As sense- and identity-building features, they are of decisive importance in the formation of motivation among students and teachers.

In attempts at school reform, the middle-level phenomena of the motivational sphere have been largely neglected. In other words, motives, the crucial driving force behind the actions of students and teachers, have been neglected. As Leont'ev (1978) put it, you cannot teach or control motives; you can only cultivate and nurture them by organizing people's lives. Notice the parallel with Ciborra's (2000) argument for the virtues of drift, presented at the end of Chapter 4:

> ... motives are formed in the life activity of the child; to the uniqueness of life corresponds the uniqueness of the motivational sphere of the personality; for this reason motives cannot be developed along isolated lines unconnected one with another. Consequently, we must speak of the problems of nurturing the motives of learning in connection with the development of life, with the development of the content of the actual vital relations of the child. ... (Leont'ev, 1978, pp. 185–186)

Studies on everyday or street mathematics (e.g., Lave, 1988; Nunes, Schliemann, & Carraher, 1993; Saxe, 1991) point to the same conclusion: The organization of the collective life activities in which the mathematical tasks are embedded is of crucial importance for motivation and successful performance. Although this realization is an important step forward, the same studies sometimes tend to evoke a less fruitful opposition between school and everyday practices. If everyday practices are idealized and school is condemned, the internally contradictory nature of both is overlooked. Activity theory calls attention to those very contradictions and the developmental potentials they entail.

There have been some recent attempts to theorize learning motivation as a contextual and sociocultural phenomenon (Salili, Chiu, & Hong, 2001; Volet & Järvelä, 2001). For example, Hickey (2003) conceptualizes motivation in terms of "engaged participation versus marginal nonparticipation." Unfortunately, Hickey's analysis, like most of the recent contextually oriented attempts, ignores the work of Leont'ev and other activity theorists. Thus, traditional Cartesian notions such as *achievement motivation* are in effect kept intact as the core of motivation.

Leont'ev's (1978, 1981) radical insight was to locate motives not in the subjects but in the *objects* of activity. Objects, in turn, are internally contradictory unities of use value and exchange value. The historically evolving internal contradictions of objects make them restless and unstable – persistently incomplete epistemic projects, to paraphrase Knorr-Cetina (1997, 1999, 2001; see also Engeström & Blackler, 2005). This is foundational for an activity-based understanding of human motivation.

Objects are not formed at will. They are shaped in and through the largely tacit "punctuation of experience" (Bateson, 1972) that is stabilized by means of the hidden boundaries of time, space, division of labor, and categorization of knowledge. To make possible a reconceptualization of the object, the hidden boundaries must be made visible and questioned.

In this chapter, I will analyze an attempt by an innovative team of primary school teachers to change the middle-level features, or the motivational sphere, of their schoolwork and classroom culture. The data used in this analysis stem from a longitudinal ethnographic study of a teacher team attempting to create and implement an integrated Global Education curriculum for grades K through 6 in a public primary school in southern California (see Buchwald, 1995, for a comprehensive presentation of the study). The case demonstrates how changes in the motivational sphere of schoolwork require questioning and crossing taken-for-granted boundaries between grade levels, classrooms, temporal units, and curricular subjects.

As a second case, I will analyze an episode in which two teacher teams in a Finnish primary school discussed and debated their ideas for innovative curriculum design from below. The data of the second case are taken from a broader longitudinal study conducted in that school (see Kärkkäinen, 1999, for a comprehensive presentation of the project). The second case demonstrates the potential power of going beyond the boundaries of a single team, of discussing and arguing with another team with a different perspective and point of view.

Common to both cases analyzed in this chapter are two questions: How can teams go beyond the confines and boundaries of their assigned tasks and routines? What is needed to make such boundary crossing fruitful and productive?

Object and Motive of Schoolwork

Leont'ev (1978, p. 52) pointed out that the concept of object is implicitly contained in the concept of activity; there is no such thing as objectless activity. An object is both something given and something projected or

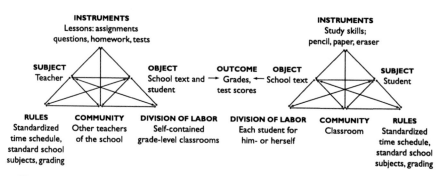

Figure 5.1. Traditional teaching and school-going as interconnected activity systems.

anticipated. An entity in the outside world becomes an object of activity as it meets a human need. This meeting is "an extraordinary act" (Leont'ev, 1978, p. 54). The subject constructs the object, "singles out those properties that prove to be essential for developing social practice" (Lektorsky, 1984, p. 137). In this constructed, need-related capacity, the object gains motivating force that gives shape and direction to activity. The object determines the horizon of possible goals and actions.

The work activity of school teachers is called *teaching*. The activity of school students may be called *school-going*:

> The essential peculiarity of school-going as the activity of pupils is the strange "reversal" of object and instrument. In societal practice text (including the text of arithmetic algorithms) appears as a general secondary instrument. In school-going, text takes the role of the object. This object is molded by the pupils in a curious manner: the outcome of their activity is above all the same text reproduced and modified orally or in written form. (. . .). In other words, text becomes a closed world, a dead object cut off from its living context. (Engeström, 1987, p. 101)

The text itself as object carries an internal contradiction:

> First of all, it is a dead object to be reproduced for the purpose of gaining grades or other "success markers" which cumulatively determine the future value of the pupil himself in the labor market. On the other hand, it tendentially also appears as a living instrument of mastering one's own relation to society outside the school. (. . .) As the object of the activity is also its true motive, the inherently dual nature of the motive of school-going is now visible. (Engeström, 1987, p. 102)

In Figure 5.1, the traditional structures of teaching and school-going are depicted as a pair of activity systems. Like any complex activity, schoolwork resembles an iceberg. Goal-oriented, publicly scripted instrumental actions are the easily discernible tip of the iceberg; the deep social structure of the activity is underneath the surface but provides stability and inertia for the system. Accordingly, the topmost subtriangles (subject–instruments–object) of Figure 5.1 represent the visible instrumental actions of teachers and students. The hidden curriculum is largely located in the bottom parts of the diagram: in the nature of the rules, the community, and the division of labor of the activity.

The activity structure depicted in Figure 5.1 is widely considered alienating for both students and teachers. It leads to encapsulation of school learning from experience and cognition outside the school (Engeström, 1991c). But the traditional structure is robust. Activity theory suggests that significant and sustainable change in the nature of schooling may not be attainable by manipulating any single component or isolated group of components of the activity systems. Change requires construction of a new object and cultivation of corresponding new motives. This, in turn, is attainable only by transforming all the components of the activity systems in concert, including and strategically emphasizing the bottom part of the iceberg.

What could replace the text as the object of schoolwork? And how could such a transformation take place in practice? I will address these questions by examining the process of planning a curriculum unit in the Global Education teacher team.

The Global Education Team

The teacher team studied by my research group was vertically integrated, consisting of five teachers responsible for five classrooms covering grades K through 6. The team was initiated and formed by the teachers themselves, with backing from the principal and a group of parents. The team abandoned regular textbooks. It aimed at creating a new curriculum integrated around the idea of *Global Education*. This was a team with a mission and a lot of "teacher agency," as Paris (1993) would call it.

The Global Education Team was preceded by some 10 years of an Alternative Education program in the same school. The two teachers of the Alternative Program were instrumental in launching the Global Education Program in the fall of 1992 after nearly a year of discussion and preparation. The idea of a team was an integral part of the new program from the beginning. The Global Education Program occupied a hexagonal building of its own on the school campus. We began to observe and record the team meetings in October 1992.

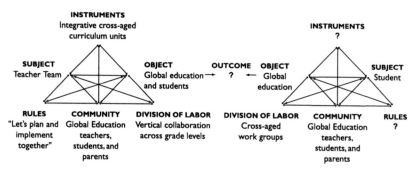

Figure 5.2. Structure of teaching and school-going activities as intended by the Global Education Team.

On the basis of interviews we conducted with the teachers of the team, the intended structure of Global Education activity systems may be sketched as follows (Figure 5.2). I emphasize the word *intended*; Figure 5.2 is not yet a picture based on observations of the actual practice of the team.

The teachers wanted to create a new kind of educational environment and experience called Global Education. In the United States, Global Education has become a broad movement in recent years, and there is a rapidly growing literature on it (e.g., Kobus, 1983; Tye, 1990; Tye & Tye, 1992). The prominence of the movement is reflected in the fact that the foreword to the book by Barbara and Kenneth Tye (1992) was written by Bill Clinton, then the governor of Arkansas.

In spite of this prominence and literature, the teachers we studied did not want to adopt or imitate any of the available programs. In their interviews, they insisted on the local hands-on creation of their own program. They made a point of not having come to the idea through literature or courses but through their own varied practical experiences and personal beliefs. They shared a belief in global responsibility and multiculturalism. But they did not offer prepared definitions of what they were trying to do.

In activity-theoretical terms, the object of the team's activity was deliberately fuzzy and emergent. Global Education was an emerging notion for the team, almost a convenient gloss or proxy for something that the team members could not quite put into words in the interviews we conducted with them. I believe that the teachers wanted to make the *complexity and increasing boundary crossing* evident in the surrounding world the new object of their schoolwork (on complexity, see Perrow, 1986; on boundary crossing, see Engeström, Engeström, & Kärkkäinen, 1995; Kerosuo & Engeström, 2003; Tuomi-Gröhn & Engeström, 2003). Instead of describing only the complexity and boundary crossing, they wanted to organize the work itself to correspond to and reflect these characteristics. They seemed to base their work on the premise that the object of schoolwork is necessarily constructed by living through the total experience of the educational process.

The team sought to cultivate the new object by making visible and redefining, if only temporarily, certain key aspects of the conventional hidden curriculum. I will focus on the team's efforts in the following aspects:

- To make visible and redefine the given division of labor for teachers and students by breaking down or crossing the traditional boundaries between self-contained grade-level classrooms; this effort was aimed at creating new ways of *grouping* the students and new ways of bounding and using school *space*.
- To make visible and redefine the given rules for teachers and students by breaking down the traditional standardized *time schedule* and by crossing the traditional boundaries between *school subjects*.

These redefinitions were in themselves deliberate measures to inject complexity and unpredictability into schoolwork. The team seemed determined to thrive on chaos. It constructed the curriculum units as complex experiences of crossing multiple boundaries. Interestingly enough, the planning of those curriculum units seemed to follow the same logic. The collaborative planning discussions in the meetings of the teacher team were characterized by features that deviated from the standards of efficient, goal-directed planning.

Features of Talk in the Planning Meetings

In the Global Education Team, instruction was loosely structured around integrated topics or curriculum units that included shorter intensive sequences of teaching in mixed-age groups, called *cross-aging* by the teachers. In the summer of 1992, the team drew up a preliminary one-page outline of the topics and activities for the coming school year. The more detailed contents and forms of work in each topic were planned in weekly team meetings as the instruction went on.

In November 1992, the integrated topic was "Harvest Celebration." The team began to discuss and plan the details of the curriculum unit on October 6. They discussed the topic in five successive meetings (October 6, 13, 15, and 20 and November 5). In November, teachers began to handle issues related to the topic in their own classes. On November 18 and 19, the teachers implemented the intensive core of their plan in cross-aged

Table 5.1. *Frequency of types of speaker exchange*

Exchange	Occurrence
Statement followed by a pause	245 (40%)
Simultaneous speech	218 (35%)
Interrupted speech	40 (6%)
Speech without preceding pause	116 (19%)
TOTAL	619 (100%)

Source: Buchwald (1993, p. 10).

groups, each teacher working with a group consisting of students from all grade levels from K through 6. On November 23, the team had a sixth planning meeting. On November 24, cross-aged instruction continued. On November 25, all 150 students gathered in a joint celebration where they presented their work and ate various foods they had prepared. On December 8, the team discussed the topic one more time in its meeting.

All in all, the planning, implementation, and evaluation of the curriculum unit lasted for 2 months and included seven team meetings. This relatively complex, multifaceted topic was the organizing unit of work of the Global Education Team. Such a unit is a cycle or a gradually unfolding web of collaborative problem solving, planning, execution, and assessment.

We videotaped and audiotaped all seven planning meetings of the team. We also videotaped the events in and around the classrooms during the 4 days of cross-aged instruction. In addition, we interviewed the teachers and the principal of the school. In the remainder of this chapter, I use only transcripts of discourse in the planning meetings as data.

A preliminary analysis of the transcripts (Buchwald, 1993; Engeström, 1994a) revealed certain interesting features of the way the teachers talked in their meetings. The first of these features was *a lack of pauses and conventional turn-taking*. There was a tremendous degree of overlap and immediate response in the teachers' utterances. The teachers frequently spoke simultaneously, expressed affirmation or disaffirmation during another's speech, or broke in to respond or continue the thought in their own words. Table 5.1, based on a large sample of discourse from three meetings, indicates the frequency of the different types of turn exchange in the teachers' talk.

During these planning sessions, fewer than half of all turns at talk (40%) were followed by a pause in the discourse. This means that conversational breaks did not occur after an individual utterance or pair of utterances but rather between clusters of statements, or flurries of talk, coming from multiple participants. A turn at talk in this team may thus be characterized as a collaborative achievement rather than an individual chance to speak.

The second feature in the teachers' planning talk was a *lack of imperative mood and prevalence of conditional statements*. There are three moods in the English language: the imperative, the subjunctive (or conditional), and the indicative. Interestingly enough, Angelika Wagner (1987, p. 165), in her study of *knots* in teachers' thinking, identifies only the imperative and indicative moods; she does not even consider the role of conditionals in teachers' dilemmatic thinking. In fact, Wagner reduces the knots in thinking to the imperative mood alone:

> A "knot" arises in consciousness if a discrepancy is detected between "what is" and "what *must* be," with consciousness reacting to this with the self-imposed injuncton "this discrepancy *must* not exist." Because the discrepancy is already there, as part of consciousness itself, thinking does indeed go around in circles without finding an exit (. . .). Hence, tension arises, with thinking quite futilely attempting to solve a problem it has created itself by continuing to imperate itself that "This *must* not be!" (Wagner, 1987, p. 168; italics in the original)[1]

According to Wagner's findings, such self-imperated knots are extremely common in teachers' thinking, as expressed in in-depth interviews and stimulated recall protocols. Although interesting and imaginative, Wagner's work displays an individualist and Cartesian bias. The knots were identified solely on the basis of monological responses from individual teachers. No data were collected from collaborative action and dialogue between teachers.

Findings from the analysis of our discourse data are quite opposite to those of Wagner (Table 5.2). There was an almost total absence of imperatives in the talk of the teacher team, and there was a striking frequency of conditionals. Conditional phrases represent more than half of the total verb forms (53%) if one counts phrases in which indicatives act as part of a conditional string. Questions and statements were worded as possibilities. Statements and recommendations were softened by conditional verbs. In general, each meeting was moved forward by conditionals: "perhaps we could. . . ."

The heavy use of conditional strings suggests a shared sense of process that includes the tracing of ideas together rather than acceptance of givens

---

[1] Knot in Wagner's specific terminology must not be confused with the concepts of knots and knotworking developed in this book as a general perspective on emerging new forms of collaborative work.

Table 5.2. *Relative frequencies of moods in the planning meetings*

Verb form occurrence	
Imperative	4 (<1%)
Conditional	485 (43%)
Indicative	516 (46%)
Indicative working as conditional	119 (10%)
Conditional working as indicative	7 (<1%)
TOTAL	1,131 (100%)

Source: Buchwald (1993, p. 14).

from outside or reliance on yes/no decisions. The co-constructed strings of conditionals are instances of joint attention to and extension of ideas, of teachers imagining together. The team worked through potential choices and their possible outcomes. Ideas did not seem to be owned by the teacher who stated them – it was not her obligation to defend them. An examination of the transcripts after the teaching of the curriculum unit reveals that very few parts of the overall plan can be traced back to a single teacher's initiative.

The third feature of the teachers' planning talk was a prevalence of *circling back and repetition* of issues. An idea or a problem was typically taken up over and over again. However, this was not a case where "thinking does indeed go around in circles without finding an exit," as Wagner put it. The issue did not return in the same form and with the same content. Repeated raising of the issue allowed it to be considered from various angles and by different teachers. Food preservation, for example, was discussed so as to express and weigh various concerns that might be relevant in shaping the topic: from conceptualization of the entire unit to dividing children into groups and selecting appropriate materials.

The entire process of planning and talking in the team meetings took the shape of a spiral, consisting of various parallel smaller spirals. It was a far cry from models of rational goal-oriented planning that proceeds in a linear order toward a predetermined destination. Rather, the teacher team's planning progressed like a vessel on a giant potter's wheel, emerging gradually as each teacher shaped it and added to it. The result was robust and sturdy in that the teachers seemed confident and coordinated during the cross-aged implementation, in spite of having no written plan at all.

These features of the teachers' planning talk – *lack of pauses and conventional turn-taking, lack of imperative mood and prevalence of conditional statements*, and prevalence of *circling back and repetition* – suggest that planning sessions themselves were already part of the emerging new object, characterized by complexity and boundary crossing.

Redefining the Division of Labor by Cross-Aged Grouping

A crucial issue for the Global Education Team in creating the curriculum unit of the Harvest Celebration was how to accomplish the cross-aging of the 150 children involved in the program. This issue was more crucial than any specific contents of the unit. In cross-aging, the teacher was to face children from the ages of 6 to 12 in her classroom, charged with providing meaningful tasks that would enable children of various ages to work together. Cross-aging is a leap beyond the confines of the self-contained single-grade classroom into the realm of unpredictable interactions. This was at the heart of what the Global Education Team wanted to achieve.

In the literature on everyday or street mathematics, it has often been pointed out how much more easily mathematical tasks are accomplished when they are embedded in meaningful practices outside the school, as opposed to their difficulty when framed as abstract assignments of school-like reasoning. The teacher team's discussion on the formation of cross-aged groups is in some sense an opposite example. In abstract terms, dividing 150 students into equally large groups, each consisting of equal numbers of students from all participating grade levels, requires elementary operations. In the concrete and complex context of creating a viable cross-aged curriculum unit, these operations became curiously difficult and awkward.

> **Global Education Team Meeting 2: Oct. 13, 1992**
> *JW:* Could we split up the rooms like, per food type?
> *BH:* Yeah.
> *LL:* Oh, yeah. We could do that. There's five rooms. What if we gave every, like one of the grains to each of the groups.
> *BH:* Classrooms, right.
> *LL:* But then, then you see, then your groups are gigantic. That means you've got thirty kids in a group!

The problem of gigantic groups was approached with the possibility of dividing each class into three subgroups with slightly different subactivities.

> *BH:* But even if you were doing one grain, maybe you could come up with, you could have three different groups doing the same grain.

And maybe come up with three different recipes. One could make a cereal.

LL: A cereal, uh huh, uh huh.

BH: One could make a pancake or you know a flatbread or something. And the other one could, I don't know, [laughs] come up with something.

LL: Make sushi [laughs]

BH: [laughs] Yeah right, come up with something.

This idea evoked an attempt to recollect an earlier experience of dividing the students into small subgroups. This, however, led to momentary confusion and a dead end.

BH: Right. Well, if each of us had a grain and we work it that maybe we had three groups, how many groups would we have to have [inaudible] do you remember, maybe ten?

LL: What groups?

BH: When we did the timeline, we had . . .

LL: Groups of four people, working to . . .

BH: What did we have? We had twenty-some groups?

LL: Well, there's about, let's see, there's five times, there's about a hundred and fifty kids.

BH: A hundred and fifty kids?

LL: More or less.

BH: And we put four kids in a group, or five. We had five kids in a group. That's five kids in a group; that's thirty groups. Oh God!

LL: Okay. That's unrealistic. If you had, if you have, if we have five teachers.

Why did the mathematical operations of dividing 150 students into five cross-aged groups seem so awkward in the teachers' conversation? Certainly the teachers knew how many students were in the program; knew that 150 students divided among the five teachers makes groups of 30; and knew the division of 30 into either five or six. In fact, all the required operations should have been automatic and smooth. However, automatic operations are dependent on the conditions of performing the actions in which they are embedded (Leont'ev, 1978, pp. 65–67). When the conditions become problematic – for instance, when we try to drive a car with an unfamiliar stick shift – the automatic operations are blocked and slowed down. For a moment, they become deliberate actions again. For the teachers, the elementary arithmetic operations were embedded in planning and problem-solving actions on a novel and problematic terrain of various contingencies and unknown consequences.

The notion of 30 subgroups was declared to be unrealistic. However, one of the teachers immediately realized that the seemingly large number was not necessarily unrealistic after all. A realistic division was constructed jointly.

> *BH:* Well, wait a minute! Thirty kids in a group. I had six in my room. It wasn't unrealistic. It was okay.
>
> *LL:* Thirty kids in one group. But I'm talking about, if we had five teachers, let's say we had five teachers participating.
>
> *BH:* 'Kay.
>
> *LL:* If we divide the kids subsequently into five groups, which gives us *thirty?*
>
> *BH:* Right.
>
> *LL:* And inside the thirty we could divide it into three groups and . . .
>
> *BH:* Right. Well, even smaller. Ten is too many.
>
> *LL:* Maybe. You could divide it into six groups . . .
>
> *JW:* So that one teacher six groups of five. That teacher, 'kay one person in that group, then somebody, you could split that thirty, the class.
>
> *?:* Right. Yes. Yes, right.

Soon the teachers returned to the issue of dividing the students into groups to summarize the provisional solution they had achieved.

> *LL:* Listen, if we had, if we had five teachers, and each teacher takes thirty kids' responsibility. And then within that thirty you've got, like, five groups of six, or whatever.
>
> *BH:* Five groups of six, six groups of five.
>
> *LL:* And let's say I have the theme wheat. Wheat.
>
> *JW:* Okay.
>
> *LL:* Okay. I need to come up with five activities that we can do with wheat. In other words. Or six, or whatever the number is.
>
> *BH:* Right, right.

However, this solution was still feeble and fragile. It was like a first draft, with little or no mutually constructed concreteness.

A few minutes later, the solution was challenged. The teachers saw that giving each student in a classroom basically the same topic would become too uniform and rigid. This led to the second major step in forming the solution. The second draft solution was a radical deviation from the first one.

> *LL:* But see, once *again* if I've got groups of six, am I gonna ask each of those six to do a little bit of research to find out what civilization used wheat? *What* am I gonna have these kids do?
>
> *BH:* Kids do?
>
> *LL:* That's right.
>
> *BH:* 'Cause usually we have a different topic for each kid.
>
> *LL:* Right.
>
> *JW:* Yea.
>
> *BH:* And this way it would be the same.

This worry about "sameness" led to a search for an alternative. A different model was gradually worked out.

> *JW:* That's why it's almost seems like to me and I don't know how we would do that exactly, but it seems like, like, I don't know . . .
>
> *LL:* Well, we might want to do it this way and that is, I still have responsibility for thirty and I still have responsibility for six groups, but I'll have a rice group, a wheat group
>
> *JW:* That's what I was thinking.
>
> *LL:* A whatever group, a whatever group, but *maybe?*
>
> *JW:* In within those thirty?
>
> *LL:* Within the thirty.

The alternative model began to gain momentum when the idea of each teacher doing exactly the same set of different activities emerged as a labor-saving solution.

> *JW:* That would work. That way you're saying, like in your classroom, you'd have all different grades, but in the sa-, in the other classroom, they'd be doing the same thing, all different recipes or whatever?

BH: Yeah, we'd all be doing the same thing but it would be just mixed cross age.

JW: Yeah, that would work.

LL: But I think, I think what we'd be smarter to do is to have all five be exactly the same.

BH: The same, exactly the same.

LL: So I'll have the same stuff going on that you have going on and you have going on.

BH: Right. We'll all do the same thing for rice. We'll all do the same thing for wheat.

LL: But we'll each have different *kids!*

BH: Except for different rooms will have different *kids* doing it.

JW: I see.

BH: 'Cause see then we could [inaudible] amount of work.

LL: But then see we could save ourselves an incredible amount of work.

JW: I see. Right.

The alternative model was drafted by three teachers; one teacher had to leave the meeting early, and another one was sick. Two days later, the entire team met again. The three teachers presented their alternative model to the two others. The discussion led to the third major step in the formation of the solution. It was a return to the first one, this time with more concreteness.

The alternative model of the previous meeting was first presented with enthusiasm and added detail.

Global Education Team Meeting 3: Oct. 15, 1992

JW: And then like LL would be in charge of just corn, and she would get all the information for *all* of us.

LL: About corn. And then one person would get all the information about wheat. And one person would get all the information about whatever. So wh- *if* we decided to do it cross-age, what we'd do is we'd, we'd fan the kids out – so what, there's five of us, right? – yeah, we'd have each each one of us in the five would have a cross-age section. So I'd have thirty kids in my room, but they wouldn't all be my own kids. Some of yours. And then inside that group, I would have [inaudible] and one about wheat and one about rice and one about corn or whatever it is. And so would you and so would you and so would you.

JW: But one teacher would only have to do all the stuff for corn.

LL: Mmhmm.

JW: And they'd give all their information to LL, to TS, to me, to you, to BH. And then you would maybe do wheat, and you'd give all your information, so we'd each have . . .

LL: It would cut down on the amount of work.

The alternative model was first questioned by TS, one of the teachers who was absent from the previous meeting.

TS: So you're like expert group, you're from experts and you would teach first the information to your own class, and then they disperse then and do it with the other kids?

LL: Well see, we could do it that way, too. And that's just another way to do it. I, I . . .

TS: One teacher does the planning and just hands it and you'd say, "Oh, you're gonna have five kids in your class doing corn and this is the activities they're doing."

JW: Right. That's what we were thinking of. That way, you could do all the research and gather everything for corn, I could do wheat, and you could do rice, you could do – I don't know, whatever – and then you we'd all give the other information to each of us. So we'd end up with four, like *I* would end up with *your* information on wheat, TS's information on rice, and then . . .

Next, JL, the other teacher who was absent, added a further question. She first received an immediate answer explaining the virtues of the alternative model.

JL: Right. So then why would you need all four, if . . . ?

JW: Because we want to cross-age.

LL: Because inside one group. If we did cross-age, inside my classroom, I would have a group for rice, a group for wheat, a group for corn, a group for whatever the grains are? So I might have four or five groups that *inside* themselves were cross-age. So the oldest kids would be, be able to read the information that I had managed to collect about corn. The oldest kids would become the experts in the group, and then help the other people do the activities about corn.

JW: See what I mean? [quietly]

JL then continued questioning the alternative model somewhat vaguely. Her doubts were now picked up and clearly formulated by JW, one of the teachers who created the alternative model.

> *JL:* I was thinking yeah. If there is like, cross-age groups but like all the kids for who are doing the wheat are in one room [inaudible] like gathering [inaudible].
>
> [*BH comes back in. There is some indistinguishable talk.*]
>
> We'll just have, just go ahead and go on. I'm not thinking exactly; that's all right.
>
> *JW:* Well, you're just thinking why, why should we have the kids, why shouldn't we just have all the wheat in one room? That's what you're saying?
>
> *JL:* That's because the expert is in that room. But . . .

LL, another originator of the alternative model, immediately adopted JL's implicit suggestion.

> *LL:* Yeah, that makes sense. We could do that way, too.
>
> *JL:* And then still have cross-age groups.
>
> *JW:* Why are we thinking corn before?
>
> *LL:* Yeah. So then you'd have, so we'd have a wheat person. And you'd have, you know, one fifth of the kids, that would be wheat?
>
> *JW:* All . . .
>
> *JL:* Right.

The teachers realized that in spite of the original intention, the alternative model would not save labor due to the burden of sharing one's special expertise across all the classrooms. A return to the first model now seemed natural.

> *LL:* That would be fine. Be easier.
>
> *JW:* Yeah, that would be fine. Yeah.
>
> *JL:* How does that sound?
>
> *TS:* And you wouldn't have to share your information with someone else.
>
> *JL:* You see, I think it would be easier if you're in the one room with the one teacher.
>
> *TS:* Yeah.

After this, the teachers drew up a list of the five different themes: rice, wheat, corn, hunting, and gathering. They then conducted a lottery to decide who got which theme. This allocation of substantive themes represented a major consolidation of the model.

A particularly interesting feature of the third step was the ease with which the originators of the second, alternative model gave up their idea and adopted the implicitly suggested return to elaborating the first model. In fact, the originators were instrumental in formulating a critique of their own model – a critique only very vaguely implied in the utterances of the two other teachers. It seems that in spite of their enthusiasm, the originators of the second model were operating in a tentative, conditional mode that kept the doors wide open to doubts and further alternatives. The behavior of the originators cannot be explained away as a desire to please senior colleagues; one of the originators (LL) was herself the most senior teacher of the whole team.

Crossing Spatial Boundaries

The creation of cross-aged groups necessarily involved a new kind of spatial movement. On the mornings of the cross-aged teaching days, the students went to their home classrooms and then left for the various thematic cross-aged classrooms to which they were assigned. This meant that on those mornings, 150 students rotated around the hexagonal building of the Global Education Program looking for their assigned rooms. At those times, the scene was that of a social whirlpool.

The fact that the teachers had abandoned textbooks as the object forced them to go out to find objects and instruments in a pragmatic way, wherever they might be available.

> *LL:* I know but I thought about walking them to my house, and just letting them go through my garden, which is a total mess. But they might be able to find some corn and stuff in there. But I can't imagine what you'd do instead. I mean I just can't imagine that much about gathering.
>
> *JW:* And then you know what um one thing may be just to assign the the certain kids in your room who will bring. And you can get like pinon nuts.
>
> *Others:* Mmhmm. Mmhmm.
>
> *JW:* And you can go, and you can just buy the stuff.

What emerges is an image of a school as an open base, or a laboratory, to which various kinds of "stuff" are being brought from the outside world for investigation and experimentation.

Redefining the Rules by Negotiating Time

> The succession of days was an endless line, gray. They ran past you. (...)
> When all the days were the same, when they recurred and recurred, and
> were planned out ten years into the future, why did you feel that time was
> passing, that it was linear, that your school days were a kind of countdown,
> that time was a train that you must and ought to be fit enough to hang on
> to? I think it was because of the insistence on achievement. Otherwise it
> is impossible to explain. (...) It only seemed as though the same subjects
> and the same classrooms and the same teachers and the same pupils came
> around again and again. In reality, the requirement was that you should,
> with every day, be transformed. Every day you should be better, you should
> have developed, all the repetition in the life of the school was there only
> so that, against an unchanging background, you could show that you had
> improved. (Høeg, 1994, p. 226)

This is the image of standardized, linear time schedules that dominates and permeates every aspect of traditional schoolwork. Time is not negotiable. It is the universal "unchanging background" of linear achievement.

The Global Education teachers' team refused to live by this notion of time. Time was turned into multiple negotiable time spans and rhythms. For one thing, they had to select and prepare for the cross-aged days.

> *JL:* When are we thinking, the sixteenth next Monday, right?
>
> *BH:* We had we had the sixteenth, seventeenth, and eighteenth. We had
> it all, right? Three full days?
>
> *JW:* I had it the sixteenth, seventeenth, eighteenth, nineteenth, twen-
> tieth.
>
> *BH:* You had it all?
>
> *JW:* I don't know.
>
> *JL:* I remember that we reserved the spot in case we didn't get it done.
> I remember now. In case we didn't get it done.

The teachers also considered how much time it would take for each teacher to prepare for the unit, how her preparation would fit with the other work she needed to do, and how that time could be reduced.

BH: I mean 'cause gathering all this material. Usually like we've done this taken *weeks*, I mean a week ahead of time and gotten all the materials. And each group had their packet, so when the kids sat down, you had all they had all the information totally directed.

JL: Well, and we *will*. I mean I know I'm gonna have stuff by the day that we start this but that's a [inaudible].

BH: We're starting it on Monday. And I got report cards, and I'm not I'm not gonna have much [inaudible].

JL: Well, that's. Today's Tuesday. I mean to me that's that's light years away.

TS: [laughing] It's not Tuesday *yet*.

The teachers also had to consider how much time should be budgeted for each subactivity.

LL: Because food preservation takes a lot of time. It'll *take* a month to make raisins.

BH: Right.

LL: Especially if the weather is like what it is.

BH: Right, what it is. And even the apples, I mean you can't do anything...

LL: Oh yeah, you can't do that overnight.

Finally, the teachers planned the presentations and the schedule for the actual harvest festival celebration.

JW: Otherwise, I don't, I don't shorter than ten minutes, they're not really gonna be able to present too much. I mean. Especially if...

BH: Well maybe if we do it in *stages*. Instead of having you know having it all in one block, having presentations maybe the first and then we go and do some eating?

?: Have two [inaudible]?

BH: Have two presentations and some eating and come back. I don't know if they, you know my kids sitting for fifteen minutes, even if they're getting up and down.

LL: Well how about if we did *three* presentations and then eat, and then come back for two presentations?

BH: Okay.

Crossing Boundaries between Curricular Subjects

As noted above, the teachers divided the topic of harvest festival into five subtopics, each of which was assigned to a teacher by means of a lottery. In other words, the teachers did not divide the work into mathematics, English, history, or other standard subjects in the cross-aged groups. Even the boundaries of the assigned subtopics were open to renegotiation.

This was demonstrated when the least experienced teacher, JW, wanted to make sure that it was okay to deviate from the plan for her hunting group by incorporating discussion of animal domestication as well as the hunting of animals.

> *JW:* So do you mind if I do animal domestication as like the next thing to hunting? Do you guys mind if I do that?
>
> *Others:* Yeah. No. We don't care what you do. Everything sounds good to me.
>
> *JW:* Because that's basically, if we're talking about grains and things like that, they're getting past the hunting. They're going into domestication.
>
> *Others:* Right. Mmmhmm. Oh, yeah. That's great.

Contradiction and Argumentation

Thus far, my analysis may give the impression that transforming the motivational sphere, or the hidden curriculum, of classroom cultures is simply a matter of good will, effort, and unanimity. Yet, early in this chapter, I argued that activity theory sees contradictions as the source of change and development. Indeed, it is now time to look into the argumentative and contradictory aspect of the teacher team's planning discourse.

In the fifth planning meeting, the model of the curriculum unit was questioned once more. This time, BH, who was assigned corn in the lottery, presented her own package of teaching the cross-aged unit and suggested that JW, and eventually the other teachers, might follow her model. BH's package was based on the preparation of poster reports in small groups.

Global Education Team Meeting 5: Nov. 10, 1992

> *BH:* Now see, if you, now like I got the thing and you could get in cooperative groups and she could do that with cooperative groups, assign an animal to each group. You could xerox it off and then you would make a poster report, and do some kind of a mural. That's what you do.

JW: Right, but I don't, I wanna do something more, I mean I . . .

BH: More?! Do you want to know how soon we have to have this ready? Plus your report cards ready? Are you nuts! More! [laughs]

JW: I wanna do something more than just a poster though. I mean if everyone else is going to be cooking things and grinding and . . .

JW rejected BH's suggestion and indicated that she wanted to do "something more" than poster reports. This nonconditional tone of discussion was unusual in the transcripts. BH responded by invoking time constraints and then by making a sales pitch for her package based on an earlier experience of teaching corn.

BH: No, no, no, no, no. Here's a list of things that we do. Now, this is what we did.

JL: But now this a corn group.

BH: Yeah, but this would be the [inaudible]. We had the cooperative groups and each. They were cross-age groups and they got together and they actually like, for instance, corn. They met each other and they made a big corn husk. For corn, a piece of corn. And they *all* put their names on it.

JW: Oh.

BH: So that was the name of the group and that would be over their station the day of the thing, but we didn't have a hundred and fifty kids. So that was how they got to come in groups. They talked about it and they all, they made this big huge piece of corn and they all put their names on it and stuff. And then. Then each group was gonna make um, let's see, they were given, they were gonna cook, they had been given a recipe and they were going to cook something for a corn-based food from a particular culture or area and I think most of them did it with Indians.

?: What'd you use, Mexico?

BH: Different places in the world that used corn. And so each group was gonna make a mural to show what the corn in their culture [inaudible]. The mural might show how they grew the corn; it might show the marketplace, if they had it on the mural. And they all painted on the mural. And then each group had a poster report that gave the title, and had a map of the area and where the corn was grown and had an illustration of life in that region, how people in that region lived and stuff – and then their recipe was on the chart. And then they cooked the recipe the day before and we ate it. So it was *not* that complicated.

BH's effort was met with little enthusiasm. In fact, JL switched the topic by asking what dates were devoted to the cross-aged instruction. However, BH did not give up. She continued presenting her package and suggesting that the others should adopt a similar structure.

> *BH:* And we could, we could have like a, you could have a rice *metate* in your room, I got a corn *metate*, and you could have whatever, what are you doing? You're doing gathering. We could do our corn together. But we could have them actually grind the grains, and see what it looks like and then they could maybe take say I'm gonna make a plastic bag and put it on your poster. You could have the grain before it was ground and the grain after it was ground.
>
> *?:* Mmhm.

At this point, JL confronted BH directly, in effect drawing a line between BH and the other teachers. She initiated a whole different line of discussion.

> *JL:* Do y-? [to BH] I know that you've got this entire packet here of stuff to do with corn. [Turning away, to the others] Do you have, do you know what you're doing for your group yet? I don't know what I'm doing.
>
> *?:* I have no idea.
>
> *JL:* Yeah. And I'm wondering, maybe what we oughtta do is . . .
>
> *?:* Oh, I . . .
>
> *JL:* What I'm wondering is if, *maybe*, if we just meet together like I know this is probably not gonna be popular, like Thursday afternoon or something. Once we've had a chance to think about what we're going to do.
>
> *LL:* Well, *I'm* really nervous about having that, I mean I don't wanna have, I need to know, before I plan this out, how many meetings we're gonna have.
>
> *JW:* Right.
>
> *LL:* That's what I need to know first.
>
> *JL:* Right. But I, I mean going much beyond that, I, I can't talk about what I'm gonna do with the kids yet because I don't even know . . .

LL: Oh yeah.

JL: ...*myself* what I'm gonna do. I have to go find something on *rice*.

Here JW stepped in and suggested that the team focus on the logistics of the actual cross-aged teaching. LL and JL joined her. So did eventually also BH.

LL: Well, if...

JW: But can we just like figure out the schedule so that we know how much we...?

LL: Yeah. How much, I need to know if I need to plan two sessions or three sessions.

JW: I know. How big is it gonna be? How how long is it gonna take?

JL: Okay. Yeah.

JW: That's kinda...

LL: Oh I think that...

JW: I think if we can decide on that, that would be great for me too.

LL: I think if we have cooking be one session, and then two other sessions.

BH: And cooking has to be the day before two other sessions, right?

But the team had not yet discouraged BH from selling her package to the others. BH took it up again, this time to be confronted directly by LL.

BH: Like if we had the same basic thing, we're gonna find out you know you're gonna work on get the grain in what region and have it region's usages because corn is used really differently in, there's a place in...

LL: But if you can do *corn* that way, but then I can't do use that same corn that way for hunting and gathering.

BH: But then you're not [inaudible] mix it up and do the corn in...

LL: I don't know. But I mean, what I mean is, is that *I* have to decide what hunting, what gathering does may be very different from what corn does.

BH tried one more time, now offering her model only for those doing the different grains. JL rejected the idea on the grounds of not knowing enough about her theme yet. LL, too, rejected it again, pointing out that each teacher might do different things.

BH: Right. But if you're doing a grain...If you're doing a grain, couldn't all the grains just be the same format and make it easier? Then we could go to the library, and we could probably find stuff together. You were doing rice, rice in China and rice in ah Turkey. They might be different. And so they would step just look at that region to s- you know...

JL: I guess what I would like to do is I need to find out, I need to get the basic information myself, so I mean I can't, I'm drawing a total blank right now, because I don't have *any* information.

LL: Yeah, because it could it could be okay like if for example like if *her* group wants to prov...present a play that just happens to talk about rice in the play, and you do poster reports for yours, and I do...

BH now redirected her effort by asking about the logistics of the final presentations at the joint Harvest Festival of all the students. The ensuing discussion revealed that the model of the unit was unclear on this point, especially for BH.

BH: How will you present this on the festival day?

JL: Well, that's what we need to others...[several people talking at once]

LL: All you need to do is to have to have some some ground rules. Like for example maybe each group has ten minutes in which to present their findings or their whatever.

BH: And we're gonna go through *how* many groups? I mean like if we have a hundred and fifty kids, that's five...

LL: There, there's *five* groups.

BH: I thought we were doing cooperative groups for each classroom!

JL: We are. But groups within have sub...

LL: Five groups. Five groups!

JL: So right.

BH: So they're only gonna present to the one class but it's five groups...

LL: No, no, no, no. See the whole...

BH: Five plus five is *twenty-five*...

LL: No it isn't, BH, it isn't, it isn't. My one group, your one group...

JL: You're gonna have subgroups within your one group.

LL: So like *corn* is gonna make a ten-minute presentation about corn.

BH: Uh huh. Uh huh.

LL: Wheat is gonna make a ten-minute presentation. Gathering will make a ten-minute presentation.

BH: Okay.

Interestingly enough, the early problem of grouping and figuring out the right numbers reappeared here. Symptomatically, BH claimed that "Five plus five is *twenty-five*," thus demonstrating again how problematic contingencies of an action may block a routine operation, leading to something that looks like an awkward error. What is even more interesting is that dialogue with the other teachers was not hampered by this error; they saw right through it. When LL exclaimed, "No it isn't, BH, it isn't, it isn't," she was not referring to the operational error but to the problematic action. The point was that not all 25 cross-aged subgroups would have 10-min presentations; only the five classes would each have 10 min, but each teacher could divide those 10 min between her subgroups as she considered appropriate. When this problem was collaboratively worked out, the object of the teachers' joint work emerged in a much clearer light.

Details of the schedule were then jointly worked out. For the team, this step resolved the problem posed by BH. There were now clear ground rules for the implementation of the cross-aged teaching sequence and the joint celebration as its culmination.

After a while, BH asked whether all the subgroups within a classroom were going to be doing the same things. This led her once more to the idea of a package, this time referring to the limited amount of time the teachers would have left to prepare diverse subactivities for the subgroups. The final rejection came from JL, who put the available preparation time in a different perspective by stating that Monday one week ahead was "light years away" for her.

The discoordination between BH and the other members of the team involved direct confrontation and argumentation by means of negating what the other participant suggested. This argumentative talk seems to reflect a contradiction between principles – saving labor by means of prepackaged curriculum materials, on the one hand, versus creating unique and personally meaningful educational experiences "from below," on the other hand.

The discoordination was not just an unfortunate setback for the team. It forced the team to focus on a serious gap in the model of the curriculum unit, namely, the missing or unclear ground rules for the final presentations on the Harvest Celebration day. In other words, elaboration and resolution of the discoordination produced a more advanced model for the joint implementation effort facing the team.

The Activity System and Its Contradictions

In Figure 5.2 I presented the intended activity structure of the Global Education Team. What do the empirical data and the analysis just presented indicate about that activity structure as it was actually practiced?

Three components of the teachers' activity system have been illuminated: the object, the instruments, and the rules. I have argued that behind the notion of Global Education, the emerging objects of the teacher team's activity may be characterized as complexity and boundary crossing. These concepts themselves are only preliminary characterizations of the educational experience in the making.

We may now distinguish between two layers of instruments in the teacher team's activity: the "what" instruments (integrative curriculum units) and the "how" instruments, consisting of oral planning primarily with the help of conditional strings and spirallike circling back on issues (on "what" and "how" instruments, see Engeström, 1990, pp. 188–189). The "how" instruments were both a strength and a weakness. The use of conditionals and circling back was tremendously robust and powerful in keeping the doors of thought open to alternatives and in providing for complex "imagining together." On the other hand, the exclusive reliance on talk as a medium could make it difficult for the team to create and maintain a collective memory to be used as a resource when similar curriculum units are planned and implemented again in the coming years. The systematic rejection of prepackaged curriculum materials seemed to be a deeply held principle in the team. But without some form of documentation designed as an alternative to prepackaging, the team members could simply become overburdened.

In the rules of the activity system, important additional rules were found. Along with the rule of doing things together, there existed the more traditional rule of individual autonomy as well as the rule of excluding written curriculum packages. These became manifest when BH's package was rejected. Packages could indeed easily become stultifying rules that standardize teachers' and students' work. On the other hand, insistence on individual autonomy may easily become an excuse for not engaging in substantive collaborative planning and teaching. That problem can be sensed in JL's insistence on her own timeline ("the way I function, that's still light years away") and her individual way of mastering the contents ("I know I'm gonna have stuff by the day we start this"). Such an approach could potentially lead to a form of teamwork where collaboration is reduced to logistical and technical coordination.

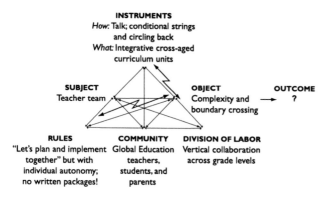

Figure 5.3. Contradictions in the activity system of the Global Education Team.

In Figure 5.3, the two lightning-shaped arrows indicate contradictions in the activity system of the teacher team. The emergent object of Global Education as a new type of educational experience was pulling the teachers into a poorly charted zone of experimentation and innovation. Insistence on talk as the only "how" tool and on the personal autonomy of the teacher as a rule seemed to have the potential to restrict and disturb the team's journey through its collective zone of proximal development. At the same time, as shown in the resolution of the discoordination between BH and the rest of the team, these same tensions were powerful sources of argumentative self-reflection and innovation.

Crossing the Boundary between Two Teacher Teams

My second case is from an elementary school in Helsinki, Finland. In the fall of 1993, two groups of teachers formed teams (Teams A and B), both consisting of five teachers. The aim of both teams was to plan and teach the local curriculum in a collaborative fashion. My research group followed the two teams for approximately 2 months. During that period, Team B planned and implemented a new curriculum unit aimed at getting to know the local community. The problem trajectory proceeded from an initial search for basic principles through a period of concrete planning to the implementation of the unit in classrooms.

Two teachers in Team A had collaborated closely for several years. At the beginning of the school year, they presented their curriculum model to the team. Team B spent their two first meetings exchanging ideas about interesting themes for collaborative curriculum units, not settling for a specific model.

The next meeting was conducted jointly with the two teams. Team A wanted to present their model to Team B. Team B was not willing to emulate Team A but was open to an exchange of ideas. In the discussion, the division of students into groups became the trigger issue.

Team A's model was based on elective courses given to selected students during each of the six periods of the school year. These elective courses were taught in small groups, with 10 students in a group. Together with their parents, students had to select one of two alternative courses offered to them. Teacher B5 questioned the rationale of the model. For her, it offered forced alternatives, not genuine choice.

> *Teacher B3:* So then you divide your students, you divide them into groups of appropriate size . . . ?
>
> *Teacher A1:* We give them two alternatives. Yes, two alternatives, which can be for instance video and soccer. They are together because both have the objective of strengthening social skills. And now they get a slip which says that we have selected for your child this and this course, and for some of them, there is video or soccer, from which . . .
>
> *Teacher A5:* Fill the selection slip.
>
> *Teacher B5:* So they select at home one or the other?
>
> *Teacher A4:* Then they select one or the other.
>
> *Teacher B5:* But what is the ideology here, since the basic idea would be to increase the child's right to choose according to his or her own interests and to progress in the direction of his or her own choice? And now, however, it's like "take this or this, but this is what you'll take."
>
> *Teacher A2:* Our point of departure is . . .
>
> *Teacher A1:* These elective courses are not for that purpose.
>
> *Teacher A2:* Yes, they are not electives in that sense. They must be in line with the objectives. They have to serve the objectives, and the selection must be based on the teacher's familiarity with the student and on educational work done together with the parents.

Team B held their own meeting immediately after the joint meeting of the two teams. In their meeting, members of Team B settled for a model of their own, based on groups of 30 students, with each group having a different theme within a shared curriculum unit. The discussion within Team B in effect continued the argument with Team A's ideas, although Team A was no longer physically present. Notice the use of reported speech as an argumentative tool by teachers B5 and B3 in the following excerpt.

> *Teacher B5:* We should probably have a discussion on the principle, to agree whether it's a problem for us that we have thirty students each. Because we have had that idea so far, but now we heard that "Aha! We will only have ten."
>
> *Teacher B3:* So now we should suddenly begin to change it.
>
> *Teacher B5:* So we are like…
>
> *Teacher B3:* Yes, but you know, I think it's to our advantage, although we have thirty. My idea of the activity is not that we tell them that "You go there, and you go here." The students will have a strong motivation for what they'll do, so that when they come for example to make their own paper or when they go somewhere, they won't start to fool around, although there are thirty kids. Instead, I feel that if we determined ahead of time what course they can take, then their motivation would be low and it would take a lot of time to get them interested in the first place.

The discussion led to a formulation of Team B's own model as distinct from that of Team A. In this model, students could choose between five different themes within the shared broader topic of a curriculum unit. Members of Team B called their model *theme teaching*.

> *Teacher B1:* There is also this difference, theirs are clearly called elective courses. Yet I think in theme teaching choice comes within the unit.… So let's stick to the name of theme teaching, and it will contain choice.
>
> *Teacher B5:* Yes, there really was a lot that somehow clarified things.…
>
> …
>
> *Teacher B3:* We have the freedom to make our own model.
>
> *Teacher B5:* We have to reflect, what are the differences and similarities between these. We really don't have to talk about elective courses.
>
> *Teacher B3:* No, we don't.
>
> *Teacher B5:* We haven't made elective courses so far. And we don't have to strive to be similar.
>
> *Teacher B3:* Yes, I think it's more like we will seek functional diversity, or a new way of working. Of course, we have objectives regarding the

contents, too, but it's more a question of students learning to work in different ways. . . .

Teacher B1: And we, too.

Teacher B3: And then to collaborate, also.

Teacher B5: Students get involved in different situations, in different groups, with different teachers and different students. So the goal is pretty social, because the contents change. Plus then, of course, the advantage of interaction between us, that we get to exchange and receive ideas as much as possible.

Here the joint meeting of the two teams was a form of boundary crossing. It did not lead to a shared concept or action plan. To the contrary, it sharpened the differences between the views held by the two teams. Teacher B5 used the argumentative question ("But what is the ideology here?") as a key discursive tool to sharpen the differences. This argumentative sharpening of differences was decisively important for the evolution of Team B's model. Team B formulated and subsequently successfully implemented theme teaching.

This case demonstrates that boundary crossing does not have to achieve mutually accepted interpretations across boundaries to be fruitful. Realization of differences and contrasts by means of argumentation may trigger significant collective concept formation on one or both sides of the boundary. Argumentation is not fruitful if there is no common point of reference. In this case, the question of dividing the students into groups functioned as a temporary boundary object or springboard (Engeström, 1987, pp. 328–331) that enabled the two teams to compare and contrast their views. It led to the fundamental questions of ideology and choice, of individualism and social interaction, and then back to the practical pros and cons of working in groups of 30.

Such stepwise alternation between theoretical principles and practical implementation seems typical of creative concept formation (Davydov, 1990). Crossing the boundary between two teacher teams led to debate and disagreement that seemed to facilitate concept formation, or theorizing "from the ground up," in Team B. Theme teaching, potentially a new theoretical concept, was formulated and put into practice.

Resources and Limits of Boundary Crossing in Teams

Like the primary care teams discussed in Chapter 4, the teacher teams analyzed in this chapter were deliberately created by the practitioners. What is unique about the teacher teams is that they were created to form an alternative to the dominant practice within their respective schools. In other words, these were teams with a mission to transform the pedagogical practices of school education from within. These teams faced the challenge of going beneath the surface in their change efforts. This meant questioning the hidden curriculum of the tacitly accepted rules and boundaries that structure the motivational sphere of schoolwork.

What place do such teams occupy in the historical scheme of Figure 1.2? On the one hand, these teacher teams had a strong craft tradition and an orientation toward autonomy. They wanted to step outside the increasingly standardized mass production of mainstream schoolwork, to create small, autonomous worlds of learning of their own. In this sense, these teams resembled the sociotechnical team concept. On the other hand, they were oriented outward, motivated to connect school learning to the world. They were willing to tackle and reconceptualize the object of schoolwork in an expansive manner. In this regard, they resembled the idea of knowedge- and innovation-driven teams. Tension between these two historically different modes of teamwork was a dominant characteristic of the teacher teams.

In their attempts to cross boundaries, both teacher teams utilized integrative cross-aged curriculum units as vehicles of change. Although the crossing of temporal, spatial, social, and disciplinary boundaries was impressive, its sustainability remained questionable due to the almost exclusive reliance on talk. The missing or weak documentation of the teacher teams reminds us of the critical observations Adler and Cole (1993; see Chapter 1) made of sociotechnical teams in industry. However, in both cases the teacher teams showed the power of contestation and argumentation as a resource of boundary crossing and innovation – something that goes beyond the typical repertoire associated with the lean production teams advocated by Adler and Cole.

The teacher teams were designed, in part, to construct new concepts and new knowledge. Their knowledge construction was limited by their weak tools and their partial clinging to the idea of autonomy. In the next chapter, I will investigate more systematically the processes and conditions of knowledge creation in teams.

6   Knowledge Creation in Industrial Work Teams

Putting Knowledge Creation Under a Magnifying Glass

In Chapter 3, I asked how innovation possibilities emerge in a team. I identified expansive transitions, moves from coordination to cooperation and communication in the way a team interacts and relates to its object. These concepts, further elaborated in Chapter 4, led to the tension between fixation and flow, or stabilization and destabilization, in a team's activity. In Chapter 5, yet another mechanism, namely, boundary crossing, was identified. All these findings may be regarded as elements or prerequisites that facilitate innovative learning and knowledge creation in work teams. But the process of knowledge creation itself remains to be explored in detail. So in this chapter I ask: How do teams learn and create new knowledge?

I define innovative organizational learning as collaborative learning in work organizations that produces new solutions, procedures, or systemic transformations in organizational practices (Engeström, 1995a). Studies of innovative organizational learning have thus far mostly produced relatively general conceptual tools (e.g., Argyris & Schön, 1978; Senge, 1990). Although it is commonly acknowledged that innovative learning at work has a complex cyclic character (e.g., Dixon, 1994), there have been few detailed attempts at theorizing such cycles and modeling their steps.

One of the most interesting attempts is the book by Nonaka and Takeuchi (1995). These authors focus exclusively on innovative learning, which they prefer to call *knowledge creation* in organizations. Nonaka and Takeuchi propose a theory of knowledge upon which they build a model of cycles of knowledge production. Their examples are primarily drawn from practices and cases of new product development in Japanese companies.

In this chapter, I compare and contrast Nonaka and Takeuchi's theory of knowledge creation with the conceptual framework of activity theory.

Activity theory is based on a dialectical theory of knowledge and thinking focused on the creative potential in human cognition (Davydov, 1990; Il'enkov, 1977).

I will first present data on two innovative learning processes – or processes of knowledge creation – that took place in successive meetings of a shopfloor work team located in a large machining plant in southern California. Then I will briefly present the theoretical framework of Nonaka and Takeuchi (1995) and apply it to the data. This exercise will demonstrate certain advantages but also certain shortcomings of the framework, calling for alternative and complementary approaches. Next, I will present a conceptual framework based on activity theory and on the theory of expansive learning (Engeström, 1987), which I will apply to the data in some detail. I will conclude with a discussion of the findings and uses of the two theoretical frameworks as toolkits for understanding innovative learning in work teams.

The Two Cases

Founded in 1927, the company in which the data were collected in 1995 was the world's leading manufacturer of midrange industrial gas turbines and turbomachinery systems. It had approximately 4,400 employees at its headquarters and manufacturing facilities in a major city in California. It had customers in nearly 80 countries and 29 sales/services offices in 14 countries.

In recent years, the company had invested heavily in teaming in all departments and at all levels of the organization. The teaming philosophy was based on the concept of self-directed work teams, systematically presented in Orsburn, Moran, Musselwhite, and Zenger (1990). The management had created a rather impressive system of training and internal support for teams.

Our field research was conducted in the Cold CAM section of the manufacturing plant (CAM = certified assembly manufacturing), where we observed, videotaped, and interviewed three adjacent production teams starting in May 1995. According to its mission statement, Cold CAM produced "components that are large and structural in nature, with surface precision and accuracies critical to engine alignment and clearances."

The data used in this chapter are from the largest of the three teams, established in 1994. In the spring of 1995 this team had 15 members, of whom 10 were machinists, 3 assemblers, and 2 welders. For purposes of production efficiency, the team was divided into two zones, Zone A and

Zone B. Zone A had six workers (including two welders and an assembler); Zone B had nine workers. The team's elected coordinator, Danny, was a machinist from Zone B. Zone A had its own zone leader, Roger (also a machinist). Zone B did not have a zone leader. The team as a whole was responsible for late parts. In the weekly team meetings, three experts with at least partially supervisory roles participated regularly: Curtis, the production engineer and area coordinator; Shawn, the resource planner; and Ron, a precision inspector.

The following analyses focus on two successive meetings of the team, held on May 30 and June 6, 1995. We videotaped both meetings, collected the written documents used in or produced to record the meetings, and conducted interviews with several participants. The analyses reported in this chapter are based on the transcripts of the videotaped conversations. Along with transcript excerpts, I will present a number of frames from the videotapes to highlight key aspects of the interaction. The frames are placed in the transcript excerpts immediately after the corresponding turns of talk. Thus, the frames are to be read as part of the transcript, not as separate figures with captions.

In the first meeting, the key issue discussed was whether or not the team should purchase new backup tooling. The new tooling was proposed by Curtis, the production engineer. The suggested new tooling (referred to as *Hertel tooling* in the transcript) would hold inserts that make the machines work. It was supposed to be more precise, more durable, and more expensive than other forms of tooling used thus far, and had been experimental at the company. In the transcripts, the term *Okuma* refers to the lathe that makes the parts, and *Mesma-Kelch* refers to an inspection machine that checks parts for discrepancies. *Department 31* refers to the team itself.

In the second meeting, the key issue was how to deal with scrap parts produced by the team. The company held ISO 9001/9002 quality system certifications, and the official policy required that scrap parts be reported in written form with the help of a Withholding Notice (referred to as *WN* in the transcript). The official procedure for handling WNs was called *corrective action*. It required that the operator responsible for the discrepant part attend a meeting outside the work team where the problem was discussed and rectified. In the transcript, the name "Crystal" refers to the precision inspector in charge of the corrective action procedure for the entire Cold CAM, and "Tony Edwards" refers to a manager of the Cold CAM.

The two cases to be analyzed represent innovative organizational learning at different levels. In the first case, the team produced a novel solution to a contested issue: whether or not to purchase new backup tools of a certain type and make. Team members initially disagreed on the issue and seemed to become deadlocked. The solution was based on a proposal to first test just one new tool in use and to decide on the purchase based on the experiences gained. I have previously called this type of outcome a *solution innovation* (Engeström, 1995a).

In the second case, the team produced a novel procedure for reporting and discussing causes of scrap parts. The team designed a procedure that deviated from the existing standard procedure in the plant. I have called these types of outcomes *trajectory innovations* (Engeström, 1995a). A solution innovation typically applies only to the specific case for which it was invented, whereas a trajectory innovation is designed to become a more or less permanent, repeatedly used procedure. Of course, it is possible that a solution innovation will subsequently be repeated in similar new situations, thus becoming a trajectory innovation. By contrast, a trajectory innovation may fail to generalize beyond the first application, thus effectively becoming a one-time solution innovation.

Using Nonaka and Takeuchi's Cycle as a Framework of Explanation

Nonaka and Takeuchi's (1995) theory of knowledge creation is based on a matrix of conversions between tacit and explicit knowledge. The matrix leads to a cyclic model of phases (Figure 6.1). The process of knowledge creation begins with *socialization*, or sharing of tacit, sympathized knowledge. The next phase is construction of explicit conceptual knowledge, also called *creating concepts*. This is followed by the phase of combining and constructing systemic knowledge, also called *justifying concepts*. Finally, the product is converted into operational and internalized knowledge. The authors divide this phase into two: *building an archetype* and *cross-leveling knowledge*. In a complex process of new product development, for example, this cycle is repeated over and over again.

I analyzed the transcripts of the two meetings in great detail with the help of Nonaka and Takeuchi's categories and found instances of all four of the basic phases depicted in Figure 6.1. In particular, creating concepts, justifying concepts, and constructing operational knowledge were relatively easy to identify. Sharing sympathized knowledge was much more difficult to find, although I finally identified two brief sequences that could be classified to represent that category.

Nonaka and Takeuchi develop and demonstrate the uses of their categories in cases of new product development that are much more global and

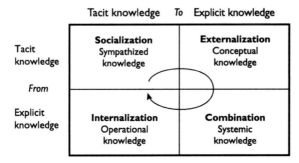

Figure 6.1. The cycle of four modes of knowledge conversion according to Nonaka and Takeuchi (1995, pp. 62, 71, and 72).

long-term than the discursive processes analyzed in this chapter.[1] The fact that it was possible to use their categories with these data indicates that the categories do have some analytical power and validity, even when applied to microlevel processes of innovative learning in individual team meetings.

Table 6.1 shows the two discussions broken into phases that follow Nonaka and Takeuchi's model as far as possible. *Turns* refers to numbered turns of talk in the discussion. The phases that could not be identified using Nonaka and Takeuchi's categories were scrutinized separately and given provisional names that try to describe their character without making any particular theoretical assumptions. These unrecognizable phases are indicated by italics in the table.

Table 6.1 reveals that two types of sequences in the team discussions could not be categorized within the conceptual framework of Nonaka and Takeuchi. I will call these sequences of *formulating/debating a problem* and sequences of *analyzing/debating a problem systematically*. Interestingly enough, the largest single chunks of discussion (measured by the number of turns of talk), namely, those consisting of turns 09–92 in meeting 1 and turns 64–175 in meeting 2, belonged to these two types that did not fit the framework.

Formulating/debating a problem covers sequences of discussion in which the participants present or argue about an issue or question to be discussed and resolved. Following is an example of a sequence where a new issue is brought to the table. A team member, Dana, initiated the new topic

---

[1] Nonaka and Takeuchi present their theory in universal terms. Yet, curiously, they all but neglect discussion of its relationship to the small cycles of continuous improvement, or *kaizen*, commonly seen as the foundation of creative renewal in Japanese companies.

Table 6.1. *Phases of knowledge-creation in the two team meetings (following the framework of Nonaka & Takeuchi, 1995; phases not recognizable within this framework are indicated by italics)*

Meeting 1		Meeting 2	
Turns	Phase	Turns	Phase
01–08	*Formulating/debating a problem*	01–12	*Formulating/debating a problem*
09–92	*Analyzing/debating a problem systematically*	13	Creating concepts
		14–19	Justifying concepts
93–99	Sharing sympathized knowledge	20–46	Constructing operational knowledge
100–132	*Analyzing/debating a problem systematically*	[47–63]	[Different topic]
		64–175	*Formulating/debating a problem*
133–153	Constructing operational knowledge	176–178	Creating concepts
154–189	*Analyzing/debating a problem systematically*	179–181	Sharing sympathized knowledge
190–200	Creating concepts	182–224	Justifying concepts
201–207	Constructing operational knowledge	225	Creating concepts
		226–239	Constructing operational knowledge

by asking what was happening with reporting scrap parts outside the team, a question discussed in the team meeting the previous week.

Meeting 2

71 *Dana:* Remember at the end of last week we were talking about going upstairs to Crystal about, uh, scrap parts?

72 *Danny:* It's actually downstairs.

73 *Dana:* Okay, well what's happening with that?

And here is an example of a sequence where participants try to formulate and define the issue through multifaceted debate.

Meeting 2

161 *Dave:* Wait, wait a second here. The, the whole thing in Zone A when Roger makes, if I scrap one of the parts that Roger's made we're doing real good on this 'cause it's happened and I have to get a hold of him and have him make the other one and it's such a more stressed team effort or these scraps want, he's either gotta catch it up with

me or vice versa. So it's not anybody getting off easy it's, it's a whole different process. I have to go, "Roger, I need to know the 103." [Des and Dana make hand movements indicating rejection]

162 *Des:* That's not the question.

163 *Dave:* And, and . . .

164 *Dana:* You're totally out there.

165 *Dave:* And, he's getting the billet out, he's documented that it's done. It's known then that otherwise we're gonna come short on your, your pieces of material.

166 *Des:* Yes, Dave. That's, that's between you and Roger and, and what Dana's about is, it's going, it's being elevated to a higher level.

167 *Danny:* It's going outside the department.

In this excerpt one of the participants, Dave, in effect argued that the present practice of dealing with scrap parts in Zone A was no problem, whereas others (Des, Dana, and Danny) argued that it was indeed a problem because Zone A was not submitted to external control, unlike Zone B. In other words, there was a debate about whether an issue was a problem or not. In these sequences, knowledge was represented as fuzzy, multifaceted *problematic*, to be somehow clarified and constrained. There was tension and pressure, but there was no clear assignment to work out or design an innovative solution.

Nonaka and Takeuchi's theory seems to take the initial existence of a fairly clear problem, task, or assignment as a given. Their cycle begins with the sharing of tacit knowledge *about a relatively clearly defined task*, captured by the authors in their notion of *organizational intention*.[2]

In the team we observed, the sequences of formulating/debating a problem were examples of *problem finding* rather than problem solving. The team may have seemed to begin with a clear task, but soon the task itself became problematized and problem construction took over. In other words, the processes of innovative knowledge creation in the team we observed emphasized much more the initial problem definition and problem construction than Nonaka and Takeuchi's model would allow.

In Nonaka and Takeuchi's model, a group of employees begins the cycle, with a clear organizational assignment in mind, by socialization, sharing

---

[2] The origination of the organizational intention is not discussed or analyzed: it is left to management as a black box.

their experiences in brainstorming camps, focused apprenticeships, and similar fields for creating *sympathized knowledge.*

> At Matsushita, team members apprenticed themselves to the head baker at the Osaka International Hotel to capture the essence of kneading skill through bodily experience. At Honda, team members shared their mental models and technical skills in discussing what an ideal car should evolve into, often over *sake* and away from the office. These examples show that the first phase of the organizational knowledge-creation process corresponds to socialization. (Nonaka & Takeuchi, 1995, p. 85)

The sequences of formulating/debating a problem were not at all like the socialization described by Nonaka and Takeuchi. The sharing of sympathized knowledge played a rather marginal part in the two meetings, certainly not the foundational role of starting the cycle, as the theory would predict. Here are excerpts from the two sequences of socialization I found in our team data.

Meeting 1
93 *Roger:* I'll, I'll agree with, I'll agree with Dana on that because I know exactly what he's talking about. But, you know just recently I found out that that Hertel's got some screws on it, on the holder that you told me, so it does flush it out that thing, and keeps the chips out of it.

94 *Curtis:* You, you, you can adjust the amount of flush.

[*All agreeing: Yeah*]

Meeting 2
179 *Nic:* I second that.

180 *Sanford:* [turning to Shawn] You're pretty good there fella, I agree with you this time.

181 *Shawn:* Thank you [pats him on the back]. That's a first.

The first of these situations occurred in the middle of an intense debate. The second occurred at the end of a debate, immediately after Shawn, one of the participants, had proposed an innovative solution to the issue at hand. Both were brief exchanges of sympathy, not the extensive socializing described by Nonaka and Takeuchi.

Analyzing/debating a problem systematically is the second category missing in the framework of Nonaka and Takeuchi. This type of discourse played a central role in the first team meeting. The following excerpt illuminates the character of this category.

Meeting 1

12 *Curtis:* [standing up] Question. If we've got a few minutes do you want to do a (quick) force field analysis right now, just on the bottom part of the board. Just say pros and cons and just [Danny: Yeah] do a little quick brainstorm here of where are the pros, where are the cons, and then just, then we can get a better idea right now where we want to head with this.

13 *Unknown Speaker:* (Project) sounds good.

14 *Unknown Speaker:* Yeah.

15 *Unknown Speaker:* If we have time, yeah.

16 *Curtis:* Do you have a pen?

17 *Unknown Speaker:* Pen?

18 *Danny:* Here's, here's a pen set right here.

19 *Nic:* Okay, who's the scribe? Curtis?

20 *Curtis:* Yeah, I'll, I'll scribe it. Okay.

21 *Nic:* _____

22 *Danny:* Pros and cons.

23 *Nic:* Pros and cons.

24 *Curtis:* Pros, cons. _____ . It's called a force field analysis, right. [Draws a twofold field on the whiteboard, the left hand side titled "Pros," the right hand side titled "Cons."] And, this is what's good about using the Hertel tooling, and then why, you know, arguments for why we don't need it. Okay, why we need it. Why we don't need it, okay. What are some of the reasons why we need it?

25 *Dana:* Time.

26 *Curtis:* Time. [Writes down "Time" on the left-hand side of the force field.]

27 *Dana:* Emphasize how much time.

28 *Curtis:* That's . . .

29 *Nic:* That's important. I mean if you ain't saving for thirty seconds or a minute, or you know, a day.

Here the problem of whether or not to buy new backup tools for the team was tackled by means of a systematic force field analysis, listing the pros and cons of each alternative solution. In the framework of Nonaka and Takeuchi, there seems to be no place for this type of discourse.[3] This is certainly not mere socialization and sharing of tacit knowledge – the procedure is explicit. But this is also not yet creation of new concepts or innovative ideas. The focus is on laying out and assessing what the members already know.

Both meetings analyzed above started with formulating/debating a problem, and both ended with constructing operational knowledge. Beyond this rather minimal similarity, the different phases observed in the two meetings did not follow any fixed order or identifiable sequential pattern. To the contrary, it seems that the different forms of knowledge suggested by Nonaka and Takeuchi may appear in many different orders and combinations in the course of a process of innovative knowledge creation.

The fundamental problem and limitation in the model of Nonaka and Takeuchi is, however, not the notion of a fixed sequential order in the cycle of knowledge creation. Such an order may always be understood as a flexible heuristic rather than a strict rule. Recall that Nonaka and Takeuchi construct a dynamic cycle out of a static matrix of four fields. These four fields are constructed on the basic distinction between tacit and explicit knowledge. Thus, the four fields, which are turned into four phases of a cycle, are essentially different modes of representing knowledge: tacit-sympathized, explicit-conceptual, explicit-systemic, and tacit-operational. The crucial question is: Are such representational modes of knowledge an appropriate basis for discerning phases and recurrent sequential patterns in processes of knowledge creation? In other words, is Nonaka and Takeuchi's leap from a matrix to a cycle justified?

I strongly doubt that a theoretically and empirically viable cyclic model can be built on the foundation of modes of knowledge representation. Modes of knowledge representation are instrumentalities, implementations of different toolkits of cognitive and discursive work. There is little evidence of any inherent order in the employment of such toolkits. Rather, they seem to be used in accordance with situationally constructed needs and opportunities, often in a probing manner and in opportunistic combinations. The few serious attempts that have been made to construct developmental models on the basis of successive representational modes, notably Bruner's (1966) *enactive*, *iconic*, and *symbolic*, have not gained much general currency. Although Nonaka and Takeuchi construct their cycle in a logical fashion, they offer little empirical evidence or compelling theoretical support for it.

---

[3] More precisely, Nonaka and Takeuchi's model has no place for debate and analysis, but their descriptive case materials do include such examples (e.g., Nonaka & Takeuchi, 1995, pp. 106–107).

Their cases seem to be partly handpicked and streamlined to fit the theory, and partly they are so ambiguous that they could be made to fit many competing and contradictory theories.

These observations lead me to the following intermediate conclusions. First, Nonaka and Takeuchi's categories may be productively used to describe different types of knowledge representation that are employed in the course of collaborative knowledge creation. Second, their framework should not be expected to be complete; in particular, it does not seem to account effectively for sequences of formulating/debating a problem, in which knowledge is represented as an open, multifaceted *problematic*, or for sequences of analyzing/debating a problem systematically, in which knowledge is represented as a problematic field to be circumscribed and dimensionalized. Third, Nonaka and Takeuchi's use of successive modes of knowledge representation may not be a viable basis for a cyclic model. Thus, it would be wise to search for and test alternative cyclic models of knowledge-creation.

Using Activity Theory and Expansive Learning as a Framework of Explanation

The situation-specific reconstruction and instantiation of the object of an activity system often takes the form of problem finding and problem definition. Simon's (1973) dictum that there are initially only ill-structured problems and that problem solving consists essentially of structuring and constraining the problem is quite appropriate against this background. What this dictum overlooks is that "one can never get it right, and that innovation may best be seen as a continuous process, with particular product embodiments simply being arbitrary points along the way" (von Hippel & Tyre, 1995, p. 12).

The mediating artifacts include both tools and signs, both external implements and internal representations such as mental models. It is not particularly useful to categorize mediating artifacts into external or practical ones, on the one hand, and internal or cognitive ones, on the other hand. These functions and uses are in constant flux and transformation as the activity unfolds. An internal representation becomes externalized through speech, gesture, writing, and manipulation of the material environment – and conversely, external processes become internalized. Freezing or splitting these processes is a poor basis for understanding different artifacts. Instead, we need to differentiate between the processes themselves, between different ways of using artifacts.

For this purpose, I have suggested four types of artifacts (Engeström, 1990). The first type is *what* artifacts, used to identify and describe objects. The second type is *how* artifacts, used to guide and direct processes and procedures on, within, or between objects. The third type is *why* artifacts, used to diagnose and explain the properties and behavior of objects. Finally, the fourth type is *where to* artifacts, used to envision the future state or potential development of objects, including institutions and social systems.

Although certain artifacts are typically used in certain ways, there is nothing inherently fixed in an artifact that would determine that it can only be, for instance, a why artifact. A conceptual model may typically function as a dynamic diagnostic tool, but it may also become a frozen definition used only as a what artifact to identify and classify phenomena. A hammer may typically be used as a what artifact for identifying objects that may be hammered (such as nails). But it may also become a where to artifact used as a symbol for workers' power.

The artifact-mediated construction of objects does not happen in a solitary manner or in harmonious unison. It is a collaborative and dialogical process in which different perspectives (Holland & Reeves, 1996) and voices (R. Engeström, 1995) meet, collide, and merge. The different perspectives are rooted in different communities and practices that continue to coexist within the same collective activity system:

> "Perspective" is a further elaboration of concepts that link activity systems to one another and to structures and dynamics of power and privilege. It allows one to speak more directly to agency in Marx's work, to the capacity of humans to apprehend the conditions of their activity and through their practice change those very conditions. (Holland & Reeves, 1996, p. 272)

As Holland and Reeves (p. 274) point out, perspective is a hedge against simplified views of context that ignore the unsettled and conflicted relations between different positions and actors. The concept of perspective opens up intriguing questions: Can and should perspectives merge? Is it possible or desirable to have a completely shared object in an activity?

The theory of expansive learning (Engeström, 1987) is based on the dialectics of ascending from the abstract to the concrete. This is a method of grasping the essence of an object by tracing and reproducing theoretically the logic of its development, of its historical formation through the emergence and resolution of its inner contradictions. A new theoretical idea or concept is initially produced in the form of an abstract, simple explanatory relationship, a *germ cell*. This initial abstraction is step-by-step enriched and transformed into a concrete system of multiple, constantly developing manifestations. In an expansive learning cycle, the initial simple idea is transformed into a complex object, into a new form of practice. At the same time, the cycle produces new theoretical concepts – theoretically grasped practices – concrete in systemic richness and multiplicity of manifestations.

In this framework, *abstract* refers to partial, separated from the concrete whole. In empirical thinking based on comparisons and classifications, abstractions capture arbitrary, only formally interconnected properties. In dialectical-theoretical thinking, based on ascending from the abstract to the concrete, an abstraction captures the smallest and simplest, genetically primary unit of the whole functionally interconnected system (see Davydov, 1990; Il'enkov, 1977; see also Bakhurst, 1991; Falmagne, 1995).

The expansive cycle begins with individual subjects questioning the accepted practice, and it gradually expands into a collective movement or institution. The theory of expansive learning is related to Latour's actor-network theory in that both regard innovations as stepwise construction of new forms of collaborative practice, or technoeconomic networks (Latour, 1987, 1988; see also Engeström & Escalante, 1995).

Ascending from the abstract to the concrete is achieved through specific epistemic or learning actions. Together these actions form an expansive cycle or spiral. An ideal-typical sequence of epistemic actions in an expansive cycle may be described as follows (see also Engeström, 1994c):

- The first action is that of questioning, criticizing, or rejecting some aspects of the accepted practice and existing wisdom. For the sake of simplicity, I will call this action *questioning*.
- The second action is that of *analyzing* the situation. Analysis involves mental, discursive, or practical transformation of the situation in order to discover causes or explanatory mechanisms. Analysis evokes "why?" questions and explanatory principles. One type of analysis is *historical-genetic*; it seeks to explain the situation by tracing its origination and evolution. Another type of analysis is *actual-empirical*; it seeks to explain the situation by constructing a picture of its inner systemic relations.
- The third action is that of *modeling* the newly found explanatory relationship in some publicly observable and transmittable medium. This means constructing an explicit, simplified model of the new idea that explains and offers a solution to the problematic situation.
- The fourth action is that of *examining the model*, running, operating, and experimenting on it in order to fully grasp its dynamics, potentials, and limitations.

- The fifth action is that of *implementing the model,* concretizing it by means of practical applications, enrichments, and conceptual extensions.
- The sixth and seventh actions are those of *reflecting* on and evaluating the process and *consolidating* its outcomes into a new, stable form of practice.

These actions bear a close resemblance to the six learning actions put forward by Davydov (1988) as constituents of learning activity that follows the logic of ascending from the abstract to the concrete. Davydov's theory is, however, oriented to learning processes within the confines of a classroom, where the curricular contents are determined ahead of time by more knowledgeable adults (Engeström, 1991b). This probably explains why it does not contain the first action of critical questioning and rejection,[4] and why the fifth and seventh actions, implementing and consolidating, are replaced by *constructing a system of particular tasks* and *evaluating* – actions that do not imply the construction of actual culturally novel practices.

The process of expansive learning should be understood as construction and resolution of successively evolving tensions or contradictions in a complex system that includes the *object* or objects, the mediating *artifacts,* and the *perspectives* of the participants. The entire ideal-typical expansive cycle may be diagrammatically depicted with the help of Figure 6.2.

The cycle of expansive learning is not a universal formula of phases or stages. In fact, one probably never finds a concrete collective learning process that cleanly follows the ideal-typical model. The model is a heuristic conceptual device derived from the logic of ascending from the abstract to the concrete. Every time one examines or facilitates a potentially expansive learning process with the help of the model, one tests, criticizes, and, hopefully, enriches the theoretical ideas of the model. In this light, it is necessary that the model of expansive learning is more detailed than, for instance, the very general sequence of *unfreezing, moving, and refreezing* suggested by Kurt Lewin (1947). When a model is too general and unspecific, it is practically impossible to test and develop it critically; almost any process will fit it.

The theory of expansive learning has often been applied to large-scale transformations in activity systems, often spanning a period of 2 or 3 years or even more (e.g., Engeström, 1991a, 1994b: Foot, 2001). In such a scale, the action phases of the expansive learning cycle are interpreted as lengthy

---

[4] This critical observation applies equally well to Nonaka and Takeuchi's theory. Only their model is not confined to the classroom. Instead, it is encapsulated by divorcing problem solving by employees from problem definition and goal setting by management.

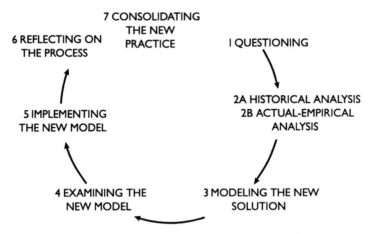

Figure 6.2. Sequence of epistemic actions in an expansive learning cycle.

periods of collaborative work dominated by a given action type (e.g., historical analysis, modeling). This corresponds roughly to the scale of events analyzed by Nonaka and Takeuchi.

In this study, the scale is radically changed. We are looking at phases and cycles that take minutes or perhaps an hour instead of months and years. Can such miniature cycles be considered expansive?

The answer is, yes and no. Miniature cycles of innovative learning should be regarded as *potentially* expansive. A large-scale expansive cycle of organizational transformation always consists of small cycles of innovative learning. However, the appearance of small-scale cycles of innovative learning does not in itself guarantee that an expansive cycle is going on. Small cycles may remain isolated events, and the overall cycle of organizational development may become stagnant or regressive or even fall apart. The occurrence of a full-fledged expansive cycle is not common, and it typically requires concentrated effort and deliberate interventions. With these reservations in mind, the expansive learning cycle and its embedded actions may be used as a framework for analyzing small-scale innovative learning processes.

Both Nonaka and Takeuchi's theory and the theory of expansive learning focus on the creation and practical application of powerful new concepts. Both theories regard knowledge creation as an escalating process.

> Thus, organizational knowledge creation is a spiral process, starting at the individual level and moving up through expanding communities of interaction, that crosses sectional, departmental, divisional, and organizational boundaries. (Nonaka & Takeuchi, 1995, p. 72)

Table 6.2. *Phases of knowledge-creation in the two team meetings (following the framework of Engeström, 1987; phases not recognizable within this framework are indicated by italics)*

Meeting 1		Meeting 2	
Turns	Phase	Turns	Phase
01–08	*Formulating/debating a problem*	01–12	*Formulating/debating a problem*
09–61	Actual-empirical analysis	13	Modeling a new solution
62–73	Questioning	14–19	Historical analysis
74–189	Actual-empirical analysis	20–46	*Reinforcing the existing practice*
190–192	Modeling a new solution	[47–63]	[Different topic]
193–203	Examining the new model	64–88	Questioning
204–207	Implementing the model	89–175	Actual-empirical analysis
		176–178	Modeling a new solution
		179–236	Examining the new model
		237–239	Implementing the model

However, whereas for Nonaka and Takeuchi (p. 72) "tacit knowledge of individuals is the basis of organizational knowledge creation," the theory of expansive learning sees different modes of knowledge representation (including the whole issue of tacit vs. explicit knowledge) as instrumentalities or toolkits that may be used in many different orders and combinations. The theory of expansive learning puts a lot of weight on the local discursive construction of a shared object and intention in knowledge-creation – something Nonaka and Takeuchi seem to take for granted, tacitly delegating it to management. It also also emphasizes the central role of contradictions and debate in knowledge-creation. The whole process is seen as energized and often radically refocused by negation: questioning, criticizing, even rejecting accepted wisdom.

In Table 6.2, the framework of expansive learning is applied to the transcripts of the two team meetings. As the table shows, the framework of expansive learning leaves three phases in the two processes unidentified. The framework of Nonaka and Takeuchi (Table 6.1) left six phases unidentified.

Interestingly, the first phase in both meetings (formulating/debating a problem) does not fall into the categories of questioning or analysis, whereas turns 64–175 in meeting 2 do fall into these two categories. In both meetings, the first phase consisted of a presentation and discussion of the issue prepared *for* the team, not initiated and constructed *by* the team.

The following excerpt illustrates this given-from-above character of these phases.

Meeting 2

01 *Danny:* Then what about that procedure for scrap parts in Zone A? That's a major issue on that side. I just...

02 *Shawn:* Here's the situation with that. The Centaur bill has cost us a hundred twenty-eight dollars apiece and the Mars bill has cost us two hundred dollars apiece. So every time you guys look down on it, every time we do like a four scrap on the first half of that shop work, we have a second operational scrap on the out. _____ we order down, we've overdrawn the variance. A hundred twenty-eight dollars on, on Centaur, two hundred dollars on Mars. The negative to that is we're not documenting the problems that are causing the scrap. A good example is uh...

The team coordinator, Danny, and the resource planner, Shawn, introduced the issue of dealing with scrap parts. Although Danny did open his turn with a question, this was immediately qualified with an authoritative statement ("That's a major issue on that side"), followed by Shawn's even more authoritative presentation of the economic costs involved. Shawn was not questioning – he was telling the others. There was an interesting twist to this when Shawn first said, "So every time *you* guys look down on it," then switched to "every time *we* do like a four scrap..."

The other unidentifiable sequence was named *reinforcing the existing practice*. In the framework of Nonaka and Takeuchi, turns 20–46 of meeting 2 fell into the category constructing operational knowledge. This would seem to correspond to implementation in the framework of expansive learning. But in this framework, the *object* is of decisive importance: implementation of *what?* The sequence covering turns 20–46 contains no new object. It contains an attempt to eliminate deviations from the accepted correct practice.

Meeting 2

22 *Shawn:* No, no what I need to have happen, what we have to have happen in terms of keeping inventory straight is when you guys, when the operator is not there and you lose a part, make a conscious decision whether or not you're going to replace it or not. If you choose not to replace it, say you have a six-piece order, you lose a ring, now it drops down to four, you almost order down to four and proceed – minus two pieces. If you determine after looking at that requirement that you need to replace it, then the requirements that you leave it

at the quantity of six, but you have to cash out the material to replace the parts that you scraped. If it's before the welding all you have to replace is the [billet], if it's at the weld you have to place the vanes and the ____

23 *Danny:* Roger?

24 *Jan:* ____

25 *Roger:* I really don't think that we need to make a conscious decision out there. If we make a scrap piece on that first half we've gotta replace it 'cause we're running the engine sets.

26 *Danny:* Yeah, well when we start on the compound we will have to.

27 *Roger:* We've got due dates for everything else, so we've got to come up with the process when it happens, how are we going to react to it? Are we going to MORC and L or are we going to scrap it and draw another piece out of the inventory?

28 *Shawn:* Behaviorally, I'd like to see you replace it. Because if you're constantly making a mistake and you're always having to go back and replace the part, you're gonna get sick and tired of doing it so you're gonna find out, okay why do we keep losing parts? Then you'll fix the process so it doesn't happen anymore. That's the behavior you're trying to create. So, if I had, if it was my decision alone I would, I would say replace the parts.

29 *?* Well, you want an engine so you've got to replace the parts.

30 *Danny:* So what we're gonna do with, we have to agree on this with MORC they'll order down and charge another billet and then all the details can go up.

31 *Shawn:* If you're going to replace a part you do not necessarily have to order it, just simply replace the part. But, you have to draw up a transaction to draw the material out of inventory. You can't just go grab a billet without you know a transaction.

32 *Roger:* And there was another ____ to that too. But, I mean I'm talking about the first side of the shop doing that. I mean you guys are gonna be getting two piece slot sizes the second, on the second side. When a piece of scrap hits you guys your key is to let us know. So we'll know one or the other engine sets comes from that, or we can replace the one part.

33 *Shawn:* Or piggyback another part on our next engine set, run three at one stage to replace it. There's some things, you know, that we could do to make up for the back half.

34 *Danny:* Okay, but for the first part of this...we'll do the MORC down, cash another billet...

35 *Shawn:* No, now listen. You're gonna replace a part you do not, do not list it in the order form. Just replace the part, but you have to do a transaction to pull the billet out of inventory.

The excerpt clearly contains operational discourse about how to proceed. But it is not about operationalizing an innovation. It is about operationalizing an already existing rule, represented by the managerial expertise of Shawn, the resource planner. We might say that this phase, as well as the initial phases of formulating/debating a problem in both meetings, are unidentifiable within the theory of expansive learning because *they are in fact nonexpansive*. In other words, processes of innovative knowledge creation are not pure. They contain both expansive and nonexpansive phases, both steps forward and digressions.

In spite of the differences, there seems to be a fair amount of similarity between Tables 6.1 and 6.2. Are the differences between the two frameworks perhaps only terminological? What added explanatory power does Table 6.2 offer?

The potential value of this framework lies in the opportunity it offers for examining closely the constitutive actions of expansive learning. Now that we have provisionally identified those actions in the discourse data, we can look at their dynamics in detail.

Questioning in Expansive Learning

The action of *questioning* is interesting in that it is all but missing in Nonaka and Takeuchi's framework. In the first team meeting, questioning erupted as a challenge in the middle of systematic analysis of pros and cons.

Meeting 1

61 *Danny:* It will utilize the initial cost of what we're already in, with you know the money we have left.

62 *Dana:* That's, that's, that's just trying to make it look good. Following along with a plan that was a bad plan to begin with. You see you disconnected...

63 *Curtis:* Well, Dana you got obviously some reasons, some strong feelings about why we shouldn't buy additional tools [turns toward Dana and point his left hand toward him]. Okay, why don't you present this side here [turn toward the whiteboard]. Why, why we don't need them?

64 *Dana:* Well I don't think we need it because what we've got now is working fine. What we've got now is working fine and I don't think we're gonna be saving any time, we're gonna be losing money . . . [Curtis writes "Working fine now" on the right-hand side of the force field on the whiteboard.]

65 *Unknown Speaker:* What have we got now?

66 *Dana:* We'll take tools out...

67 *Unknown Speaker:* Who's taking the tool out?

68 *Danny:* Let him finish.

69 *Curtis:* Shhhh.

70 *Dana:* We're supposed to be taking the tool out but now if, if, if we ain't taking it out and that's you know we ain't doing it right then.

71 *Unknown Speaker:* Why? It's working fine. We're not taking them out.

72 *Dana:* Well wait 'til you scrap a part. We've all seen that. It happens and we've been in this room many times saying...

73 *Curtis:* Hey, hey we won't talk about scrapping parts, we're talking about tools here, okay.

The challenge presented by Dana, a machinist, was straightforward: "a bad plan to begin with." Instead of engaging in a verbal fight or struggle over authority, Curtis, an engineer and area coordinator, used the force field on the whiteboard as a mediating artifact, transferring Dana's argument into an externalized, jointly observable form on the whiteboard. Externally, the analysis of pros and cons continued. However, after Dana's challenge, the dynamic of the discussion was changed. There was a tension that demanded a resolution. The exact contents of the tension were not clear at the outset. Much of the subsequent cognitive and discursive work in the meeting was devoted to turning the fuzzy tension into an analytically manageable problem.

Meeting 2

64 *Dana:* How 'bout the Zone B, how are we gonna write up the scrapped parts in Zone B?

65 *Curtis:* Most of the time those parts are going to be so costly, you know....

66 *Nic:* It's gonna be scrap.

67 *Danny:* The value of it is a lot higher than the...

68 *Curtis:* Most of the time it's either going to be scrap or repair.

69 *Shawn:* At that particular point we still need to have a replacement procedure. How are we going to replace the part in the engine set and that's what we have to work on in the zonings.

70 *Nic:* [inaudible]

71 *Dana:* Remember at the end of last week we were talking about going upstairs to Crystal about, uh, scrap parts?

72 *Danny:* It's actually downstairs.

73 *Dana:* Okay, well what's happening with that?

74 *Nic:* Everybody wanted to do it.

75 *Danny:* We voted on it.

76 *Roger:* It's all on.

77 *Danny:* Nine to six.

78 *Dana:* Well, at the end of last meeting, at the end of last meeting, we didn't finish voting and we said we'd carry it on to the following meeting.

79 *Jan:* No we didn't. [Several participants disagreeing: "No" "we voted"]

80 *Danny:* They voted how...

81 *Dana:* No I was here!

82 *Roger:* Timeout. Do you want to vote, vote now?

83 *Danny:* No, [whistle] Roger!

84 *Dana:* If that's the case, no see what is, what is the um, what is the, what is the pros out of taking it up to Crystal? I mean what, did we do a pro and con list?

85 *Jan:* We did this last week... from last week. Let's get the minutes from last week.

86 *Dave:* I don't ever get the chance to scrap a part and go...

87 *Jan:* We have all the pros and cons Dana.

88 *Dana:* No we didn't do one on this, Jan, you must have been sleeping, 'cause we didn't do this.

Here Dana's challenge came first in the form of questions ("how are we gonna write up...?" and "what's happening with that?"). When other participants maintained that the issue was closed in the preceding meeting, Dana argued that the issue was not closed. Roger (turn 82) suggested a re-vote; Dana (turn 84) responded by suggesting the employment of a pro and con list as a mediating artifact. Jan (turn 85) wanted to use last week's minutes as evidence, then (turn 87) argued that "we have all the pros and cons." Again, the atmosphere was electrified, although the exact contents of the tension were not yet clear.

In both meetings, the action of *questioning* was initiated by one participant but accomplished through collaborative argumentation. Basically these were actions of *collective refocusing*, though the new object was captured only in a fuzzy and ambiguous form. In the first meeting, the focus was shifted from mere technical comparison of features to an underlying opposition of alternative policies ("a bad plan to begin with"), although the shape of these alternative policies remained unclear at this point. In the second meeting, the focus was shifted from an operational maintenance issue that had nothing to do with scrap parts (turns 49–63) to reopening the issue of scrap parts and corrective action. Most participants thought this was already closed and left behind as an issue of simply reinforcing the existing policy (Zone A does only internal corrective action because the parts are cheap; Zone B does external corrective action because the parts are expensive).

Analysis in Expansive Learning

The actions of *analysis* are also missing in Nonaka and Takeuchi's framework.[5] In our data, *historical analysis* appeared only in meeting 2.

Meeting 2

14 *Shawn:* Maybe Curtis and Des can shed some light on how that quality, how that affects the quality report.

15 *Curtis:* Well, favorably, if you don't write it up you . . .

16 *Des:* Well that's what we've been doing in the past if you remembered, right up to the . . . Then John started to get upset because the inventory was so long he'd pull them down.

17 *Curtis:* People were going along accounting for all the pieces there were extra pieces, then all the sudden a ring was thrown out then another piece was grabbed.

18 *Danny:* The first and second are a little different.

19 *Curtis:* We asked okay, everybody write it up so that we can make sure we can account for all the material and, uh of course our quality

---

[5] Again, in their case descriptions Nonaka and Takeuchi do indicate that management may engage in historical analysis when formulating the organizational intention. But this happens before and outside the cycle of knowledge creation.

managers were the ones to account for everything. But then again, uh, we have said officially and unofficially that if, uh, the cost of parts is less than the cost of WN that we would go the variance route rather than writing it up. But, then again we have SPC which help document the problem.

History was used here to clarify the origination of the present policy. Interestingly, the dilemma and tension of the meeting, which would emerge only later, when Dana initiated the action of questioning, was implied in the way Curtis (the area coordinator) hesitated in his historical account: "*But then again*, uh, we have said officially and unofficially that if, uh, the cost of parts is less than the cost of WN that we would go the variance route rather than writing it up. *But, then again . . .* "

Actual-empirical analysis was used extensively in both meetings. In meeting 1, it was structured with the help of a mediating artifact, the force field analysis, which took the physical shape of a matrix of pros and cons. During the analysis, the object of analysis itself was renegotiated and revised.

Meeting 1

24 *Curtis:* And, this is what's good about using the Hertel tooling, and then why, you know, arguments for why we don't need it. Okay, why we need it. Why we don't need it, okay. What are some of the reasons why we need it?

. . .

113 *Curtis:* This is, this is for buying more Hertel tooling or not buying it. Reasons for buying it, reasons for not buying it, okay.

. . .

120 *Shawn:* So without the Hertel tooling, the down time is three to four minutes. [Unknown speaker: Right.] Without the Hertel tooling the _____ is not applicable, is that what I understand?

121 *Unknown Speaker:* Yeah

122 *Dave:* But we're still gonna stay with Hertel.

123 *Shawn:* Yeah, without the Hertel tooling we're running just fine as we are. Is that a true statement?

124 *Nic:* That's what they're saying. Some people are saying.

125 *Jan:* But you already have a . . . investment with Hertel right?

126 *Danny:* Well, a lot of it yeah. We have those impact . . . already. That's a high dollar cost that we have, we're not using.

127 *Roger:* We bought Hertel and we bought the Mesma-Kelch, at least that's my understanding, to implement Hertel and the tools right there at your machine. (Active) tools we just never did it before. We've been three years down the line . . . we always did it with the . . .

128 *Dave:* Curtis, this isn't really compare Hertel against another tool though?

129 *Curtis:* No, no this is just, we're using Hertel tooling, it's just, it's just the way . . .

130 *Dave:* Either way we're gonna use the Hertel tooling, so either way we need backup tools. Regardless whether people have changed the insert in the machine or not.

Also, the mediating artifact, the force field analysis matrix, was revised in the middle of the analysis.

Meeting 1

154 *Curtis:* [Has added a second twofold field on the whiteboard, to the right from the original one; the original is titled "Hertel tooling"; the new one is titled "As-Is"] Here and over here. I had a brain lapse, this is really how you do one of these things. Here's the Hertel tooling,

here's how it is, here's the pros and cons for Hertel, here's the pros and cons for As It Is, so I kind of separated them out. So here's Hertel tooling we got: it's gonna reduce time um, with the new method it's supposed to be more accurate but it's gonna require torque, actually it should say it's gonna require torque, that should be on this side, torque wrenches.

Although the force field matrix gave structure to the analysis, it created problems of its own. It did not differentiate between specific descriptive features and general principles as possible pros and cons. It seemed almost too easy to throw in some feature as a pro or a con without explaining why it should be interpreted as such. This led to ambiguous interpretations, such as the following one.

Meeting 1

105 *Woo:* I have a con. Saving money.

106 *Danny:* Okay.

107 *Curtis:* Save...money [writing the words on the bottom of the right-hand side of the force field]. As a con?

108 *Jan:* That's not a con.

109 *Woo:* Yeah.

110 *Danny:* That's too.

[Several participants mumbling]

111 *Curtis:* This is, this is Hertel...

112 *Unknown Speaker:* Full blown.

113 *Curtis:* This is, this is for buying more Hertel tooling or not buying it. Reasons for buying it, reasons for not buying it, okay.

[Overlapping conversation]

114 *Jan:* Save expenses?

115 *Curtis:* [pointing at the bottom of the right-hand side of the table] Yeah, we got that right here [wipes off the last line from the bottom of the right-hand side of the force field].

116 *Danny?:* It would be save expenses, yes.

117 *Curtis:* Now saying, uh [Jan: Save the budget] or the cons, the cons for Hertel tooling is that it's [Danny: Expensive] more expensive than. _____ [writes down "more $" at the bottom of the right-hand side of the force field]

118 *Dave:* Not necessarily. Less expensive, I guess...

119 *Curtis:* Well I was doing one process against the other, um, the best that I could.

Correspondingly, the outcomes of the force field analysis were far from conclusive. The analysis resulted in evolving lists of pros and cons from which the team could not derive a clear-cut solution.

Meeting 1

156 *Curtis:* Okay, um we're gonna gain visual management and we'll start using the Mesma-Kelch properly, presetting. The cons for that is, is yeah that we're gonna have to use torque wrenches, it's very sensitive to torque which of course your accuracies then are very dependent upon that torque. Uh, your Z dimensions are up. You take that in and out you have room, room for chips to get in there and air um, you gotta, depend on good flushing because it says never to blow the air directly in to the adapter, um so that repeatability is in question and it costs a lot more money to go that way.

157 *Roger:* I've got another pro here Curtis when you get a chance.

158 *Curtis:* Okay. And then so far what I have for As Is, um we don't need the torque wrenches, it's more accurate right off the Mesma-Kelch and it's doing just fine. The, the con is it, it just takes more time than if we just had to change the one piece of the tool. . . . So, that's kinda what I've got out of it so far.

The inconclusive, almost endless nature of the force field analysis led Curtis, the area coordinator, to press repeatedly for some sort of closure to the discussion.

Meeting 1

172 *Curtis:* Anyway, from this information, do you think we're at a point where we can make a decision or do you still think it's like (six to one half a dozen hen or a rock in a hard spot) type of thing?

. . .

185 *Curtis:* Yeah, you've got a lot of scribbling on that page. Anyway, do you think we're at a point where we can make decision, or do you think we can table this and go on to a little bit more research? From, from what I read here we've got people going both ways so it looks like we need to have Emmit either do us a little more proof. . . .

186 *Frank:* . . . we're gonna have people going different ways six months from now.

187 *Roger:* Well, what I think we've gotta do is, is we gotta, we gotta make a decision on one way or another and do it. [Frank: There we go.] Not say, "Well, I don't like it so, but I'll use it and . . . "

The response from Frank and Roger increased pressure toward a solution immediately rather than delay. Though seemingly constraining, this kind of pressure toward a decision may in practice facilitate innovation rather than compromise (Perrow, 1984).

In meeting 2, actual-empirical analysis took a different shape. It became a struggle between *principles*, much more explicitly than in meeting 1. This difference was probably to a large extent a consequence of the different nature of the issues discussed. However, the use of the force field matrix as a mediating artifact may also have played a role, as indicated previously.

The analytical debate spanning turns 89–175 was basically a confrontation between two major principles of work organization: *individual responsibility and accountability* versus *equal responsibility and fairness*. After the questioning sequence, Curtis, the area coordinator, began to justify the practice of an individual corrective action procedure that required reporting scrap parts outside the team. Curtis invoked the principle of individual responsibility and accountability ("report on their *own* mistakes") – only to receive an immediate rebuttal from Dana, who invoked the principle of equal responsibility and fairness ("the first half *too*").

Meeting 2

89 *Curtis:* Let me, let me give you a good reason 'cause my boss asked for the [ME's] to be out of the loop, but he wants the ____ people to go and report on their own mistakes.

90 *Dana:* Okay, well then you have the first half too, why are you trying to hide something from your boss?

A little later, Curtis explicated the principle of individual responsibility more fully.

Meeting 2

106 *Curtis:* Well, the whole point is not to have to report it to Danny or have Danny go. The whole point is that each person takes care of their own problem. They do all the paperwork and take it to the meeting themselves.

Not long after that, Dana tried to explicate the principle of equal responsibility, only to receive an individualist rebuttal from Curtis.

Meeting 2

120 *Dana:* No, but if you're gonna do it you might as well do it all the way through. You're saying, this is what you're saying well if the first half scraps a part they just have a meeting in Zone A.

121 *Curtis:* Well, why don't you become a member of Zone A instead of Zone B?

Dana did get support from some of the team members, most notably Des, who repeatedly paraphrased and clarified Dana's point.

Meeting 2

132 *Des:* What Dana's saying is quite true, he's, what Dana is concerned about here . . . The guys in Zone A, they can scrap a part. They can just let . . . What Dana's thinking is, they scrap a part, just slide it aside, ignore it and run on.

133 *?* And let me tell you that's what I used to do.

134 *Des:* In Zone B they have to go through all this paraphernalia and procedure. That's not to say that the people in Zone A still have to report.

135 *Dana:* Exactly.

And again:

Meeting 2

149 *Des:* The people in Zone A still have to report and they still are responsible for the parts that they scrap. All I'm saying is, I agree with Dana. Dana's idea here is there's favoritism being portrayed by one side in other words the, the individuals in, in Zone A are getting off light when they scrap a part. Whereas the operators in Zone B are getting hit hard. And . . .

150 *Roger:* How are they getting hit hard?

151 *Shawn:* 'Cause they have to report and the people in Zone A don't.

152 *Danny:* Let him finish.

153 *Roger:* Well, I mean what's so hard about going to a meeting and saying I screwed up here and this is the problem.

154 *Des:* Wait a minute, hold on Roger. I'm only relating what, what, what Dana. I'm trying to interpret what Dana's ideas are. With regards one side has to go to a meeting and the other, the other side doesn't. Am I right Dana?

In themselves, the two principles are logically fully compatible: Individual responsibility can apply to everyone equally. In this case, their incompatibility was caused by a subprinciple attached to individual responsibility, namely, the subprinciple of *cost-efficiency*.

This subprinciple was enforced as a reservation: If individual responsibility becomes too costly, that is, if the external corrective action procedure costs more than an average scrap part, then full individual responsibility is not applied. The team was divided into Zone A and Zone B. Parts handled in Zone A were cheaper than those handled in Zone B: thus, the principle of individual responsibility was fully applied only to workers in Zone B – which in turn violated the principle of equal responsibility.

Meeting 2

125 *Curtis:* No Dana, list . . . , listen to this the whole reason for not writing up a part is because the cost of processing a WN, writing it up and processing it costs more than the part that's the whole reason for not doing it.

126 *Dana:* Your boss tells you to write a WN and you say no [raises his hand toward Curtis]. That's what I heard today.

127 *Shawn:* What you're saying is . . .

128 *Curtis:* I told . . .

129 *Dana:* Why don't you tell your boss all that?

130 *Curtis:* I told you my boss wants us to write WNs but for the exception of cost.

131 *Roger:* It costs more to write a WN than it is to scrap it.

The principle of equal responsibility also carried two subprinciples: *nonredundant reporting* and *not being singled out outside the team.* The first of these subprinciples was explicated by Nic.

Meeting 2

105 *Nic:* What I do, what I would like, can I say something [what I, can I] I don't agree, I didn't vote on this. I voted but I voted in the negative. I personally, myself think it's, it's kinda redundant, uh, the guy makes a scrap, uh, he makes the corrective action, he reports that to Danny, he reports it to the ME's and that should be enough, that's internal now, now he's got to take more time out to go to another meeting and report the same thing that he's already reported twice and talked about to somebody else.

The second subprinciple was explicated in a debate between Dana, Roger, and Curtis, joined by several others a little later.

Meeting 2

155 *Dana:* You're, you're exactly right now it just, now these guys see it like we just go to a meeting and they document it for improvement purposes. Well if that's what you guys believe, you know that's not what's happening. You get your name documented several times, someone's gonna take note how you guys are scrapping parts so.

156 *Roger:* Your name will be documented no matter if you go to the meeting or not.

157 *Dana:* No it ain't, no, not 'cause it ain't a WN. It might be in Curtis's file but it ain't up to the manager, it's not in front of a WN.

158 *Curtis:* The only person who takes any action is me anyway, okay. So no matter what happens all action is taken through me. So whether it's recorded in that meeting it makes no difference [Dave, Sanford and Shawn all raise their hands and want to speak.]

159 *Sanford:* Wait a minute, the other ones should have to, too.

160 *Dana:* Exactly.

161 *Dave:* Wait, wait a second here. The, the whole thing in Zone A when Roger makes, if I scrap one of the parts that Roger's made we're doing real good on this 'cause it's happened and I have to get a hold of him and have him make the other one and it's such a more stressed team effort or these scraps want, he's either gotta catch it up with me or vice versa. So it's not anybody getting off easy it's, it's a whole different process. I have to go, "Roger, I need to know the 103." [Des and Dana make hand movements indicating rejection.]

162 *Des:* That's not the question.

163 *Dave:* And, and . . .

164 *Dana:* You're totally out there.

165 *Dave:* And, he's getting the billet out, he's documented that it's done. It's known then that otherwise we're gonna come short on your, your pieces of material.

166 *Des:* Yes, Dave. That's, that's between you and Roger and, and what Dana's worried about is, it's going, it's being elevated to a higher level.

167 *Danny:* It's going outside the department.

168 *Des:* Yeah, it's going outside the department and it actually is being documented, registered and all that good stuff.

169 *Dana:* And it's like . . .

170 *Curtis:* There's never been anybody disciplined out of that quality meeting, never not once at all.

171 *Des:* I know.

172 *Sanford:* Yeah, but humiliated...

173 *Danny:* I take it in case you were in Zone B, you were in Zone B and you did spit out a few WN's back to back and you had to report and your name was written on that WN maybe it's time to switch over to A side for awhile.

174 *Shawn:* No, no that's not the situation.

175 *Danny:* I don't know, I don't know, it is an issue that doesn't seem fair.

This sequence was not mediated by graphic artifacts such as the force field matrix used in meeting 1. Words and gestures were the primary mediating artifacts in this debate. Beyond that, verbally formulated principles were employed as decisive *why* artifacts. This whole debate is an example of analysis in the important sense that general principles were separated analytically from various descriptive details and explicated in such a way that the central disagreement became evident.

Modeling a New Solution in Expansive Learning

In both meetings, the new solution was formulated in a brief sequence almost as a sudden flash of insight. In meeting 1, the solution – testing just one new machine in practice before deciding on the purchase – was suggested by Dana, supported by Roger.

Meeting 1

187 *Roger:* Well, what I think we've gotta do is, is we gotta, we gotta make a decision on one way or another and do it. [Frank: There we go.] Not say, "Well, I don't like it so, but I'll use it and..."

188 *Dana:* Well, why don't... Oh, excuse me...

189 *Shawn:* May I ask a question? [Roger I guess so] Maybe... just ask the question, how many people would support it, is there anyone that's like thumb's down against doing it? Is there anybody that's like really...?

190 *Dana:* Well, why don't we do this. We've got enough backup tools for one machine, right?

191 *Shawn:* Can we answer my first question please? Do have anybody in this room that is dead set against it?

192 *Dana:* [smilingly] Well, why don't I, why don't I answer this one first [Roger watches Dana intensely, smiles and groans encouragingly] and then yours will be like the second. Okay, why don't we try it at one machine, we've got enough back-up tools, and then see how, how it works.

This sequence was remarkable in that Dana made his suggestion in spite of first having been fairly forcefully overridden by Shawn, the resource planner (turns 188 and 189). In turn 192, Dana basically recaptured the initiative by force, with significant vocal and mimetic encouragement from Roger. Roger's support had a dual function: It encouraged Dana, and it gave immediate weight to his suggestion in the eyes of other participants. The new solution was a joint achievement.

A careful analysis of previous events reveals that the new solution was not, after all, a sudden flash of insight. Before becoming formulated, Dana's idea was silenced at least once before in the course of the meeting.

Meeting 1

174 *Roger:* Dana had an idea here. Because I said we had the money.

175 *Dave:* You know it's not tool-wise, it's . . .

176 *Unknown Speaker:* And then we can get Curtis, get Curtis to write out a check.

177 *Curtis:* Yeah I'll use my Visa card.

178 *Dave:* So that option kinda went right out the window, huh.

179 *Unknown Speaker:* Is that a Gold Card?

180 *Curtis:* No...

181 *Unknown Speaker:* It won't handle it then.

182 *Curtis:* I don't, I don't carry that kind of a balance on my card.

In turn 174, Roger began to introduce Dana's novel idea. But the initiative was taken by others, who started joking about purchasing the tools with Curtis's Visa card. Instead of re-mediating the discourse toward a solution, joking here diverted it from the emerging new idea.

In meeting 2, the new solution was modeled equally briefly, this time by Shawn, the resource planner. He introduced the principle of *teaming* as a way out of the deadlock between the principles of individual responsibility and equal responsibility.

Meeting 2

176 *Shawn:* Can I tell you my thoughts on it? Part of the teaming concept here is us being all accountable to one another and as a team being accountable to the organization. And, I agree with the, with what Dana's saying to have one team member have to go up there and say, "I screwed up," and it's not a tough, not a grinder where we happen to lose parts, no matter who's over there or on the third Okuma because of some of the, the...

177 *Nic:* Then it's dimensions...

178 *Shawn:* Then you have the same three or four people going up there you know saying, "I screwed up, I screwed up." And my opinion, this is my opinion. If, if we have a representative of the team going he can say the operator made this mistake here's the corrective action, without putting a name tag on who did it 'cause in the scheme of teaming that's really not relevant. Now if there's a problem that is from, say it's Dana who keeps scrapping the part. The team says, "Hey Dana, you need to pay more attention," 'cause it's just, it's just pure neglect. Then the team takes care of that problem. Not the organization, that's what. That's how I perceive it.

Shawn's suggestion was powerfully mediated by the rhetorical device of reported speech. This device was used to make vividly concrete both the negative ("I screwed up, I screwed up") and the positive ("Hey Dana, you need to pay more attention") alternative.

Again, careful examination reveals that the solution had antecedents in the discussion. At the very beginning of the meeting, Danny, the team coordinator, suggested the notion of *internal corrective action*, although at that point conservatively, limited to Zone A, where even management did not demand external corrective action due to its costs.

Meeting 2

13 *Danny:* That's for inventory reasons. What about quality, uh corrective action reason. I was thinking in terms of going ahead with the corrective action sheet or form that we normally do for the building. And have it like an internal corrective action setup so, you know we don't just take these parts off and throw 'em in the trash and sit back down and forget about it. So, you know, we can speak about it in this meeting or maybe Zone A meeting, when we scrap a part we'll talk about that corrective action and how to prevent it and all that kind of stuff. That way quality is improved and then what you spoke about to take care of inventory. And we keep it within our department, nobody else needs to know.

Notice that Danny used the protective argument "nobody else needs to know" rather than pushing offensively for the team principle. He did not even mention the word *team* at this point. This anticipatory but premature attempt at modeling the new solution was left without a collaborative response and elaboration. However, the term *internal corrective action* was picked up later and played a decisive role in the conceptualization of the solution – though invested with conceptual content different from that suggested by Danny.

As pointed out earlier, Nic then argued for internal corrective action to avoid redundant reporting (turn 105). However, he too failed to invoke the teaming principle. Thus, the contradiction between the two major principles of individual responsibility and equal responsibility remained unsolved.

Examining the New Model in Expansive Learning

In both meetings, the new solution model was collectively *examined* immediately after its formulation. In meeting 1, this involved only one reservation from Curtis (turns 193 and 195). Roger immediately began to concretize the model – again, notice the use of reported speech (turn 197). After that, the conclusion was evident and Curtis, too, expressed his approval (turn 201).

Meeting 1

193 *Curtis:* We still need to buy the screen gauge.

194 *Dana:* The what?

195 *Curtis:* To qualify your torque wrenches in there. You can't, can't do it without investing some money.

196 *Dana:* Well...

197 *Roger:* Let's talk to Emmit. He's got an idea here [pointing at Dana]. Let's talk to Emmit say, "Emmit let us have one of these things on consignment" [Dana: There you go], see if, see if, see if the system works and if, and if we see the system working we'll go ahead and purchase it, and if not they'll have it back...

198 *Jan:* That does make a lot more sense.

199 *Danny:* That makes a lot of sense.

200 *Roger:* You know he's got, he's got one machine back there we can do back and forth.

201 *Curtis:* All right, I think the story's coming to an end here.

202 *Danny:* All right, yeah. So we'll go with that.

203 *Roger:* Does everybody else agree?

In meeting 2, the examination was more critical and comprehensive. First, Shawn's model received warm support from Nic, Sanford, and Dana.

Meeting 2

179 *Nic:* I second that.

180 *Sanford:* [turning to Shawn] You're pretty good there fella, I agree with you this time. [Abe has his hand up]

181 *Shawn:* Thank you [pats him on the back]. That's a first.

182 *Abe:* Okay, hey if everybody on the A team agrees with this process, I think it's okay. But, the guys on the B team don't, well, I mean, I don't know.

183 *Dave:* _____

[Several participants talking]

184 *Dana:* That's how I feel that's how it should be done.

The discussion soon took the shape of a debate between Curtis and Shawn.

Meeting 2

200 *Curtis:* Okay, to this point for the most part, somebody like Des or myself and over the last couple of years it had been a management team member going to the meeting, okay and they have asked to have those who actually create the WN to go and report on the WN because they better than anybody, know exactly what happened and if it happened to them maybe they're the ones who can come up with the idea of how to avoid it again. If, if I was out there and made a piece of scrap and knew exactly what I did to cause it, maybe I could come up with the best solution of how I can avoid doing it again. And that's the whole idea behind having people go report their own corrective actions, not to say, "Hey I'm in trouble something _____." It's "What can I do to make it better so I don't do this again and help other people avoid doing it." That's the whole purpose.

201 *Shawn:* We all agree with what you're saying in terms of documenting the corrective actions. The issue here is in dealing with the operator in terms of his, you know, it's very uncomfortable for a lot of people to go up there and say, "I screwed up." There is a soft skills side of the business here that Dana's talking about. If, if Roger scraps out fifteen parts on the first Acuma then never had to talk about it, he scraps out one part on the Grinder but he has to report on it. It, it does create you know a sense of, uh, I'm not sure what the word is, but unfairness and being uncomfortable for some people. If they're writing [Curtis tries to interrupt] the issue, the issue if they're writing the corrective actions, right. If Dana scraps out a part, and he, and he still writes a corrective action, then who cares who reports what the corrective action is. That's . . .

Here both Curtis and Shawn used reported speech. Soon enough, Shawn also employed the mediating device of analogy.

Meeting 2

210 *Shawn:* Let me give you an analogy, let me give you an analogy. If, if we're a baseball team and you're the short stop and you make a critical error that costs your, your team the game, does the short stop go to the President or the, the GM and say you know, "Next time, next time I'm gonna get my butt and watch the ball into the glove," and he already knows he made a mistake. He already knows he made an error, he already knows he's gonna, he's gonna you know to work

harder at being better, more efficient and some positions in baseball you're gonna have more errors because there's a lot more action than a short stop for example, versus a right fielder who'll over the course of the season make three or four errors.

The decisive artifact turned out to be the principle of teaming. This began to become clear when Nic made what was for him an unusually long and forceful statement.

Meeting 2

215 *Nic:* Just real, real briefly uh, you know when John, uh Shawn was talking before about the team. It's just, it's just kinda similar to me with Des' little [sheet] then going to this other guy and outside the team, [indicating "outside" by raising his right hand] you know, this is, this

is the team we have our, we're trying to develop our own business. [Enforcing his idea by repeatedly pushing, almost pounding his right hand down toward the table; Dave rests his head on the tabletop as if falling asleep] We have to address, I, I feel we have to address

these issues within ourselves at the Acuma team, at the ... team, at the Zone B team, the A team work together and like we were talking about before, sure if Dana just, just Dana as a name, right now makes three, four of the same mistakes of course we're gonna say, "Hey, what's happening guy, you know you can't do this." But the fact is to write that corrective action, talk to the team about it as we do, you know we can always talk about these things and then go to somebody outside the team [raising his hand to indicate "outside"], that including Tony Edwards. I have never seen Tony Edwards come through the shop and look at all the processes and all that [shit] and I'm sure Crystal doesn't know what the whole process and problems we have so, it, to me they're, they're outside looking in [again raising his hand to indicate 'outside']. We're the people that need to solve these problems as a team and I just, that's the way I feel. We don't need to go outside the circle.

Nic's statement added the important aspect or variable of *expertise* to the examination. If external corrective action involves reporting to people who do not know the local process, why not keep the reporting inside the team, where the expertise exists? The distinction between inside and outside was made the crux of the matter by means of corresponding significant hand gestures.

Roger, who was initially opposed to the new model, changed his mind and suggested a compromise whereby Zone A would also do external corrective action but not write up a formal WN. Roger's compromise received a mixed response.

Meeting 2

217 *Roger:* Okay, uh I'm gonna go with Dana, uh I mean our problem here, shhh [Nic: Right] our problem here seems to be for Zone B has to go to corrective action ____. Side A or B on this side doesn't have to go. Why don't we set something up with, with Crystal, we fill out the corrective actions. We don't create WN's 'cause it will cost us money. We do have to go to the meeting and come up with the corrective action . . . parts that come out of the job, or a spin on the second op, or we put the wrong punch in it. We can have the corrective actions, it's, I don't see any problem with it.

218 *Danny:* You wanna have a corrective action for Zone A down there, you're saying.

219 *Roger:* Yeah, Zone A.

220 *Shawn:* That would make it more fair.

221 *Roger:* I mean that's, that's what I hear it's not fair, now this would be fair.

[Overlapping talk]

222 *Danny:* Well, well not really because you'd still have WN's to document and . . . in the system with in, in the [subdescriptor] has your . . . number on it so although you will be, um, doing the corrective action in front of Crystal and them. I know it's not fair.

223 *Roger:* Well, I mean we're not getting our hands slapped we're not getting beat, we're not getting fired for it. Curtis is sitting here saying that what they're looking for is a corrective action . . . and that's what we're gonna be doing, we're gonna be trying to get a corrective action, that's all it is.

Being uncertain of the implications of Roger's compromise proposal, Danny, the team coordinator, turned to Ron, the team's expert on corrective action. This brought the examination to a close.

Meeting 2

224 *Danny:* Ron's, Ron's the guru with that corrective action.

225 *Ron:* Um, that won't work. For one if you report on any WNs in that meeting, and it's minutes to that meeting, okay guy . . . comes

down and looks for that WN or a corrective action is found and he says, "Well why wasn't a WN written?" That's a hit against ISO, number one. Number two, number two, uh, if you want to go to some type of form of _____ [raising the forefinger of his right hand as if an instructor; participants keenly focusing on Ron] I suggest that I'd think again.

That actually, we as a team, we can [repeatedly pushing or pounding his right hand down toward the tabletop; participants keenly focusing

on Ron] vote to be taken out of the loop of corrective action and do internal corrective action and return our corrective actions to Tony Edwards straight from the group. That way we can face the issues of on the first Acuma on the first side without writing a WN and then we don't have a whole bunch of admins. But we have our internal corrective actions for the first side and then we have the ones who, that we have WN documentation, that we have to get Tony to sign off. So that way we're dealing with both issues, we're dealing with the third and the issues of the first as a team, as a team [pushing or pounding his right hand down toward the tabletop] and that way every time something happens on the first you have, not a WN but maybe some type of sheet, "Okay, here's what happened," and you fill out a corrective action "This is what happened" and then we'll address that in our internal corrective action.

Ron first seemed to represent the viewpoint of management, referring to the demands of the ISO. This move was needed to point out that Roger's compromise was not viable. After that, Ron forcefully reformulated Shawn's model of internal corrective action and the team principle behind it. The crucial distinction between outside and inside was again expressed with the mediating hand gestures used earlier by Nic. After Ron's authoritative input, participants expressed general agreement and a decision was reached quickly.

Implementing the New Model in Expansive Learning

In both meetings, the *implementation* of the new model was a rather technical and brief ending sequence of the discussion. In meeting 1, the only substantive step toward implementation was a summary of the decision formulated by Curtis.

Meeting 1
204 *Curtis:* So, so the end to this conversation is we're going to ask Emmit [Dana: Did you get that on film? General laughter and overlapping talk in an approving tone] for a straight gauge on consignment, or until we can prove for ourselves that this system will work for us, and then if so we will write him the check for____, otherwise it's you have it back and we don't want anything to do with it.

In meeting 2, Ron was appointed as the person, together with team coordinator, Danny, to take the team's proposal forward.

Meeting 2

237 Danny: Why don't we put Ron up ... Ron, Ron do you want to take part of that, take action on that and I'll help you, together. . .

238 Ron: I know we have team power, but how much team power do we have?

239 Danny: Well, let's find out. So if you have something by next week, let us know what the progress is. Next maybe, you'll have something, maybe. All right, put him down for next week.

Ron's question (turn 238) was prophetic. After an initial positive response, management eventually turned down the team's proposal for full-scale internal corrective action.

Conclusions

In both of the team meetings just analyzed, the team constructed a problem and an innovative solution to it. In what sense was there innovative learning and knowledge creation?

The first solution was to test a single tool in practice before deciding to purchase a whole set of similar tools. This does not seem to be a particularly original idea. Yet, there was disagreement on the benefits and drawbacks of the new tools, and no consensus was in sight. The only reasonable decision seemed to be postponement of the decision – in itself no guarantee of anything better. The testing solution was clearly novel for the team. It may have remained a one-time innovation. On the other hand, it may also have provided a model and a resource for proceeding in other similar situations.

Whether sustained learning in the classical sense (similar stimulus situation – novel behavior) actually took place is an open issue. The occurrence of similar situations was not at all unlikely: Technological investments are often debated in such a rapidly developing field. It is quite possible that in such an event the team worked with more options than *yes*, *no*, and *delay* – the three alternatives it started out with in the first meeting analyzed.

As to knowledge creation, the actual implementation of the innovation, that is, the practical testing of the single new tool, was itself the embodiment of new knowledge in this case. It was very much "knowledge in the world" (Norman, 1988) or "between people" (Engeström et al., 1995), not necessarily conceptualized or internalized "knowledge in the head" of any particular individual.

The second solution was to adopt a new procedure of internal corrective action for the entire team for dealing with scrap parts – a trajectory innovation meant for permanent use. This was a deliberate deviation from the accepted company policy. Had this innovation been accepted by management, the reporting (corrective action) behavior of the team would certainly have become qualitatively different from what it had been and what it was expected to be in the organization. Because the proposal was rejected, the innovation remained a potential innovation only. However, it was given a name (*internal corrective action*) and conceptualized to such a degree that it gained some stability in the discourse, thinking, and practice of the team. At least potentially, it became a new mediating knowledge artifact in the local activity. When an innovation is rejected but has conceptual coherence and need-based anchoring in the daily realities of a collective activity system, it is not likely to disappear completely. Reappearances in modified forms are much more likely, although difficult to trace.

Both meetings testify to the importance of critical questioning and rejection of the accepted wisdom as a triggering action in innovative learning. Tjosvold and Tjosvold (1994) emphasize the importance of "constructive controversy" in teamwork. Bartunek and Reid (1992) discuss the positive potential of conflicts in organizational change. Although a related phenomenon, questioning is a more specific action than the global notions of controversy or conflict. It is an action of challenging and negating the prevalent authoritative view or policy, much in line with what Litowitz (1990) aptly characterized as "just say no."

Both meetings also demonstrate the crucial role of object/problem construction in innovative learning. The initial existence of a shared problem or task can rarely if ever be taken for granted in work teams. In fact, actions directed toward constructing a shared understanding of the problem took the lion's share of both discussions. The innovative solution itself seemed to emerge as a final burst after the painstaking period of object construction.

The formation of a shared object is a major collaborative achievement. It is above all an analytical achievement, involving the formation and use of historical explanations, systematic comparisons, and explanatory principles. Here the theory of expansive learning differs very clearly from Nonaka and Takeuchi's theory of knowledge creation. The latter emphasizes socialization and sharing of sympathized, tacit knowledge as the step leading to an innovative solution. In the theory of expansive learning, and in the data analyzed earlier, such a phase has no prominent role. There are at least two possible explanations that may mediate this difference. First, analysis is never purely conceptual and explicit; it always includes more tacit and experiential aspects. Second, Nonaka and Takeuchi may refer to groups that have little shared experiential background to begin with, being selected from different departments of a company. In such case, the socialization phase may indeed be necessary. This, however, in no way diminishes the importance of subsequent or parallel analytic actions.

In the two meetings, an array of mediating artifacts was used. The primary *what* artifacts included above all talk and gestures used to construct the object/problem and its solution. Reported speech and analogy were among the rhetorically powerful *what* artifacts used in the meetings. Joking about purchasing the new tools was used in meeting 1 in a way that diverted the discourse from the emerging innovative solution – an instance that may be seen as an antidote to optimistic assumptions about the innovation-facilitating potential of humor (Hatch & Ehrlich, 1993). In the second meeting, the significant hand gestures indicating "outside" and "inside" were used by two participants in the decisive phase of examining the new solution model.

A number of seemingly fixed and finished theoretical concepts, obviously obtained from above through training and instruction, were also used as *what* artifacts in the meetings. These included concepts used to convey authority, such as *ISO* ("That's a hit against ISO"), but also concepts used as tools appropriated for practical use, such as *inventory*. Some concepts, like *continuous improvement*, might be in the middle, in the process of becoming increasingly everyday for the participants. The seemingly fixed and finished character of these concepts should not be taken for granted either. *Corrective action* was obviously a theoretical concept from above. But the team transformed it into the idea of *internal* corrective action, which gave it an entirely different meaning.

The *how* artifacts included numerous forms of meta-talk that were used to guide and constrain the discussion. Here are a few examples:

Meeting 1
08 *Nic:* Wait a minute, one person at a time . . .

. . .

87 *Curtis:* Okay, don't, don't argue [Dana: Oh yeah, that's a good point, that's a good point] who's right and who's wrong let's just get the ideas up.

Meeting 2
119 *Danny:* We're getting personal, we're getting personal. Come on . . . let someone else have a chance.

. . .

147 *Des:* Well can I speak without being interrupted?

. . .

154 *Des:* Wait a minute, hold on Roger. I'm only relating what, what, what Dana. I'm trying to interpret what Dana's ideas are.

The *how* artifacts in these examples might be named "one person at a time"; "don't argue about who's right and who's wrong"; "let's not get personal"; "one can speak without being interrupted"; and "interpreting what someone else said is not the same as defending that opinion." These are actually procedural rules with different degrees of generality. "One person at a time" is a very general rule in institutional conversations, whereas "don't argue about who's right and who's wrong" applies specifically to a type of discussion in which the group tries to to produce ideas rather than decide on their validity. One could say that procedural rules such as these remain rules as long as they are implicitly constraining the discussion. They become active tools as soon as they are deliberately used by participants in order to maintain or redirect the course of the discussion.

In the second meeting there was a particularly curious example of metatalk.

209 *Curtis:* This is a debate.

Taken separately, this statement looks like a simple what artifact. However, one might argue that in the context of the discussion, it was used as a shorthand how artifact to confirm that now certain procedures are valid, namely, those of a debate.

The *why* artifacts included the force field analysis in the first meeting and the principles and subprinciples in the second meeting. The force field analysis is aimed at elucidating justifications for a choice between two alternatives. In other words, it should yield *why* artifacts that can be used to reach a decision. In meeting 1, the force field analysis seemed to yield mainly descriptive *what* artifacts that were difficult to interpret in any convincing or conclusive manner. Thus, a tool such as this does not inherently determine how it is used – descriptively or analytically. In the second meeting, the general principles were explicated largely as a response to the persistent and aggressive questioning initiated by Dana. He first demanded that a force field analysis be conducted on this issue, too. He then provocatively and repeatedly used the why question.

90 *Dana:* Okay, well then you have the first half, too. Why are you trying to hide something from your boss?

. . .

129 *Dana:* Why don't you tell your boss all that?

Interestingly, in both meetings the solution models were jointly obtained only in spoken discourse. The later written minutes were constructed by the minutes keeper only. The available graphic tools (whiteboard, overheads) were not used to explicate the solutions and examine them collectively. Thus, the crucial newly produced *where to* artifacts remained fairly vague and ambiguous.

Even though research on work teams has increased greatly in recent years (see Beyerlein & Johnson, 1994; Beyerlein, Johnson, & Beyerlein, 1995), very few studies have focused on detailed analyses of discourse in the team. This is probably due in part to the difficulty of analyzing relatively long multiparty conversations that are embedded in practical activity. The preceding analyses indicate that innovative learning processes in teams may not be harmonious brainstorming sessions or situations where "members think alike" (Rentsch & Hall, 1994). To the contrary, in the two meetings different perspectives disagreed and entered into the debates. In meeting 1, the perspective proposing the purchase of new tools and the perspective questioning the purchase collided. In meeting 2, the perspective advocating individual responsibility/accountability and the perspective advocating equal responsibility/fairness collided.

These perspectives were not merely individual-psychological properties. In both cases, one perspective was more anchored in the community of management and supervision, whereas the other perspective was more anchored among the shopfloor workers. However, this distinction alone would be greatly oversimplified. In meeting 1, the purchase of new tools was both supported and criticized by the workers. In meeting 2, the perspective of individual responsibility was initially strongly supported by the workers of Zone A but criticized by Shawn, one of the representatives of the community of management and supervision. The demarcation lines were permeable from the beginning and remained so. In both cases, the solution went beyond the initial perspectives – a new team perspective emerged. Yet, it would be an exaggeration to claim that the new perspective was unanimously shared. Reservations were expressed and played with.

Meeting 2

235 *Danny:* Okay, everybody agree? Thumbs up. Thumbs up. Anybody disagree?

236 *Unknown speaker:* [Jokingly] I think somebody's disagreeing.

Interestingly, the perspectives were not fixed in the sense of stable alliances between individuals. The relationship between Roger and Dana is a case in point. In meeting 1, Roger and Dana were the closest of allies, especially toward the end of the discussion, when together they pushed for the innovative solution. In meeting 2, Roger and Dana were in opposite camps from the beginning, to the point of launching personal attacks.

Meeting 2
191 *Roger:* Dana you're not listening to what I'm saying. You're getting mad because you don't want to go to the meeting period.

192 *Danny:* Stop getting personal.

193 *Roger:* Well it is, it is a personal thing. You've gotta get personal when it's a personal thing, that's all there is to it.

Toward the end of the meeting, Roger changed his mind and suggested a compromise solution. The perspectives as collective formations were robust enough to allow individual movement between them.

Meeting 2
217 *Roger:* Okay, uh I'm gonna go with Dana, uh I mean our problem here, shhh [Nic: Right] our problem here seems to be for Zone B has to go to corrective action _____.

But what gave Ron the authority to bring the discussion to a nearly unanimous close in the second meeting? It would be easy to speculate about his position and special expertise. However, there may be another explanation. The new innovative model of internal corrective action was constructed in several steps of conceptual evolution and enlistment of social support. This stepwise progression could be expressed as a chain of key actors and actions:

Danny [modeling] -> Dana [questioning] -> Des [actual-empirical analysis] -> Shawn [modeling] -> Nic [examining] -> Ron [examining] -> Danny [implementing]

This representation makes evident the collaborative and constructive nature of innovative learning and knowledge creation. Ron could bring the discussion to a close not just by virtue of his personal authority but also because sufficient collective weight had developed step-by-step behind the innovation and simultaneously because the innovation itself had been shaped to an acceptable degree of coherence.

This is in line with both Nonaka and Takeuchi's theory and the theory of expansive learning. The two theories do not have to be seen as mutually exclusive or hostile. Nonaka and Takeuchi's emphasis on the alternative *modes of representing* knowledge and the transitions between them offers important insights that may be overlooked within the theory of expansive learning. On the other hand, the theory of expansive learning, based on the dialectics of ascending from the abstract to the concrete, offers a new framework for analyzing the interplay of the *object* under construction, the mediating *artifacts*, and the different *perspectives* of the participants in a progression of collectively achieved actions. Perhaps the theory of expansive learning can be regarded as a basis for defining the phases of a cycle, whereas Nonaka and Takeuchi's categories are useful in defining the alternative modes of representation available to the participants as complementary instrumentalities in each phase of the cycle.

Deriving the phases of the cycle of knowledge creation from modes of knowledge representation has led Nonaka and Takeuchi to exclude questioning and analysis from their cycle. These actions are tacitly delegated to management. Had the authors analyzed small cycles of innovative learning in work teams, they would have realized that such a split between problem construction and problem solving, or intention and realization, is unrealistic. No matter how clear the intention and assignment may be for management, the object will be creatively reconstructed by those who are supposed to solve the problem. This creative reconstruction often involves questioning, confrontation, and debate. If this is overlooked, the important dimension of power will be artificially separated from object-oriented collaborative work and innovative learning in work organizations.

7   Teams, Infrastructures, and Social Capital

In Chapters 3 and 4, I developed and used the concepts of coordination, cooperation, and communication to characterize the different modes
of interacting and relating to the object in teams. In Chapter 5, I expanded
the picture with the concept of boundary crossing. Cooperation, communication, and boundary crossing seem to be productive but fairly short-lived
episodes of innovative interaction. What all these concepts are missing is
stability. Now it is time to ask: Can teams develop and sustain some sort of
durable capability to interact and solve problems in a productive and proactive manner? In other words: What could be the nature of social capital in
teams?

I define *social capital* as the glue that makes communities more than the
sum total of their individual members. Social capital is a collective good, not
the private property of those who benefit from it. I take a sociocentric view
that focuses on what makes communities work. In other words, I search
for factors that enable collective actors to sustain themselves, to perform
beyond routine expectations, and to reorganize themselves when needed.

My thesis is that social capital should not be understood exclusively as
intangible network relations between actors, or as equally intangible norms,
values, beliefs, or mental processes. I suggest that social capital is firmly
rooted in and practically inseparable from certain types of tangible material
structures and artifacts – including the materiality of human beings as bodily
actors. If the intangible aspects are separated from their material basis, social
capital easily becomes mystified, just as psychology and cognitive science
have mystified so many allegedly strictly mental structures and properties
(Hutchins, 1995; Keller & Keller, 1996).

To examine the material and artifactual basis of social capital, I will
again use the model of the complex mediational structure of human activity systems (Engeström, 1987, p. 78). The model highlights three central

subsystems within human activity: distribution (mediated by division of labor), exchange (mediated by rules), and production (mediated by tools). I will identify three types of materiality of social capital characteristic of the three subsystems respectively.

To concretize my argument, I will examine data from an intervention project within a relatively large telecommunications service provider company in Finland (hereafter called TC). During 1999, our research group conducted a series of intervention sessions called Competence Laboratories (see Ahonen et al., 2000; Virkkunen & Ahonen, 2004) in different work teams of the company aimed at helping the practitioners identify problems, emerging challenges, and expansive new solutions in the competency base of their work community. Much of the work in the Competence Laboratories turned out to focus on the formation of social capital in the teams.

In this chapter, I will use data from one work team and its Competence Laboratory, namely, the call center team responsible for the telephone sales and first-line customer support of the Internet connection packages offered by the TC. The work team (hereafter called the Internet Team) was founded in September 1998. At the time of the Competence Laboratory sessions (August 1999), it consisted of 15 members whose average age was in the early 20s.

Human Activity Systems as Carriers of Social Capital

Communities need infrastructures to exist. Infrastructures are so embedded in everyday life that they tend to disappear. As Bowker and Star (1999, p. 33) point out, "the easier they are to use, the harder they are to see." According to these authors, infrastructures are characterized by a historical process of development of many tools, arranged for a wide variety of users, and made to work in concert; a practical match among routines of work practice, technology, and larger-scale organizational and technical resources and a rich set of negotiated compromises that are both available and transparent to communities of users (Bowker & Star, 1999, p. 34).

Bowker and Star refer to Becker's (1982) analysis of art worlds and Clarke and Fujimura's (1992) study of biological research as examples of infrastructures. The latter case is particularly instructive:

> The purpose of the volume was to tell the history of biology in a new way – from the point of view of the materials that constrain and enable biological researchers, Rats, petri dishes, taxidermy, planaria, drosophila, and test tubes take center stage in this narrative. The standardization of

genetic research on a few specially bred organisms (notably drosophila) has constrained the pacing of research and the ways the questions may be framed, and it has given biological supply houses an important, invisible role in research horizons. (. . .) A starkly different view of the tasks of laboratory biology emerges from this image. (. . .) The supply chain, techniques, and animal handling methods had to be invented along with biology's conceptual frame; they are not accidental, but constitutive. (Bowker & Star, 1999, p. 36)

Marx argued that the original foundation of communities is earth, "the inorganic body" of a given group of people:

These *natural conditions of existence*, to which he [the producer] relates as to his own inorganic body, are themselves double: (1) of a subjective and (2) of an objective nature. He finds himself a member of a family, clan, tribe etc. – which then, in a historic process of intermixture and antithesis with others, takes on a different shape; and, as such a member, he relates to a specific nature (say, here, still earth, land, soil) as his own inorganic being, as a condition of his production and reproduction. (Marx, 1973, p. 490)

Marx (1973, p. 490) further pointed out that "the abstraction of a community, in which the members have nothing in common but language etc., and barely that much, is obviously the product of much later historical conditions." Following Marx, the land to which a community attaches itself as its own inorganic body may be regarded as an early form of infrastructure. Recall that Bowker and Star characterize infrastructure as displaying a rich set of negotiated compromises that are both available and transparent to communities of users. That this is indeed the case with regard to land is amply illustrated, for instance, by the "songlines" of Australian Aboriginals, the invisible pathways connecting up all over Australia (Chatwin, 1987; Rumsey & Weiner, 2001).

Turning attention to infrastructures is illuminating. But to gain an analytical understanding of the formation of social capital, the notion of infrastructure needs to be located in human practice. To accomplish this, I propose the concept of *activity systems*. Figure 7.1 depicts the basic mediational structure of a human activity system. What is the place of infrastructure in this model?

I suggest that infrastructure is embedded in different ways and serves different purposes in the constituent subtriangles of an activity system: production, distribution, exchange, and consumption:

Production creates the objects which correspond to the given needs; distribution divides them up according to social laws; exchange further parcels out the already divided shares in accord with individual needs; and finally, in

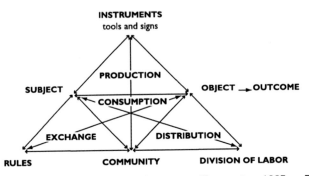

Figure 7.1. The human activity system (Engeström, 1987, p. 78).

consumption, the product steps outside this social movement and becomes a direct object and servant of individual need, and satisfies it in being consumed. Thus production appears to be the point of departure, consumption as the conclusion, and distribution and exchange as in the middle. (. . .). (Marx, 1973, p. 89)

From the point of view of community formation, putting production first may not be adequate. Leakey and Lewin (1983, p. 120) argue that "sharing, not hunting or gathering as such, is what made us human":

(. . .) the invention of a primitive container – the first carrier bag – transformed the early hominids' subsistence ecology into a food-sharing economy. The digging stick may have come before or after the carrier bag, but, important though it was, it lacked the social impact of the container: the digging stick may have made life easier, but it didn't usher in an entirely new life-style. (Leakey & Lewin, 1983, p. 127)

This justifies examining the *infrastructures of distribution* first in analyzing the formation of communities and social capital. After that, I will discuss infrastructures of exchange and production. I will not discuss infrastructures of consumption here because in the context of corporate work units they do not seem central.

Distribution Infrastructure: Service Networks

The prototypical material foundation of distribution in human activity systems is public works, the physical structures and facilities developed to provide water, waste disposal, power, transportation, and similar services to facilitate the achievement of common social and economic needs and objectives (Hoy, Robinson, & Armstrong, 1976). Public works include

Figure 7.2. Invisible distribution networks in the making: Wall Street 1917 (Keating, 1994, p. vi).

such infrastructure systems as streets, water pipelines, electricity networks, and telephone cables, to name just a few. Most importantly, public works are crucial achievements and stabilizing characteristics of communities (see Figure 7.2):

> Public works history is concerned with both physical structures and the people who build and maintain them. We can physically explore the landscape of public works – even if that would require digging down to tunnels and conduits. At the same time, communities of individuals build these projects. They are the products not of single individuals, but of groups of individuals working together. (...) Their development and financing tell us a great deal about a community. The amount of public support needed to create an infrastructure system can be staggering, and the process of reaching consensus on such projects can reveal the innermost sensibilities of a community. The physical structures that make up public works, as well as methods of administration and financing, allow us a glimpse of what constituted

the slippery concept of community, both today and at points in the past. (Keating, 1994, pp. 7–8; see also Tarr & Dupuy, 1988)

In a corporate setting such as that of TC, an obvious type of distribution network is that of Intranet applications designed to distribute company information to work teams and individual employees. From the point of view of social capital, an important question is, to what extent are such applications motivated as preconditions for dealing successfully with the object of the activity? The more concretely the work community connects the infrastructure to the object of the productive activity, the more likely it is that the infrastructure will contribute effectively to the formation of social capital. An infrastructure that is seen as an end in itself or as something serving only the nurturing of team spirit in the work community is not likely to have such an impact.

The Internet Team decided to create an Intranet application for its own use. Within 2 months a couple of team members created a prototype of the application, and it was quickly adopted as a central means of making useful information available to the team members. The application was called The List. It contained (1) a description of the organization, (2) photos and personal introductions of the members of the team, (3) descriptions of their tasks, (4) descriptions of the products and services offered by the team, (5) contact information for relevant other units and persons within and outside the company, (6) descriptions of key competitors, and (7) a glossary of important terms. What amazed us about this solution was the quickness of its creation and the no-nonsense attitude displayed by its youthful creators and users. It was simply something needed to accomplish the objective of the team. The team member responsible for the creation of The List explained its purpose.

> *Team member 1:* The aim of the intra is that it should become a knowledge portal which can be utilized by employees as they work the phones and through which new employees receive much previously undocumented material. In other words, things which would not be explained because they are so self-evident to employees who have worked here longer.

Many Intranet solutions remain alien to and underutilized by large groups of employees because they were initially designed and implemented from above, without careful consideration of the work routines and interaction patterns on the shop floor. Such infrastructures are not likely to be effective foundations for social capital formation.

Figure 7.3. The first whiteboard in its setting at the Internet Team.

In the Internet Team, the distribution infrastructure was an entirely home-grown project constructed from below. This is nicely reflected in the fact that the team members decided very early on to construct two large whiteboards (Figures 7.3 to 7.5) as complementary outlets of information. Such necessary redundancy was justified by the member responsible for the construction of the whiteboards.

> *Team member 2:* Hopefully it will be made use of. It is on the rear wall, pretty visible, and at least you get from it quickly such information as "what was that fax number?" or similar things. In other words, it contains the names and contact information of the most important persons and our most important collaboration partners. And then we have a second whiteboard which is located above the sofa. It is a so-called calendar model, so we put on it important events and announcements of the month or the day. Everyone can put on it items that you feel are important for you or for the others. It has been functioning pretty well, you find on it what you need, and it has been real good to new employees, you get the information instantaneously. (. . .)
>
> *Team leader:* You can probably think about it in relation to the intra, so that the intra contains complete information . . .
>
> *Team member 2:* Yes.

Figure 7.4. Closeup of the first whiteboard: contact information.

Figure 7.5. The second whiteboard: important events.

> *Team leader:* ... and this is kind of a shortcut, if you have several appli-
> cations open at the same time, for instance, then you can get it by a
> quick glance at the rear wall. And you can also put there alarms for
> acute things.

The second whiteboard was particularly interesting. It contained calendar-type items that were not included in The List. Thus, it was not just a shortcut; it added another dimension to the information distribution.

We followed the implementation of the solutions created by the Internet Team for 2 months, a period too short for assessing the routinization of the use of the new infrastructures. This is obviously a crucial issue. The potential for social capital formation of the infrastructure depends on its becoming embedded in the daily practices and routines of the community.

Finally, infrastructures are vulnerable, subject to wear and tear as well as potentially to becoming outdated by developments around them. In other words, infrastructures require maintenance. The creators of The List were clearly aware of this.

> *Team member 1:* All of you, if you notice in the intra something that needs to be added or something that may be incorrect or outdated, please inform me immediately so I will update it as soon as I can. And I have planned that I would reserve some five hours a week from now on for updating it. So if you have suggestions I should have time available.

Exchange Infrastructure: Rule Collections

Infrastructures of exchange consist of rules and procedural norms of social interaction. Their material carriers and embodiments are manifold. Locks and alarm systems that regulate and sanction access to physical space are good examples. Bruno Latour (1992) uses the example of speed bumps, inanimate embodiments and guardians of the moral order that regulate and sanction the behavior of drivers.

Rules typically come in interconnected sets or collections. Locks and alarms are tangible parts of a collection of rules regulating access and movement in a physical space. Speed bumps are tangible parts of the collection of traffic rules. They are typically complemented by visual signs as well as written formulations stored in rule books.

As an outcome of discussions in the Competence Laboratory, members of the Internet Team decided to create an explicit collection of rules for their work community. The rules were formulated, discussed, and stored in The List. As they were formulated, they did not evoke strong feelings or debates. Again, the matter-of-fact nature of their adoption was somewhat striking to us. After all, rules epitomize power and constraint.

A careful scrutiny of the rules reveals a possible reason for their easy acceptance. These rules were very specific, object-oriented, practical, and to a large extent embodied in material artifacts. Here are a few examples.

- Keep tab of the calls you answer, and transfer the numbers at the end of the day to the M1 folder in the "M1 calls" worksheet.
- Lock the telephone and turn it to the 3300 series at the end of your shift.
- During the day shift there are always two persons working the phones and one person on site. Additional need is assessed situationally.
- Papers to be destroyed [should be placed in] the "to be destroyed" box. [The] Saturday shift takes care of emptying the box.
- The access pass card is always kept in plain view. If one forgets it at home, one signs off a visitor pass card which is kept in plain view.
- Important papers are kept behind locks.
- Office desks are kept clear of extra papers.

These rules were formulated in nonmoral language. Altogether there were 45 rules, of which only 4 (exemplified by the first 2 in the preceding sample) used the personal pronoun *you* or the adjective *your*, so often dominant in corporate rule books meant to evoke a feeling of personal moral responsibility. The majority of the rules were stated in the passive form to avoid personalization: "If one forgets it at home, one signs off a visitor pass which is kept in plain view." Coercive imperatives such as *must* were not used. Not a single one of the rules included the threat of sanctions. And there were no negative "don't" rules among the 45.

On the other hand, the rules displayed a consistent orientation to and dependency on specific material artifacts: *folder, worksheet, phones, 3300 series, papers, box, access pass card, visitor pass card, locks, office desks*. In a similar vein, specific material bodies, identified by their functional roles, were also mentioned: *two persons working the phones and one person on site, Saturday shift*.

Production Infrastructure: Tool Constellations

Configurations of ideas, implements, and materials needed to perform a task may be called *constellations*. As Keller and Keller (1996, p. 90) emphasize, "these elements, mental and material, are equally critical."

> The specialized components of a constellation are often the ideas formulated as hypotheses regarding the means to attain a particular end. Any

given tool may be a constituent in numerous constellations, with the goal and logic of each particular step defining the use to which the implement is put. It is important to note that the ideas constituting the mental components of a constellation often include procedures for correcting or repairing deviations from the image of the desired outcome of a particular step in production. Therefore, tools may well be used in multiple ways even within a given constellation. (Keller & Keller, 1996, p. 103)

A constellation may gain permanence as it becomes routinized:

Constellations may be ephemeral, held together only as long as relevant for production, or they may endure as techniques or recipes in the stock of knowledge with tool assemblages potentially realized in the organization of the shop. (Keller & Keller, 1996, p. 106)

Constellations turned into recipes are a particular type of *secondary artifacts* (Wartofsky, 1979). They are typically textual procedural representations, instructions, or algorithms that display a standard sequence of steps to be taken when performing a task.

The Internet Team community constructed a set of such recipe-like constellations for their most common tasks. These ranged from the use of telephones to the handling of customer orders, technical defects, and cancellations of contracts.

The Internet Team displayed the pattern of infrastructure formation observed earlier with regard to distribution and exchange. The recipes were motivated by object-driven production needs. They were formed from below, primarily by two members of the team who took the assignment to collect, formulate, and store the recipes in The List. They were immediately put into use by the employees in their daily practice – though we did not have the opportunity to follow their routinization. The two members responsible for their creation also took responsibility for their maintenance and updating, inviting the other members of the team to contribute improvements.

Consequences of Materiality: Temporal Dynamics of Social Capital

I have suggested that social capital in organizations is foundationally dependent on and partially engraved in infrastructures. Infrastructures are to a large extent tangible material networks and constellations. There are at least three relevant types of infrastructures, namely, infrastructures of distribution (service networks), infrastructures of exchange (rule collections),

	MOTIVATION	FORMATION	ROUTINIZATION	MAINTENANCE
DISTRIBUTION INFRASTRUCTURE	*Object-driven*	*Constructed from below*	**?**	*Assigned responsibilities*
EXCHANGE INFRASTRUCTURE	*Object-driven*	*Constructed from below*	**?**	*Assigned responsibilities*
PRODUCTION INFRASTRUCTURE	*Object-driven*	*Constructed from below*	**?**	*Assigned responsibilities*

Figure 7.6. Matrix for assessing social capital as cycles of infrastructure formation.

and infrastructures of production (tool constellations). Each one has its own forms of materiality.

The Internet Team of the TC was a new organizational unit. When the Competence Laboratory offered the members of this team the chance to analyze and redesign their work arrangements to facilitate competence development, they opted for infrastructure construction. All three types of infrastructure were effortlessly articulated and made visible as the employees speedily created and adopted them. At first, this struck us as odd, given the pertinent observation that "the easier they are to use, the harder they are to see." What made it so easy for the Internet Team to articulate and construct their infrastructures?

The answer may lie in the general temporal dynamics of social capital. I hypothesize that new organizations and teams, in particular, face pressures of infrastructure formation as they struggle to establish themselves as coherent and sustainable communities.[1] At this stage, infrastructures are necessarily articulated – the very lack of needed infrastructures and the very act of building them make them visible (see the Wall Street of the early days in Figure 7.2). The key issue is *motivation*. Infrastructures are often introduced and motivated as ends in themselves, as representatives of moral and ideological values, or as support for cohesion for the sake of cohesion. However, they can also be motivated as ways to facilitate the community's work on its object. In the latter case, infrastructures are

---

[1] It should be pointed out that infrastructures also necessarily become visible when a community is falling apart or being destroyed. When Sarajevo was being destroyed by constant shelling, its infrastructures became painfully visible foci of attention in the inhabitants' struggle for daily survival.

articulated in a matter-of-fact manner – they don't seem to be a big deal. Their disappearance starts at the point of their conception and articulation.

The temporal dynamics of social capital may be depicted as movement from motivation to formation to routinization to maintenance. These steps of cyclic movement give us a heuristic for assessing social capital as a dynamic process rather than just a structural property. This heuristic is represented in the form of a matrix in Figure 7.6. Perhaps in future studies the steps of infrastructure formation may be brought together with the learning actions of the expansive cycle discussed in Chapter 6.

In the cells of Figure 7.6, the texts in italics refer to the findings concerning the Internet Team at TC. Admittedly this is a rather unusual case in that the local work community was permitted and encouraged to construct its own solutions. Observing the routinization and maintenance of those solutions over a longer period of time would certainly make the now optimistic picture look much more rough and problematic.

The most important lesson from this process is, however, that it might indeed be useful to analyze social capital in work organizations and teams as a process of infrastructure evolution with distinctive steps and actions that can be monitored and deliberately reshaped.

8   From Iron Cages to Webs on the Wind

The six case studies presented in the preceding chapters yield a contradictory picture of teams in work organizations. On the one hand, a close analysis of teams in action often reveals moments of innovative potential and productive problem solving. On the other hand, these moments seem to be just that: passing moments with little evidence of sustainability and durability.

Creative moments seem to be typical of new teams still searching for their routines. When teams persist as stable units, their very durability seems to destroy innovativeness and the capacity to learn, at least in the case of the television production team analyzed in Chapter 2. What is perhaps more troubling is the finding, well illustrated by the machinist team analyzed in Chapter 6, that when reasonably mature teams attempt to create innovative solutions, they easily end up in conflict with the overall managerial strategy and rules of the larger organization, which can turn their innovations into frustration.

The literature on work teams is saturated with questionable success stories and normative guidelines for management. Against this background, it is refreshing to read critical studies of teams. However, as I will show, critical team studies tend to fall into the opposite trap of condemning teams as a management conspiracy. In this chapter, I will try to take the contradictory character of teams seriously, seeking a more dialectical and forward-looking approach, with an emphasis on implications for learning at work.

The Contradictory Character of Work Teams

The normative managerial view depicts learning in work teams as a well-planned process of acquisition of skills for collaboration, communication, and planning (e.g., Katzenbach & Smith, 1993; Orsburn et al., 1990). Teams are seen as training grounds for making workers responsible for the continuous monitoring of the output and quality of production, as well as for multiskilling and cross-training of workers to enhance flexibility. Part of the deal offered to workers is that teams will give them an opportunity to learn useful and marketable skills.

In critical studies of teams, on the other hand, the focus is typically on issues of power, control, and ideological values of management (see Ezzamel & Willmott, 1998; Parker & Slaughter, 1988; Sewell, 1998). James Barker's (1993) paper "Tightening the Iron Cage: Concertive Control in Self-Managing Teams" is a case in point. Barker uses the notion of *concertive control* to depict the type of managerial power embodied in self-managing teams. Concertive control is based on the internalization of managerial values:

> Workers achieve concertive control by reaching a negotiated consensus on how to shape their behavior according to a set of core values, such as the values found in a corporate vision statement. (p. 411)

In Barker's account, the formation of teams as "tightening of the iron cage" takes the form of gradual acceptance and consolidation of corporate values. "Slowly, the value-based norms that everyone on the team once 'knew' became objective, rationalized rules that the team members could easily understand and follow" (p. 425). In other words, explicit corporate values and goals are first taught to the teams as tools. As they gradually become habitual routines, they are transformed into rules that are no longer consciously used but automatically followed. This view depicts learning in work teams as stepwise internalization of management values and norms. In effect, teams exist to teach workers to control themselves and each other.

These two opposite views of the learning potential of work teams are important in that they make it clear that workplace learning is a contested terrain. Well-intentioned general theories of experiential learning, apprenticeship learning, action learning, and so on will have very limited impact if they ignore the ideologically loaded nature of and struggle between managerial and critical views of team learning. Furthermore, this debate makes it clear that the nature of workplace learning is crucially dependent on the character of work organization: To understand learning in teams, we must understand teams.

This chapter provides an intermediate balance of the findings gained in the preceding chapters. The central findings may be condensed into three

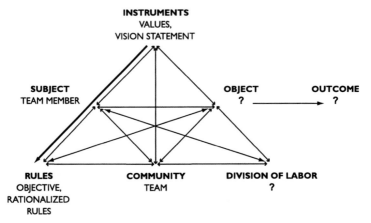

Figure 8.1. Formation of teams as tightening iron cages.

theses. For the first, I argue that self-organizing work teams are relatively complex and inherently contradictory formations where both power and learning are largely outcomes of locally constructed ways and means for dealing with the contradictions. Second, I argue that it is misleading to treat teams as monolithic or uniform formations. To the contrary, the nature and potential consequences of teams are dependent on the particular historical type of production in which they are embedded. Finally, as the third thesis, I argue that the stereotypical view of teams as uniform formations may blind us to the fluid forms of knotworking that are rapidly becoming more relevant and interesting than supposedly stable teams as forms of organizing work.

The First Thesis: Teams Should Be Analyzed as Multiply Mediated, Object-Oriented Activity Systems

In Figure 8.1, the iron cage account of team formation is schematically depicted with the help of the by now familiar model of an activity system. The basic process of team formation is reduced to the adoption of managerial values and their transformation from tools into rules. Accounts such as that of Barker do not give much information about the object and outcomes of the team's work or the division of labor within the team. These appear as largely irrelevant technical details from the point of view of power, thus the question marks in Figure 8.1.

But even Barker's own examples indicate that something else is going on. Objects – commodities as contradictory unities of use value and exchange value – are produced for customers. Quotes from two workers illustrate this:

> I work my best at trying to help our team to get stuff out the door. If it requires overtime, coming in at five o'clock and spending your weekend here, that's what I do. (Barker, 1993, p. 422)

> Under the old system, who gave [a] hoot if the boards shipped today or not? We just did our jobs. Now, we have more buy-in by the team members. We feel more personal responsibility for the product. (Ibid.)

An immediate interpretation might be that these are ultimate manifestations of concertive control: The workers have internalized the corporate values so as to discipline and motivate themselves more effectively than any manager could.

However, as Barker notes in passing, the company he studied was struggling desperately and almost went under, so that in mid-1990, lay-offs reduced the number of teams from three to two. According to Barker (1993, p. 423), "the power of their values helped the teams navigate this difficult period." He gives no direct evidence for this claim. I suggest that instead of managerial values internalized by the workers, we should seek an explanation for the workers' strong motivation in the object of their work.

What do I mean by *object*? The two preceding quotes give a preliminary answer. The first worker talks about getting "stuff out the door." The second worker talks about "the boards" and "the product." These are material objects produced in the plant. As material objects, they have use value for their eventual users and exchange value in the market. In other words, they are internally contradictory sources of pride and revenue.

Certainly time pressure threatens the quality of the product, but there is also pride in being able to ship boards to the customer on time. Certainly most of the revenue is appropriated by the owners of the plant, but by producing those products in a competitive manner, the workers also keep their jobs. Self-managing teams typically bring these issues much more into the conscious collective focus of the workers than did previous production arrangements. Teams become directly responsible for the quality, quantity, and the timely output of their products. As a Finnish post office worker (see Engeström, Virkkunen, Helle, Pihlaja, & Poikela, 1996) struggling with the formation of a team put it: "Do we want more work – or no more work? Now we have to think and talk about hard questions like this." This is learning – but not the kind typically recognized by either the managerial or the critical account.

The motivation generated by a collective focus on the object of work is resistant to the effects of managerial values. The language used by the teams may be more or less saturated by the managerial values vocabulary, but commonly the vocabulary given from above is soon partly abandoned and partly reinterpreted to fit the challenges involving the object. Hart-Landsberg and Reder's (1995) study of teams in a manufacturing plant provides an example (see also Engeström, 1999a). Management had implemented a reward system for "bankable ideas," small improvements suggested by workers and teams. Sean, a parts assembly worker, reflected on his experiences as follows:

> If people try to go through [official] channels [it won't work]. . . . Individuals think you can just hand over an idea. But you can't. We also need to be able to talk to engineers. The only reason I didn't talk to the engineer myself is they wouldn't tell me who he was because I would've ripped his head off. It took 6 to 8 months from the original idea to finally getting it in. The bankable system is still used – now the only problem is finding an engineer who has some time to do it. I came up with a tooling idea – an engineer has to draw it up. We have five or six team engineers. You get to know which ones deal with which gears. They are usually receptive but look like "Oh God, another thing to do."! (Hart-Landsberg & Reder, 1995, pp. 1033–1034)

Reflecting on contradictions in talk is typically manifested in dilemmas such as the "but" structure in Sean's last sentence (Billig, Condor, Edwards, Gane, Middleton, & Radley, 1987). The energy in this utterance does not come from the managerial term bankable ideas. It comes from the real material contradiction between the objective need for and possibility of improvements and the equally objective obstacles in the production pressure and division of labor, which make the improvements very difficult to realize.

How precisely do teams make contradictions in the object more accessible to the workers? In Chapters 3 and 4, I identified three steps or modes in the opening of the object by teams, which I called coordination, cooperation, and communication. I will now return to these modes in order to translate them into the conceptual framework of the triangular model of activity used repeatedly in this book.

The first mode, coordination, refers to the elimination of gaps and unnecessary overlaps in production. Teams typically achieve this by studying the production process and skill profiles of the workers, by eliminating artificial obstacles to flexible collaboration, and by cross-training and multiskilling the workers. Barker (1993) points out that the teams he studied

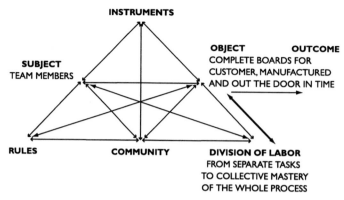

Figure 8.2. Object-oriented coordination in Barker's (1993) team.

"had to merge, or consolidate, a variety of differing perspectives on how to do good work":

> For example, the new team members knew the separate activities involved in circuit board production, but they did not know how to control their individual efforts so that they could complete the whole process themselves. (p. 420)

The structure of the coordination mode is depicted schematically in Figure 8.2.

Coordination commonly yields fairly quick results in terms of productivity increases. But these improvements also tend to flatten out and stagnate relatively soon. The television production team analyzed in Chapter 2 is a case in point. Highly routinized coordination had become a way of masking troubles in the team.

The second mode, cooperation, shifts attention from gaps and overlaps to more proactive handling of disturbances and quality improvements in the process and the products. Efforts are triggered by unexpected failures and breakdowns, as well as by customer complaints or other quality problems. Only limited results can be achieved by once-and-for-all solutions; involvement must become much more dynamic and continuous than in coordination. Figure 8.3 depicts the structure of cooperation. To illustrate this step, I again borrow an example from Hart-Landsberg and Reder (1995, p. 365; see also Engeström, 1999a, for an extended analysis).

> The Rexford, a machine for grinding metal bars into components for automobile accessories, "crashed." Teresa was just concluding her first week operating it. Team members milled around, trying to figure out the cause

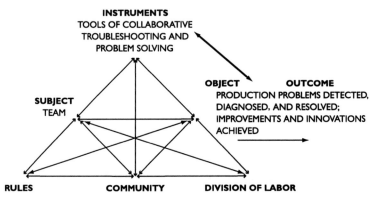

Figure 8.3. Object-oriented cooperation in a team.

of the crash. To anyone who was listening, Teresa expressed her guilty feelings: "It had to have something to do with the operator." Jeff disagreed. "The same thing has happened to all of us." Then he warned her that the tooling experts assigned to troubleshoot this problem probably would tease her as they teased all operators involved in such breakdowns. Immediately an expert arrived and took Teresa aside to talk to her. Later another young machinist of the team, Carrie, told the observing author that the problem of Teresa's machine had *not been* her fault: It was the machine's. "Some of the best machinists come out from a situation where the machine crashes all the time," Carrie maintained.

In the aftermath of the breakdown, an item on the team meeting agenda was: "Update on the Rexford." Chuck, the team's oldest worker, with years of experience operating and fixing the machine, recounted that after the crash he had "rebuilt," "remade," "realigned," and "recentered" all the Rexford parts which had been "wiped out really bad," "burnt up," "shoved back," and "had gullies in them." After participants stopped chuckling at the extent of Chuck's chores, he asserted, "It's not Teresa's fault." But Teresa still seemed worried about her culpability: "It was only the second time I've loaded bars . . . but Emily loaded a similar bar [with no resulting breakdown]."

Participants then launched into a technical analysis of bar size and developed a new recording procedure for tracking undersize bars to prevent future breakdowns. Thus the team's response to the breakdown was to support Teresa and attempt to improve the production process by creating a new type of written record.

This example demonstrates how both power and learning can grow out of mastering the object. In this case, the team took over the task of diagnosing and preventively redesigning the problematic work procedure, something that traditionally was handled by engineers. In other words, the team not

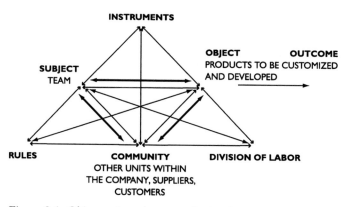

Figure 8.4. Object-oriented communication in a team.

only improved the production of the object and the tools needed for it, it also challenged the division of labor and authority between workers and engineers. More detailed examples of the cooperation mode, and its difficulties, were presented and analyzed in previous chapters of this book, starting with cooperative problem solving in a court of law (Chapter 3) and in primary care medical teams (Chapter 4).

The third mode, communication, emerges as a team gets involved in a network of customization and product development, which requires constant interaction and exchange with other units within the organization as well as with suppliers and customers. In other words, the team must open up outward, cross boundaries, and reflect upon itself as an actor in a network (Ancona, 1990; Ancona, Bresman, & Kaeufer, 2002; Ancona & Caldwell, 1992; Kenney & Florida, 1993; Victor & Boynton, 1998). The structure of communication is depicted in Figure 8.4.

In Chapter 3 of this book, the judge tried to initiate reflective communication with the attorneys but failed. The first case in Chapter 4 also exemplifies how easily the crucial object was covered with a "blanket" or "muffler" and attempted communication turned into pseudocommunication. In Chapters 5, 6, and 7, we saw flashes of reflective communication in which the team not only expansively redefined its object but also self-consciously reconceptualized its own ways of working and dividing the labor.

My first thesis can now be restated. An activity-theoretical analysis opens up the possibility that something quite different from corporate values may motivate teamwork and team learning, namely, the objects of the productive work, with all their internal contradictions and precisely because of them. No matter how much managerial hype and values talk are associated with them, the bottom line is that self-managing teams are created to deal with gaps and overlaps in production, with quality problems and breakdowns, and with challenges of customization and product development on the shop floor – in other words, for the purposes of object-oriented coordination, cooperation, and communication.

Object-oriented teamwork necessarily generates production competency and collective expertise that provide new grounds for practical contestation of managerial values and rules, as well as the existing division of labor and authority. If critical studies of teams ignore this, they patronize and underestimate workers and miss the possibilities of emancipatory development from below in work practices.

However, moving from coordination to cooperation and communication is by no means automatic. It is a huge learning challenge commonly overlooked by both managerial and critical accounts of teamwork. I return to this challenge in the final section of this chapter.

The Second Thesis: The Nature of Teams Depends on the Historical Type of Production in Which They Are Implemented

Both the managerial and critical literatures mostly treat teams as a uniform phenomenon. Historical differences between different types of teams are all but wiped out. Again, Barker provides an example:

> Although self-managing teams have gained much of their popularity in recent years, they are not a new phenomenon. Research and writing on the subject originally dates from Trist's study of self-regulating English coal miners in the 1950s and includes the Scandinavian experience with semiautonomous teams and early U.S. team experiences, most notably the Gaines Dog Food plant in Kansas. The contemporary version of the self-managing team concept draws on both the past experiences with teams in Europe and the U.S. and the more recent influence of Japanese-inspired quality circles in Western organizations. (Barker, 1993, p. 413)

In other words, according to Barker, from the early 1950s on, the same basic idea has been around. Subsequent developments are just versions of this concept.

From an activity-theoretical point of view, this is patently untrue. Teams have qualitatively different objects and activity structures, and thus quite different potentials and consequences, depending on the historical type of production within which they are implemented.

In Chapter 1, I presented a tentative basis for a historically oriented analysis of teams, condensed in Figure 1.2. I now return to this historical

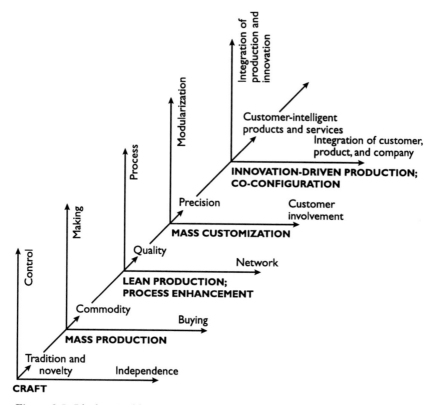

Figure 8.5. Ideal-typical historical types of production and their internal tensions.

framework and present a more detailed chart to describe the field of transformation in the organization of work (Figure 8.5).

On the one hand, Figure 8.5 depicts *a progression from craft production to
mass production, to process enhancement/lean production, to mass customization,
and to innovation-driven co-configuration.* Each of these ideal-typical modes
is driven by its own central object and motive: from tradition and novelty to
commodity, to quality, to precision, to customer-intelligent products and
services (see Victor & Boynton, 1998).

On the other hand, Figure 8.5 indicates two dimensions that are crucial
in the strategic decisions faced within each of the ideal-typical modes of
production. The vertical axis represents *internal orientation,* and the horizontal axis represents *external orientation.* In craft production these two
dimensions are the tension between control and independence. In mass
production the tension is between making and buying. In lean production the dimensions take the form of process development and network

development. In mass customization they are modularization and customer involvement. Finally, in co-configuration the internal orientation involves integration of production and innovation inside the organization, whereas the external orientation means integration of the customer, product, suppliers, and producer. Although in each mode both dimensions are necessary and mutually dependent, there is an inherent tension between them. These tensions are simultaneously sources of trouble and sources of learning.

As I described in Chapter 1, in mass production environments sociotechnical team concepts were developed and experimented with largely as means to alleviate alienation among workers (see Ketchum & Trist, 1992, for a contemporary overview). In the sociotechnical literature, the object of teamwork is typically depicted as the team's own autonomy. The objects of actual production tend to be taken for granted.

When Japanese competition forced Western companies to focus on quality and process enhancement, teams quickly gained a strategic role for management. These teams are not just a variation of the basic idea proposed by sociotechnical theorists. They have a radically different object and accountability for production.

Returning to the distinctions between coordination, cooperation, and communication sketched earlier, lean production and process enhancement mainly require coordination and cooperation from teams. The main learning challenge is in the acquisition and implementation of tools and techniques of collaborative continuous improvement.

The focus shifts to reflective communication in environments of mass customization and, in particular, innovation-driven co-configuration. These differences are crucial for our understanding of teams. When product development and continuous customer-driven reconfiguration of products become pervasive aspects of shop floor work, the notion of a relatively stable team with clear boundaries becomes increasingly problematic, if not obsolete.

This increasing instability of teams is manifested in the hybrid and transitional character of many of the teams analyzed in the preceding chapters. The court example of Chapter 3 is a case in point, worth repeating here:

> The basic institutional framework of the trial represented hierarchical, standardized mass production. But the judge was an active proponent of the delay reduction program and the so-called independent calendar adopted as reform programs by the court. Both were reforms aimed at streamlined, cost-effective case management, or movement toward market-oriented mass production. However, the judge's attempt to reach reflective communication by means of the issues conference went beyond those

top-down programs. It was an example of a bottom-up innovation aimed at informal and dialogical teamwork, ready and willing to modify the rules and standards situationally in the interest of reaching mutually acceptable solutions.... The persistent lecturing style in the judge's approach to the attorneys represents the heavy tradition of autonomous craft, dominated by the personal characteristics and authority of the individual master practitioner.

Similar hybridity was found in the health care teams analyzed in Chapter 5:

At the macro level, the health care teams analyzed in this chapter represent deliberate attempts to break out of the confines of standardized, hierarchical mass production toward autonomous groups responsible for substantial improvement of processes and enhancement of quality of care. But in both cases, the identity and mission of the team were ambiguous with regard to the tension between sociotechnical and lean production models, discussed in Chapter 1. The emphasis on team autonomy and self-sufficiency resembles sociotechnical models, whereas attempts at networking beyond team boundaries resemble lean production models.

Vulnerable hybridity also was found in the teacher teams studied in Chapter 6:

On the one hand, these teacher teams had a strong craft tradition and an orientation toward autonomy. They wanted to step outside the increasingly standardized mass production of mainstream schoolwork to create small, autonomous worlds of learning of their own. In this sense, these teams resembled the sociotechnical team concept. On the other hand, they were also oriented outward, to connect school learning to the world. They were willing to tackle and reconceptualize the object of schoolwork in an expansive manner. In this regard, they resembled the idea of knowedge- and innovation-driven teams. Tension between these two historically different modes of teamwork was a dominant characteristic of the teacher teams.

The Third Thesis: Fluid Forms of Knotworking Are Becoming More Interesting Than Supposedly Stable Teams as Forms of Organizing Work

The very notion of an iron cage implies stability and rigidity. In Barker's (1993) analysis, teams are depicted as well-bounded structural nodes in the organization, disciplining and controlling their members through their pervasive presence and peer pressure.

In reality, we seldom see such stability and closure in teams. Teams are constantly fading away, getting mixed with and overlapped by other parallel patterns of organizing, and being reconfigured to fit changing production requirements. The television production team analyzed in Chapter 2 was dissolved soon after our study. The court team analyzed in Chapter 3 was a transitional and temporary attempt initiated by an individual judge. The primary care teams analyzed in Chapter 4 have changed their forms and functions many times since we collected our data. The first teacher team analyzed in Chapter 5 has been amazingly resilient, whereas the teams in the second case dissolved and changed shape after our study. The machinist team analyzed in Chapter 6 ceased to function soon after our study, and the organization of work within the company has been reconfigured several times since then. The call center team of Chapter 7 has been continuously changing its membership and modes of functioning due to rapid turnover in the workforce, frequent introduction of new product and service generations, and radical fluctuations in the profitability and market position of the company.

This flux becomes increasingly prevalent as we witness organizations moving from lean production to models of mass customization and co-configuration. One can hardly avoid the conclusion that teams are but one probably overrated form among a growing multitude of fluid forms of organizing collaborative work. The iron cage begins to look more like a temporary and patched-up tent in a windy landscape – or a web on the wind (Nardi & Engeström, 1999).

In a series of recent studies (Engeström et al., 1995, 1999; Haavisto, 2002; Hasu & Engeström, 2000; Kerosuo, 2006; Puonti, 2004; Seppänen, 2004; Toivainen, 2003), my colleagues and I have encountered numerous examples of work I call *negotiated knotworking*. The notion of *knot* refers to rapidly pulsating, distributed, and partially improvised orchestration of collaborative performance between otherwise loosely connected actors and activity systems. Knotworking is characterized by a movement of tying, untying, and retying together seemingly separate threads of activity. The tying and dissolution of a knot of collaborative work is not reducible to any specific individual or fixed organizational entity as the center of control. The center does not hold. The locus of initiative changes from moment to moment within a knotworking sequence. Thus, knotworking cannot be adequately analyzed from the point of view of an assumed center of coordination and control or as an additive sum of the separate perspectives of individuals or institutions contributing to it. The unstable knot itself needs to be made the focus of analysis.

The rise and proliferation of knotworking is associated with ongoing historical changes in organizations. Victor and Boynton's (1998) concept of co-configuration is particularly interesting from the point of view of knotworking:

> When a firm does co-configuration work, it creates a product that can learn and adapt, but it also builds an ongoing relationship between each customer-product pair and the company. Doing mass customization requires designing the product at least once for each customer. This design process requires the company to sense and respond to the individual customer's needs. But co-configuration work takes this relationship up one level – it brings the value of an intelligent and "adapting" product. The company then continues to work with this customer-product pair to make the product more responsive to each user. In this way, the customization work becomes continuous.
>
> ... Unlike previous work, co-configuration never results in a "finished" product. Instead, a living, growing network develops between customer, product, and company. (Victor & Boynton, 1998, p. 195)

A hallmark of co-configuration is *customer intelligence*. To achieve it, a company must continuously configure its products and services in interaction with the customer. Victor and Boynton (1998, p. 197) name medical devices and computer software systems as two leading industries where co-configuration is being implemented. The authors emphasize that co-configuration is more than just smart, adaptive products:

> The application of configuration intelligence to the product creates a system of customer, product or service, and company. The complex of interactions among all three, as a product or service adapts and responds to the changing needs of the customer, is the underlying, dynamic source of value.... With the organization of work under co-configuration, the customer becomes, in a sense, a real partner with the producer. (Victor & Boynton, 1998, pp. 198–199)

Victor and Boynton give us a model of three interdependent components, or *actants*, to use Latour's (1996) terminology: customer, product/service, and company. What is missing in this picture is interdependency between multiple producers forming a strategic alliance, supplier network, or other such pattern of partnership that collaboratively develops a complex product or service (Alter & Hage, 1993; Moody, 1993). This extension adds to the complexity of interactions in co-configuration work. Against this background, knotworking may be seen as the emerging interactional core of co-configuration.

To sum up, we can name six criteria of co-configuration: (1) an adaptive product or service; (2) a continuous relationship between the customer, product/service, and company; (3) ongoing configuration or customization; (4) active customer involvement; (5) multiple collaborating producers; and (6) mutual learning from interactions between the parties involved. Various historical layers of team formation typically coexist with emerging forms of knotworking.

Knotworking is related to the rise of temporary groups (Meyerson, Weick, & Kramer, 1996). However, temporary groups are understood as one-time formations created for the purpose of completing a task with a clear deadline. Knotworking, by contrast, is a longitudinal process in which knots are formed, dissolved, and re-formed as the object is co-configured time and again, typically with no clear deadline or fixed endpoint. In temporary groups, the center still firmly rests in a definable, bounded group. In knotworking, the center does not hold.

Knotworking poses qualitatively new learning challenges to work communities. The relatively stable standard procedures of cooperative continuous improvement are not sufficient. Rapid negotiation and improvisation with constantly changing configurations of partners gain central importance. On the other hand, these quick, pulsating negotiations have to be embedded in a radically extended time perspective – the entire life trajectory of the product or service (Engeström, Puonti, & Seppänen, 2003).

Teams and Expansive Learning at Work

One of the most illuminating analyses of the learning implications of teams is Robert Ginnett's (1993) study of airline crews. Ginnett had the opportunity to observe and compare the performance of two kinds of captains: those assessed by check airmen as being exceedingly good at creating highly efficient teams (HI-E captains) and those who received low ratings on this same ability (LO-E captains). The performance Ginnett observed was a formal crew briefing before the first leg of a new crew complement, conducted in the terminal 1 hour before departure. The most interesting finding had to do with how the captains talked about the crew boundaries:

> The HI-E captains worked both in the briefing and at other opportunistic times to expand the relevant team boundary and to make the boundary more permeable. They always talked about "we" in terms of the total flightcrew, as opposed to some of the LO-E captains who referred to the cockpit crew as "we" and the flight attendants as "you." The HI-E captains also worked to create a larger vision of the relevant work group – one that exceeded the bounds of the aircraft. They took pains to include (at least psychologically) gate personnel, maintenance, and air traffic controllers as part of the group

trying to help them – not as an outside hostile group trying to thwart their objectives. One HI-E captain routinely reminded the crew that the passengers could be a relevant part of their team if the crew made the effort to listen to passengers, particularly if they were expressing some concern about the aircraft. (Ginnett, 1993, p. 87)

Teams acquire and develop routinized patterns of performing and interacting. These may be called *scripts, stable roles,* or *shells.* Ginnett found that the best captains kept "elaborating and expanding" these routines:

> They expand the existing shell and create new ways to operate within and outside its boundaries. They are the ones who expand and create new opportunities for constructive interactions among crew members. (Ginnett, 1993, pp. 96–97)

Within an activity-theoretical framework, such expansive moves may be conceptualized as transitions from role-centered coordination to task-centered cooperation and to self-reflective communication (Engeström, 1992). In Ginnett's data, such moves were initiated by skilled captains who had the courage to deviate from the routine by "disavowing perfection": "They make a statement suggesting they don't know something about a particular issue even though the information is often quite readily available.... They are open about dealing with their own vulnerabilities" (Ginnett, 1993, p. 90).

In teams where authority is more distributed, these expansive transitions typically require that one or more members of the team begin to confront and reject the established routine or prevalent practice. Closely related to Klein's (1998, pp. 244–249) notion of *team metacognition* and Tjosvold's (1995) notion of *constructive controversy,* such *actions of questioning and negation* are crucial for innovative learning. They make the script and the boundaries of the team visible and open to alternative possibilities. A team embarks on *expansive learning* when it engages in questioning, reflective communication, and redesign of its own way of working, including its boundaries and its relations to outsiders such as other teams or clients (Engeström, 1987, 1995a).

In Chapter 3, I observed expansive transitions from coordination to cooperation and attempted communication in a court team. In Chapter 6, I analyzed in detail small, potentially expansive cycles of learning and knowledge creation in a team of machinists. Elements or buds of such learning also were observed in Chapters 4, 5, and 7. In other words, teams seemed to come to the threshold of expansive learning. But these attempts were short-lived and often thwarted by subsequent events inside and outside the team. The very nature of this type of learning as a prolonged process that expands in social space, involving increasingly diverse actors across organizational boundaries, makes single well-bounded teams insufficient as sites of expansive learning.

In the next and final chapter, I explore the emerging landscape of organizing collaboration and learning at work beyond teams.

9   Knotworking and Agency in Fluid
Organizational Fields

In this chapter, I make an attempt to hybridize three relatively separate fields of inquiry: (1) theories and studies of collective intentionality and distributed agency,[1] (2) theories and studies of social capital in organizations, and (3) cultural-historical activity theory.

I argue that employees' collective capacity to create organizational transformations and innovations is becoming a crucially important asset that gives a new, dynamic content to notions of collaborative work and social capital. In philosophy, sociology, anthropology, and cognitive science, such capacity is conceptualized as distributed agency or collective intentionality (e.g., Barnes, 2000: Meggle, 2002). The problem with theories of intentionality and agency is that they are seldom grounded in empirical observations or interventions in people's daily realities and practices at work.

Theories and studies of social capital in organizations, on the other hand, have largely focused on the value-generating potential of social ties, network relations, and trust (e.g., Lesser, 2000: Lin, Cook, & Burt, 2001). Issues of agency and intentionality have remained marginal in this literature. Furthermore, this literature has not dealt with issues of transformations in work and emergence of new organizational forms. On the other hand, there are indications of emerging interest in issues of volition, intentionality, and energy as organizational assets, evidenced, for example, in the recent papers by Ghoshal and Bruch (2003) and Cross, Baker, and Parker (2003).

---

[1] Collective intentionality and distributed agency are two fairly separate though overlapping fields, collective intentionality being mainly a topic for analytical philosophy and cognitive science and distributed agency being mainly debated by sociologists, anthropologists, and social philosophers. Because a thorough review and comparison of these two fields is impossible within the scope of this chapter, I take the liberty of moving across their boundaries without much warning.

I suggest that cultural-historical activity theory can serve as a challenging mediator between agency and intentionality, on the one hand, and social capital, on the other hand. Intentionality and agency were central concerns in the founding texts of the cultural-historical approach in the 1920s. For Vygotsky (1999, pp. 64–65), voluntary action "probably distinguishes man from the animals which stand closest to him to a greater extent than his more developed intellect." A number of recent studies inspired by activity theory have focused on problems of agency in organizational transformations (e.g., Blackler, Crump, & McDonald, 2000; Blackler, McDonald, & Crump, 1999; Engeström, 2000, 2004; Uden & Engeström, 2004), as well as on the forms and formation of social capital (Engeström, 2001).

There is a good reason to bring together and hybridize the three fields. The purpose of this chapter is to examine the possibility that current changes in work organizations may create historically new features of collective intentionality and distributed agency. Understanding these new features is important if we are to give viable content to the emerging notion of collaborative capital (Beyerlein, Beyerlein, & Kennedy, 2005) or, as I will suggest, *collaborative intentionality capital.*

I will build my argument in six steps. First, I briefly introduce the notions of emergent interactive intentionality and distributed agency recently put forward by a number of scholars. Second, I present five principles of cultural-historical activity theory as potential enrichments, or perhaps challenges, to the existing literature. Third, I take up the historicity of agency, focusing in particular on historical changes currently visible in work organizations and asking what might be the contours of agency in new network- and amoeba-like organizational forms. Fourth, I analyze a fictional example of distributed agency, namely, a recent detective novel by Tony Hillerman. Fifth, I analyze some data and findings from my own fieldwork in health care settings. Finally, I sum up the outcomes of the analyses and propose a tentative conceptual framework for future studies of agency as a learning challenge in a landscape of knotworking.

Emergent Interactive Intentionality and Distributed Agency

Searle's (1990) notion of *we-intentions* has served as a springboard for interesting attempts to conceptualize collective intentionality. The recent philosophical arguments of Bratman (1999) and Tuomela (2002) are two prominent examples. The two also exemplify the difficulties of overcoming cognitivsm and individualism. Bratman practically equates intentions with plans, whereas Tuomela prefers to see intentions in terms of goals.

In contrast to these views, Gibbs (2001) argues that intentions are emergent products of social interaction. The interaction may take place between multiple humans or between a human actor and his or her tools and material environment. People assign meanings, intentions, goals, and plans to their ongoing interactions as they occur. Thus, actions are not primarily results of privately held, internalized mental representations. In a similar vein, Fogel (1993, pp. 124–125) discusses the development of intentionality in terms of *participatory future* and *anticipatory directionality*: "direction is not a static initial condition, not an executive giving orders that guide action, it is a fluid part of a dynamic perception-action system."

In sociological studies of agency, a similar move may be observed. Barnes (2000, p. 55) points out that the successful execution of routine collective practices always involves the continual overriding of routine practices at the individual level. An orchestra playing a familiar work serves as an example: "Any description of these activities as so many agents each following the internal guidance of habit or rule would merely describe a fiasco." What is needed is constant mutual adjustment and alignment, agreement out of difference.

Pickering (1995, pp. 21–22) characterizes intentionality in human practice as a *dance of agency* or *dialectic of resistance and accommodation*. As active, intentional beings, scientists tentatively construct some new machine. They then adopt a passive role, monitoring the performance of the machine to see whatever material agency it might capture. "Symmetrically, this period of human passivity is the period in which material agency actively manifests itself. Does the machine perform as intended? Has an intended capture of agency been effected? Typically the answer is no, in which case the response is another reversal of roles (. . .)."

Gell (1998, p. 21) pushes this argument further:

> Anti-personnel mines are not (primary) agents who initiate happenings through acts of will for which they are morally responsible, granted, but they are objective embodiments of the *power or capacity to will their use*, and hence moral entities in themselves. I describe artefacts as "social agents" not because I wish to promulgate a form of material-culture mysticism, but only in view of the fact objectification in artefact-form is how social agency manifests and realizes itself, via the proliferation of fragments of "primary" intentional agents in their "secondary" artefactual forms.

Gell (p. 23) adds the important observation that the concept of agency implies "the overcoming of resistance, difficulty, inertia, etc." That, however, should not be confused with control.

Ciborra (2000) points out that in organizations, agency is typically framed in terms of control. But we live in a runaway world (Giddens, 1991) in which the technologies and organizations we create keep drifting, generating unintended, sometimes monstrous consequences. This calls for a notion of distributed agency not obsessed with control: "What if our power to bring to life sophisticated and evolving infrastructures must be associated with the acceptance of the idea that we are bound to lose control? And that any attempt to regain top-down control will backfire, lead to further centrifugal drifts, and eventually impede our making sense and learning about how to effectively take care of the infrastructure?" (Ciborra, 2000, pp. 39–40). Ciborra suggests a reframing of agency in terms of drift, care, hospitality, and cultivation.

Perhaps the most radical accounts of distributed or *fractured* agency are to be found in the works of Deleuze and Guattari (1977, 1987) and Latour (1993, 1996, 2004). Schatzki (2002, p. 205) provides an eloquent summary of these *posthumanist* views:

> Consider the practice-order bundle that is the day trading branch office. This complex of traders, managers, technicians, rooms, computers, computer network, power system, potted plants, and day trading, managerial, repair, and other practices converts electricity, computer graphics, trader savvy, and money into (1) commissions that subsidize expansion of the firm, (2) greater visibility or notoriety for the branch office in the firm, and (3) waste products such as used paper, burnt-out wiring, and carbon dioxide. If such actions as making commissions, projecting an image, and producing waste are grouped together, the actor that performs them, that is to say, the substance to which they are attached, is the practice-order bundle (the branch office). More precisely, the actor that performs these actions is this bundle treated as a unit. If, by contrast, such actions as scanning a computer screen and keeping a diary, or such doings as straining a trader's eyes and crashing, are grouped together, the actors involved are the traders or computers, respectively. These agents, too, are networks taken as units. For Latour and Callon, consequently, an ascription of agency, as in Deleuze and Guattari, is an instantaneous apprehension of multiplicity. By considering different congeries of action, moreover, agency can be seated in any component of a network, as well as in the network as a whole.

Although I endorse the general ideas expressed in these multiple strands of theorizing, I also feel that they are often relatively vague and partial. For instance, talk about "practice-order bundles" seems more metaphorical than analytically rigorous. Above all, as a student of real work practices and organizations, I wonder how one might use such conceptualizations in detailed empirical field studies and interventions.

Thus, I will try to spell out a few key principles of cultural-historical activity theory as a potential contribution to increased systematicity, and also as a challenge to some possible limitations or gaps in the approaches mentioned earlier.

The Contribution of Activity Theory

If intentions are emergent and not reducible to individually held mental representations of goals and plans, how do we explain the persistence and durable guiding power often associated with collective intentions? Shweder (1991, pp. 74–76) attempts to explain this with the notions of *intentional worlds* and *intentional things*. However, the explanation is somewhat circular: "Intentional things are causally active, but only by virtue of our mental representations of them. Intentional things have no 'natural' reality or identity separate from human understandings and activities. Intentional worlds do not exist independently of the intentional states (beliefs, desires, emotions) directed at them and by them, by the persons who live in them" (pp. 74–75). This leads Shweder to maintain that there is no logical requirement that the identity of things remain fixed across intentional worlds. Shweder seems to conceive of intentional worlds and intentional things mainly as situated achievements without much historical inertia and dynamics of their own.

Understanding the durability of collective intentions seems to require a historical concept of object. Vedeler (1991) points out that infant intentionality may be best explained as striving after external objects, as object-directedness. On a larger scale, Knorr-Cetina (2001) discusses the tremendous motivating power of incomplete but durable epistemic objects – such as markets-on-the screen – for entire professional groups. In these views, objects do have historical dynamics and trajectories of their own. These trajectories and dynamics stem from the fact that objects are constructed by much more multilayered, temporally and spatially distributed actors and forces than just the human participants observably present in a given situation.

As pointed out in Chapter 1, in cultural-historical activity theory Leont'ev (1978) distinguished between goal-oriented individual or group actions and object-oriented collective activity. The latter is a product of division of labor. Leont'ev's classic example is a tribal hunt in which some individuals chase the animals while others wait in ambush and kill them.

The action of chasing the game away makes no sense if it is separated from the overall activity and its object. Leont'ev argues that there is no activity without an object. The object carries or embodies the true motive of the activity. Activities are systemic formations that gain durability by becoming institutionalized. But activities take shape and manifest themselves only through actions performed by individuals and groups.

In complex activity systems such as today's work organizations, it is difficult for practitioners to construct a connection between the goals of their ongoing actions and the more durable object/motive of the collective activity system. Objects resist and bite back: they seem to have lives of their own. But objects and motives are hard to articulate: they appear to be vague, fuzzy, multifaceted, amoeba-like, and often fragmented or contested. The paradox is that objects/motives give directionality, purpose, and meaning to the collective activity, yet they are frustratingly elusive. The activity of health care is a case in point. Without the object of illness there would be no hospitals and health professionals. But despite its pervasive presence, illness is very hard to define, it does not follow the mental representations of professionals and patients, and it certainly does not disappear no matter how well one does one's work (Engeström, 1995b; Engeström & Blackler, 2005; Engeström, Puonti, & Seppänen, 2003).

In practical actions, objects and motives are stabilized, temporarily "closed," by means of auxiliary artifacts – tools and signs. Vygotsky described this artifact-mediated nature of intentional action as follows:

> The person, using the power of things or stimuli, controls his own behavior through them, grouping them, putting them together, sorting them. In other words, the great uniqueness of the will consists of man having no power over his own behavior other than the power that things have over his behavior. But man subjects to himself the power of things over behavior, makes them serve his own purposes and controls that power as he wants. He changes the environment with the external activity and in this way affects his own behavior, subjecting it to his own authority. (Vygotsky, 1997, p. 212)

Vygotsky (1997) pointed out that voluntary action has two phases: a design phase in which the mediating artifact is (often painstakingly) constructed and an execution phase that typically looks quite easy and almost automatic. Classic examples of mediated intentionality include the use of an alarm clock to wake up early in the morning to master the conflict between motives of work and rest. Vygotsky's examples of voluntary action focus on individual actors. This must not be interpreted as neglect of collective intentionality. According to Vygotsky's famous principle, higher psychological functions appear twice: first interpsychologically, in collaborative action, and later intrapsychologically, internalized by the individual. The interpsychological origins of voluntary action – and collective intentionality – are found in rudimentary uses of socially shared external prompts, reminders, plans, maps, and so on.

Mediating artifacts such as an alarm clock typically serve as signs that trigger a consequential action. They are mediators of action-level decisions. But humans also need and use mediating artifacts to stabilize future-oriented images or visions of their collective activity systems. Language and various semiotic representations are needed to construct and use such *tertiary artifacts*, as Wartofsky (1979) called them. Human agency gains unusual powers when the two, future-oriented activity-level envisioning and consequential action-level decision making, come together in close interplay (Engeström, Engeström, & Kerosuo, 2003). Ghoshal and Bruch (2003, p. 53) provide a nice example from organizational practice:

> Thomas Hill was a midlevel manager in a U.S.-based pharmaceuticals company. Comfortable in his job as head of Central European sales, Hill suddenly faced the possibility of becoming the Indian subsidiary's general manager. After days of internal battles, Hill asked two colleagues to debate the pros and cons in his presence. "I was distanced because the struggle took place outside of me," he recalls. "And yet it made the facts and my inner situation crystal clear." The colleagues continued the discussion until Hill was sure what he wanted. Impressed, he now uses the process regularly for tough decisions.

In activity theory, contradictions play a central role as sources of change and development. Contradictions are not the same as problems or conflicts. Contradictions are historically accumulating structural tensions within and between activity systems. The activity system is constantly working through tensions and contradictions within and between its elements. Contradictions manifest themselves in disturbances and innovative solutions. In this sense, an activity system is a virtual disturbance- and innovation-producing machine.

The primary contradiction of activities in capitalism is that between the use value and exchange value of commodities. This contradiction pervades all elements of our activity systems. The work activity of general practitioners in primary medical care may serve as an illustration. The primary contradiction, the dual nature of use value and exchange value, can be found by focusing on any of the elements of the doctor's work activity. For example, instruments of this work include a tremendous variety of medicaments and drugs. But they are not just useful preparations for healing; they are above all commodities with prices, manufactured for a market, advertised, and sold for profit. Every doctor faces this contradiction in his or her daily decision making in one form or another.

Activities are open systems. When an activity system adopts a new element from the outside (for example, a new technology or a new object), it often leads to an aggravated secondary contradiction whereby some old element (for example, the rules or the division of labor) collides with the new one. Such contradictions generate disturbances and conflicts, but also innovative attempts to change the activity. The stiff hierarchical division of labor lagging behind and preventing the possibilities opened by advanced instruments is a typical example. A typical secondary contradiction in the work activity of general practitioners would be the tension between the traditional biomedical *conceptual instruments* concerning the classification of diseases and correct diagnosis, on the one hand, *and* the changing nature of the *objects*, namely, the increasingly ambivalent and complex problems and symptoms of the patients, on the other. These problems, more and more often, do not comply with the standards of classical diagnosis and nomenclature. They require an integrated social, psychological, and biomedical approach that may not yet exist.

Contradictions are not just inevitable features of activity. They are "the principle of its self-movement and (. . .) the form in which the development is cast" (Ilyenkov, 1977, p. 330). This means that new qualitative stages and forms of activity emerge as solutions to the contradictions of the preceding stage of form. This, in turn, takes place in the form of "invisible breakthroughs," innovations from below:

> In reality it always happens that a phenomenon which later becomes universal originally emerges as an individual, particular, specific phenomenon, as an exception from the rule. It cannot actually emerge in any other way. Otherwise history would have a rather mysterious form. Thus, any new improvement of labour, every new mode of man's action in production, before becoming generally accepted and recognised, first emerge as a certain deviation from previously accepted and codified norms. Having emerged as an *individual exception* from the rule in the labour of one or several men, the new form is then taken over by others, becoming in time a new *universal norm*. If the new norm did not originally appear in this exact manner,

it would never become a really universal form, but would exist merely in fantasy, in wishful thinking. (Ilyenkov, 1982, pp. 83–84)

Activity systems take shape and get transformed over lengthy periods of time. Their problems and potentials can only be understood against the background of their own history. History itself needs to be studied both as the local history of the activity and its objects and as the history of the theoretical ideas and tools that have shaped the activity. Thus, medical work needs to be analyzed against the historical background of its local organization and against the more global history of the medical concepts, procedures, and tools employed and accumulated in the local activity.

To sum up, five principles of cultural-historical activity theory seem relevant for the study of collective intentionality and distributed agency. These may be called (1) the principle of object orientation, (2) the principle of mediation by tools and signs, (3) the principle of mutual constitution of actions and activity, (4) the principle of contradictions and deviations as source of change, and (5) the principle of historicity. The last one, historicity, requires that I now turn briefly to the changing landscape of agency in work organizations.

Agency in Hierarchies, Markets, Networks, and Beyond

Many recent attempts to analyze historical change in work organizations (e.g., Powell, 1990) have condensed the current landscape into three major forms: hierarchy, market, and network. In this view, organizations in capitalist society have been built either on the principles of centralized hierarchy (for example, large vertically integrated corporations and big bureaucracies) or on the principles of the market (typically more agile companies seeking to exploit new opportunities). Hierarchies are strong in developing the standardization needed in traditional mass production, but they are limited by their rigidity. Market organizations are strong in their flexibility, but they are limited by their excessive competitiveness, which tends to exclude collaboration and reciprocity.

In a simplified form, we might characterize the nature of agency in hierarchies with the imperatives "Control and command" for management and "Resist and defend" for workers. In an ideal market organization, this dualism melts into one overriding imperative: "Take advantage and maximize gain."

Powell and many others point out that these two classic forms of organizing work in capitalism are increasingly being challenged or even replaced by various forms of networks in which different organizations or organizational units seek new innovations by means of collaboration across traditional boundaries. In network organizations, the imperative would be "Connect and reciprocate."

The rate of alliance and partnership formation in work organizations has exploded in recent years. Firms no longer compete as individual companies; instead, they compete as rapidly changing constellations of companies that cooperate to succeed. In virtually all sectors of the economy, alliances have reshaped the interactions of companies. Although partnerships and alliances are clearly spearheads toward the future, they are also full of tensions and thus are extremely difficult to sustain and manage (Spekman, Isabella, & MacAvoy, 2000).

Partnership and alliance formation typically takes place in multiorganizational fields (Scott, Ruef, Mendel, & Caronna, 2000). In activity-theoretical terms, these may be called *distributed multiactivity fields or terrains*, bound together by partially shared large-scale objects. The mastery and/or cultivation of such "runaway objects" urgently requires new forms of distributed and coordinated agency.

As I pointed out in Chapter 8, my research groups have been particularly interested in what we call negotiated knotworking as an emerging way of organizing work. In knotworking, collaboration between the partners is of vital importance, yet it takes shape without strong preterminded rules or central authority. The concept of a *network* is somewhat problematic as a framework for understanding knotworking. A network is commonly understood as a relatively stable web of links or connections between organizational units, often materially anchored in shared information systems. Knotworking, on the other hand, is a much more elusive and improvised phenomenon.

Knotworking is similar to the *latent organizations* described by Starkey, Barnatt, and Tempest (2000, p. 300) in that it "persists through time as a form of organization that is periodically made manifest in particular projects," remaining dormant until market or user demand presents an opportunity or necessity for the organization to reanimate itself as an active production system. However, Starkey et al. (p. 300) argue that latent organizations "come to exist when a central broker reconstitutes the same creatively unique set of agent partners on a recurring project basis." This is clearly not the case in the knotworking settings we have analyzed. As pointed out in Chapter 8, in these settings the center does not hold.

In Chapter 8, I connected knotworking to the mode of production that Victor and Boynton (1998) characterize as co-configuration. However, the notion of co-configuration does not capture the profound implications of what is called *social production* or peer production. Benkler (2006, p. 59) summarizes this phenomenon as follows:

> A new model of production has taken root; one that should not be there, at least according to our most widely held beliefs about economic behavior. It should not, the intuitions of the late-twentieth-century American would say, be the case that thousands of volunteers will come together to collaborate on a complex economic project. It certainly should not be the case that these volunteers will beat the largest and best-financed business enterprises in the world at their own game. And yet, this is precisely what is happening in the software world.

The Open Source movement in software production (e.g., DiBona, Ockman, & Stone, 1999) is often used as the prime example of new forms of community-based work and social production that go beyond the limits of bounded firm-based models (Lee & Cole, 2003; see also Weber, 2004). According to Lee and Cole (2003, p. 639), the key to the "knowledge expansion" witnessed in the Linux kernel development is, besides its openness and nonproprietary nature, the norm of critique:

> In the Linux development community we observe a peer review process as a structured approach to generating criticism of existing versions, evaluating these criticisms, and eliminating 'error,' while retaining those solutions that cannot be falsified.

Lee and Cole (p. 641) report that between 1995 and 2000, they found 2,605 people in the Linux community "development team" that adds features and fixes bugs. Over the same period, they found 1,562 people on the "bug reporting team" that reports, documents, or characterizes bugs. In addition, the authors found that 49% of the bug reporting team also performed tasks of the development team and that 29% of the development team performed tasks of the bug reporting team. The sheer size, openness, and fluctuation across boundaries of this community make the use of the term team somewhat ludicrous.

Authors like Howard Rheingold (2002) have begun to prophesize *smart mobs* as radically new forms of organization made possible by mobile technologies. Initial conditions of such "swarm" or "amoeba" organizations were nicely captured by Rafael in an essay discussing the overthrowing of President Joseph Estrada in the Philippines in 2001:

> Bypassing the complex of broadcasting media, cell phone users themselves became broadcasters, receiving and transmitting both news and gossip and

often confounding the two. Indeed, one could imagine each user becoming a broadcasting station unto him- or herself, a node in a wider network of communication that the state could not possibly even begin to monitor, much less control. Hence, once the call was made for people to mass at Edsa, cell phone users readily forwarded messages they received, even as they followed what was asked of them. Cell phones then were invested not only with the power to surpass crowded conditions and congested surroundings brought about by the state's inability to order everyday life. They were also seen to bring a new kind of crowd about, one that was thoroughly conscious of itself as a movement headed towards a common goal." (Rafael, 2003, p. 403)

Clearly, such a smart mob has no single, permanent center. Mobile technologies make it possible for each participant potentially to be a momentary center. Rafael's example underlines the importance of a shared goal. But the emphasis on the goal also implies the problem. Because goals are relatively short-lived, smart mobs also seem to be very temporary organizational forms.

However, there are amoeba-like organizations that are not limited to the pursuit of short-term goals. Two quite resilient examples are the activities of birding (e.g., Obmascik, 2004) and skateboarding (e.g., Borden, 2001). These might be also called *wildfire activities*, as they have the peculiar capacity to disappear or die in a given location and suddenly reappear and develop vigorously in a quite different location or in the same location after a lengthy dormant period. Although participants in these activities commonly use mobile technologies to communicate with one another and to broadcast information about their objects (rare birds, good skating spots), these activities are much older than mobile phones and the Internet. Birding has a history of several hundred years, and skateboarding dates back at least to the early 1970s. Two additional features need to be mentioned. Both birding and skateboarding are peculiar combinations of leisure, work, sport, and art. And they both have consistently defied attempts at full commercialization, offering ample opportunities for entrepreneurship but not becoming dominated by commercial motives.

What might be the nature of collective intentionality, or distributed agency, in knotworking and social production? I will now turn to cases, first a fictional one, to examine this question.

A Fictional Case: Hillerman's *The Sinister Pig*

The classic mystery novel concentrates intentionality and agency in the individual master detective (e.g., Poirot, Maigret), often supported by a slightly shadow-like sidekick (e.g., Holmes and Watson) and working on an equally individual master criminal or crime. The historical evolution of the genre has led to increasingly complex configurations and plots, yet the focus on an individual or dyadic central agent has stubbornly remained.

Tony Hillerman's mystery novels, located in the Navajo Reservation of New Mexico, demonstrate the evolution of detective mysteries in a nice way. Hillerman's first three books had a senior Navajo tribal police officer, Joe Leaphorn, as their central hero. The next three books elevated a junior officer, Jim Chee, to the position of central agent. In the subsequent books, Leaphorn and Chee worked together in an often ueasy alliance. In his memoir, Hillerman muses on this as follows:

> Luck, for example, caused me to put Chee and Leaphorn in the same book. I was on a book tour promoting the third of the books in which Jim works alone. A lady I'm signing a book for thanks me and says:
> "Why did you change Leaphorn's name to Chee?"
> It took a split second for the significance to sink in. A dagger to the heart. I stutter. I search around for an answer, and finally just say they're totally different characters. "Oh," says she, "I can't tell them apart."
> I am sure there are writers self-confident enough to forget this. What does this old babe know? But that was not to be for me. Like what St. Paul called his "thorn in the flesh," it wouldn't go away. I decided to put both characters in the same book to settle the issue myself. I tried it in *Skinwalkers*. It worked so well I tried it again in *A Thief of Time*. Hurrah! It was the breakout book! (Hillerman, 2001, pp. 298–299)

An author's encounter with a reader, such as the one described by Hillerman, does not have to be characterized as luck. It may also be thought of as a relatively probable and common opportunity for knotworking – a point Hillerman himself seems to imply when he writes that he's sure that "there are writers self-confident enough to forget this." In terms of distributed agency, we might say that this step in Hillerman's writing resulted from knotworking between the fictional subjects of Joe Leaphorn and Jim Chee and the real (?) subjects of the lady and Tony Hillerman.

Hillerman's recent book, *The Sinister Pig* (2003), steps radically beyond this dyad. The field of actors developed in the book may be diagrammatically depicted as in Figure 9.1. In the diagram, the unbroken two-headed arrows indicate relatively strong relationships of collaboration, whereas the dotted two-headed arrows imply a weak collaborative relationship. Lightning-shaped two-headed arrows indicate hostile relationships. The letters A, B, and C signify that the actors represent three different law enforcement

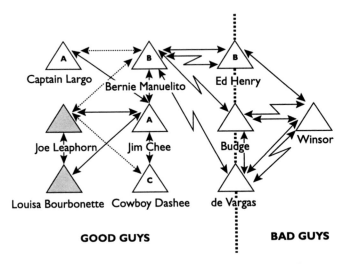

Figure 9.1. Network of distributed agency in *The Sinister Pig*.

agencies,[2] namely, the Navajo tribal police, the Border Patrol, and the Bureau of Land Management, respectively. The gray triangles signify unofficial actors who represent no institutional agencies.

A few interesting features are immediately evident in Figure 9.1. First, the good guys are not a group in which everyone collaborates with everyone else. There are two very different hubs among the good guys: one frontline-oriented around Bernie Manuelito, the other more distant-from-action around Jim Chee and Joe Leaphorn. These two hubs are connected through a strong relationship between Chee and Manuelito, a weak relationship between Manuelito and Leaphorn, and weak mediation by Captain Largo. Second, there are three relationships that are both collaborative and hostile, indicating a radical switch in the nature of the interaction at some point. Third, three actors are placed on the boundary between the good and the bad, indicating serious ambiguity and uncertainty. Fourth, three different law enforcement agencies are involved. And finally, along with official representatives of different agencies, individuals with no official status are involved in the work.

From the point of view of activity theory, what kind of agency and intentionality is involved in Hillerman's book? To answer this question, I will examine *The Sinister Pig* with the help of the five principles of activity theory presented earlier.

---

[2] The term *agency* appears here, interestingly, in its formal institutional sense. One of the central points of Hillerman's novel is that such official agencies gain real agency only through the often deviating actions of flesh-and-blood people.

The first principle, *object orientation*, calls attention to the object of the activities under scrutiny. In criminal investigation, the object is a suspected crime. In *The Sinister Pig*, the crime is widely distributed in time and space. Initially the focus is on a murder case, but it gradually drifts to suspected smuggling of narcotics over long distances across the Mexico-U.S. border through abandoned oil pipelines. This widely distributed and highly ambiguous nature of crime as object is not at all unrealistic. My student Anne Puonti recently published her dissertation on collaboration between authorities in the investigation of economic crimes. She points out that whereas a traditional crime always takes place at a certain time and place, economic or white-collar crime is typically committed over an extended period of time, and nobody can point to an exact time at which the boundary between legal and illegal was crossed. Nor can an exact place for economic crime be determined: The perpetrator may have a permanent residence in one location, the company may be found somewhere else, and company property may even be located in other countries (Puonti, 2004).

The second principle, *mediation by tools and signs*, asks us to look at the artifacts involved in the activities under scrutiny. The sinister pig itself turns out to be a crucial artifact, a mobile module originally used to clean oil pipelines, now converted into a container for the illegal drugs. The pig is a tool for the bad guys, but it also serves as a boundary object, an emblematic semiotic mediator by means of which Leaphorn begins to formulate a theory of the crime.

> (...) Chee shook his head. "I'm way behind you on that connection."
> Louisa had poured their coffee, a mug for herself, had joined them at the table, but had politely refrained from getting into this discussion. Now she cleared her throat.
> "Of course he's behind, Joe. Who wouldn't be? Tell him about your pig theory." She smiled at Chee. "As Joe sees this situation these are very sinister pigs."
> Leaphorn looked slightly embarrassed.
> "Pig is the name pipeline maintenance people use for a device they push through the pipes to clean them out. (...)" (Hillerman, 2003, p. 153)

For both the bad guys and the good guys, the functioning of the central artifact, the pig, is dependent on a constellation of supporting artifacts, primarily mobile phones and maps (on tool constellations, see Keller & Keller, 1996, and Chapter 7 of this book).

> "When we get about an hour from El Paso, I'm making some calls," Winsor said. "You take care of dealing with getting my plane parked. I'll meet a

man I need to talk to at the administration building. You brought your cell phone?"

"Always. And the pager." (Hillerman, 2003, p. 146)

"There's more I want to explain," Leaphorn said. "I want you to take a look at an old map I dug up."

Now Chee snorted. "A map! Have I ever discussed anything with you when you didn't pull a map on me?" (Hillerman, 2003, p. 150)

The third principle, the *mutual constitution of actions and activity*, prompts us to inquire into the relationship between situated consequential decisions and future-oriented visions. In *The Sinister Pig*, the coming together of activity-level envisioning and action-level decision making is vividly described in two subsets of encounters. The first one is that between two bad guys, Budge de Baca and Diego de Vargas:

"I don't know what he thinks. But I think that if we kill her, he has it figured out so he'll get away with it. But if he has it figured right, she is a federal cop. The federals will catch us, wherever we go. Not give up until they do. And then they either kill us or we die in a federal prison somewhere. And, of course, that's exactly the way he hopes its will work out. He wouldn't want us around anymore."

Diego sighed. "Yes," he said. "It would be true also among those where I've always worked."

"The way it happens in Washington, my patron is rich and powerful, and his roomful of lawyers and very important friends let the police know that our rich and powerful boss is innocent. He just came out here to shoot an African antelope for his trophy room. And he had me put his special trophy hunting rifle back there in the storage place to show them evidence that that's the truth. And then he says he was betrayed by two low-class scoundrels who already are wanted by the police."

"Yes," he said. "That sounds like it would be in Mexico too."

"I think there is a way out of this for us," Budge said.

"Tell me," Diego said. (Hillerman, 2003, pp. 187–188)

"What's the trouble?" he asked. "Worried, or is it love sick?"

"Worried," Chee said. "How am I going to get Bernie to quit this damned Border Patrol job and come on home?"

"That's easy," Cowboy said.

"Like hell," Chee said. "You just don't understand how stubborn she is."

(...)

"If you want her to come home, you just say, 'Bernie, my sweet, I love you dearly. Come home and marry me and we will live happily ever after.'"

"Yeah," Chee said. (Hillerman, 2003, pp. 191–192)

These two exchanges of future-oriented envisioning move at the level of activity systems. In the first one, Budge and de Vargas, anticipating the critical action assigned to them, envision their future fate as members of the criminal activity system led by Winsor. The envisioning leads toward a preliminary committment to new action – but due to interruption, an action plan is never formulated and the new action is subsequently improvised. In the second example, Chee and Dashee, also anticipating critical actions ahead of them, envision Chee's future life activity. In this case, the very actions of seeking out Officer Manuelito are driven by the activity-level envisioning – which itself is articulated only as the critical actions unfold.

The fourth principle, *contradictions and deviations as source of change*, invites us to examine systemic tensions in the activities under scrutiny. The two excerpts just cited also exemplify the key contradictions operating in Hillerman's novel. The first contradiction is embedded in the criminal activity system, which depends on unquestioning obedience from subordinates but at the same time puts the subordinates at unacceptable risk in demanding violent actions from them. This is, of course, the classic contradiction that has made it possible for law enforcement officers to use lower-level members of organized crime as informants. The tension pushes Budge and de Vargas to take actions that deviate radically from the script devised by their boss.

The second contradiction is embedded in the professional activity systems of Officers Chee and Manuelito. This is the equally classic tension between crime as invasive object and the pursuit of personal happiness. Much of today's crime drama and fiction is built around this tension between the official and the personal in police work. In Hillerman's story, the contradiction pushes Jim Chee to deviate radically from the rules of his institutional agency. In effect, his quest to solve the crime blends with his personal quest to find Bernie Manuelito. This drives him to move far beyond his jurisdiction with the help of a friend, Cowboy Dashee.

The fifth principle, *historicity*, tells us to explore the successive and intersecting developmental layers, including the emergent new ones, in the activities under scrutiny. Hillerman provides a lot of material for this, and his previous books set a historical stage for viewing changes at work in law enforcement. Joe Leaphorn, the legendary individual, is retired and stays in the background. Jim Chee is not at the center of frontline action either. The focus drifts to the female officer, Bernadette Manuelito, and eventually the climax takes place without a clear individual or dyadic hero, largely facilitated by unanticipated actions of the two bad guys, Budge and de Vargas. All in all, the center does not hold. Different actors put their spoons in the soup, none of them having the whole picture or complete information about what the other actors are doing. Historically, this is amplified in the image of the multiple institutional agencies involved:

> (. . .) and she missed the arrival of an SUV occupied by Drug Enforcement Agents, and the resulting dispute over which of the agencies had jurisdiction, which was eventually resolved by the arrival of someone representing Homeland Security, who declared himself in charge of the FBI, the DEA, the Border Patrol, the Department of Land Management, and the Najavo Tribal Police. (Hillerman, 2003, pp. 220–221)

So, what do we learn about distributed agency and collective intentionality from these five excercises?

In Hillerman's story, there is no fixed and stable center of control and command, individual or collective: The center does not hold. Yet, the job gets done, and various inviduals and subgroups contribute to the achievement in an intentional and deliberate manner. Moreover, it does not seem satisfactory to characterize the process simply as an accidental aggregation or combination of individual and subgroup efforts. There is a strong attempt among all participants to grasp and resolve the complex whole, even though it seems hopelessly beyond the limits of each participant's horizon of understanding and capability.

In the story, the job gets done by means of numerous seemingly separate or weakly connected strings of actions that take place over an extended period of time and far apart from one another in geographical space. But again, they are not completely disconnected. Partial connecting information, or hints and clues, do circulate and connect the various actions. Although often inefficiently, partially and belatedly, the different actors do seek interconnections and they do reciprocate.

The intention, or the goal, or the idea of what is actually being accomplished emerges in bits and pieces spread among the dispersed actors over the course of the events, to become fully and jointly articulated only after it is all over. This after-the-fact articulation and stabilization also apply to control and command, as is made evident in the last excerpt presented earlier.

But why bother about a mere fictional detective story? I submit that fiction is often more sensitive to the changing landscape of societal life than are our everyday descriptive accounts or scientific analyses. The change in Hillerman's fiction provides one window into thinking of change more generally. Let me now try to open another window, this time grounded in longitudinal and interventionist field research in health care organizations.

An Empirical Case: Knotworking in the Care of Chronically Ill Patients in Helsinki

Can distributed, networked agency be purposefully cultivated? What kinds of tools and collaborative arrangements are needed to facilitate it? How does it manifest itself in situations of collaborative decision making and problem solving? I will devote this section of the chapter to these questions, using examples from a series of longitudinal intervention studies we conducted in the multiactivity field of health care in the city of Helsinki, Finland (see Engeström, Engeström, & Kerosuo, 2003).

Scott and his coauthors (2000, p. 355) conclude that "much of the interest and complexity of today's healthcare arena, compared with its condition at mid-century, is due not simply to the numbers of new types of social actors now active but also to the multiple ways in which these actors have become interpenetrated and richly connected." Medical work is no longer only about treating patients and finding cures. It is increasingly about reorganizing and reconceptualizing care across professional specialties and institutional boundaries. This *clinical integration* is not easily accomplished. As Shortell and his colleagues (2000, p. 69) state, "overall, clinical integration for the management of people with chronic illness is still largely a promise in search of performance."

In other words, the shape and implications of spatiotemporally distributed work and expertise are still fragile and open, literally under construction. When professionals perform such work and discourse, they also give shape to it. Thus, a methodology is needed that allows us, in an anticipatory manner, to explore and make visible the potentials and problems of constructing and performing this emerging type of work.

To meet this challenge, we recently arranged a series of joint "laboratory sessions" for medical professionals involved in the care of patients with multiple chronic illnesses in the city of Helsinki. For such a session, one of the participating physicians was asked to select a patient and prepare a presentation of the patient's care trajectory. The patient attended the session, along with physicians and nurses representing different specialties and clinics involved in the patient's care. The session was aimed at improving coordination and collaboration among the parties. The physician presenting the case was asked to prepare drafts for (1) a care calendar summarizing the important events in the patient's care trajectory, (2) a care map depicting the key parties involved in the care, and (3) a care agreement summarizing the division of responsibilities among the caregivers involved. We gave the physician simple one-page templates for each of these representations, but the participants were invited to modify and redesign them according to their preferences.

This procedure generated two kinds of data. First, the physician preparing the case usually invited the patient to a consultation where they discussed the patient's care to prepare for the presentation. Sometimes the physician invited a key colleague from another clinic to join in this consultation or arranged a separate meeting with one or more relevant colleagues. A researcher from our group videotaped the preparatory consultation and collected copies of the documents used or prepared in it. The researcher was also available if the practitioners or the patient wanted to discuss the arrangements of the forthcoming laboratory session. Second, we videotaped the laboratory session itself and collected copies of the documents presented or produced in the course of the session. Here are three examples from discussions in three different laboratory sessions, each with a short analysis.

Example 1

Heart specialist: Who, in your opinion, should from the point of view of the care of the heart deficiency take the initiative with regard to producing the care plan? Who is responsible, who makes it or sees to it that it is made?

Administrator physician: As I see it, it is still the expertise of the cardiology clinic to make the plan.

Heart specialist: Yes, it should be, but there must be a specified person in the cardiology clinic...

Administrator physician: Yes.

Heart specialist: ...a man or a woman who does it. The clinic as such doesn't do anything.

Administrator physician: No, it doesn't. I'm getting there, I am of course looking at the only one who is present here, with burning eyes...

[*laughter*]

Researcher: You've been put in charge of quite a lot, you know.

Administrator physician: And then it's Mary, too, in that this is kind of pressure, if Mary is indeed the personal physician...

...

Administrator physician: Yes, it is so that the personal physician is here under the pressure that the plan will be made....

The first example illustrates the importance of *contradictions*. It contains an attempt to assign initiative and responsibility to identifiable participants. The patient has a serious heart deficiency, and the discussion has led to a point where the participants realize that this condition is not properly under anyone's responsibility for care. The heart specialist represents the Cardiology Clinic but he has not treated this particular patient, and due to the constant rotation of physicians at the clinic, he is uncertain if he will ever have a chance to deal with this patient. So the first contradiction surfaces: The Cardiology Clinic has the needed expertise, but as the heart specialist says, they need "a man or a woman who does it. The clinic as such doesn't do anything." The specialist can offer no continuity of care.

To provide continuity of care, the focus shifts to the patient's personal physician, a general practitioner (GP) in the local primary care health center: "the personal physician is here under the pressure that the plan will be made." This reveals the second contradiction: The personal GP can provide the required continuity of care, but has little authority and often limited competence in matters of specialized medicine.

Example 2

Chief physician: So, will you be first, as the physician responsible for her at the primary care health center, and then we will add ...

Consulting physician: Here we are kind of documenting what is already in place, but *if we had a similar case* where these contacts had not yet been created, *this would serve as sort of a model* from which other patients could benefit.

Chief physician: It would be very important *if we had a situation* where the patient's personal physician is changed, the previous doctor would go on a leave, and the next doctor would come for half a year. *In such cases this has great importance*, so that the doctor knows ...

[the patient's primary care GP signs the care agreement and starts to hand it back to the chief physician]

Chief physician: Please let the patient also sign it, while you are at it....From the signatures one sees that there are several people involved....

The second example illustrates the importance of mediating artifacts as well as the coming together of activity-level visions and action-level decisions. It contains a situation in which the laboratory session has led to drafting of a shared care agreement for a patient. The different professionals involved in the care of this patient, and the patient herself, are now ready to sign the care agreement; they are controlling their own behavior with the help of an external tool they have created. While signing the crucial artifact, the professionals discuss it. In the excerpt, I have used italics to identify segments of future-oriented activity-level envisioning. These envisioning segments are formulated by means of hypothetical language: "if we had a similar case," "if we had a situation." At the same time, the participants are making consequential action-level decisions: "So, will you be first," "Please let the patient also sign it." The last decision, in which it is realized that the patient also needs to sign the agreement, illustrates the importance of object orientation. This small but extraordinary realization was possible because the patient – the embodiment of the object of medical work – sat in as a knotworking partner with the medical professionals.

Example 3

Researcher 2: What are we going to do with this agreement, what will be done with it now?

Researcher 1: Isn't it so that O [the GP] will follow the situation at this point...

Researcher 2: ...Yes but this...

Researcher 1: ...because there aren't clearly identified partners yet, before these are cleared up, these ongoing examinations and tests and their results.

GP: Yes, we still miss the signatures, so...

Researcher 2: Well.

Researcher 1: Or what do you have in mind?

Researcher 2: Well, I just asked, what do you think, now that such a document has been prepared, so...

Researcher 1: Or all this groundwork, yes.

Researcher 2: Groundwork, what will be done with it. And now that O [the GP] refers R [the patient] to different places, would it be good if those different places to which she sends her for a specific problem, if they got to know about this whole picture in which this specific is...?

GP: Well, do I understand correctly, that I'd attach to it [the referral] this whole bundle, if someone there wants to quickly glance through it. How much would it then...? If I'm completely honest, having worked as a replacement for a specialist at one time, I sense that the less extra [paperwork] one got beyond one's own specialty the happier most colleagues were. So what is the standpoint of the seniors here...?

Researcher 1: This is an interesting question when there is so much material coming from the personal physician.

GP: Does it make a difference for how the process gets started in that end [in specialized hospital care]? Because if one learns this, [...] so that one just learns to use this tool, then one just does it. Surely at some point this will be moved from paper-and-pencil over to the other type...

Researcher 1: ...Soon, over to Pegasos... [*computerized medical records system currently being implemented in the primary health care system of Helsinki*]

GP: ...yes, so surely it will be much easier in there...or somehow to pick it up from there. Or maybe some aid might do it there, or something like that...

Nephrologist: But in my opinion, when someone has done this work, this will be useful for all.

Researcher 1: There is no reason not to send it all with a small statement, telling that "here is background information which may be helpful, and I am ready to discuss if needed," something like this.

Researcher 3: I think H [researcher 2] was thinking, "why not attach this care agreement to the next referral."

GP: Yes, but in my opinion it would also require these care calendars.

Researcher 3: Aha, those should be added to it, yes.

Researcher 1: Those calendars were clearly very important tools for you when you sorted through all of this.

GP: Yes, that's how I started to make sense of the reality in which the lady had lived the years before returning to Finland and after it.

Researcher 1: Yes.

GP: It was not easy in the first consultation. I kind of thought when I was writing down those calendars that if I only had had this kind of a tool then. So that I would have been able to arrange these issues at once according to some jointly agreed-upon model. I experienced this as very good.

Researcher 1: Right, yes.

GP: I mean, the first contact is heavy because there are so many things, and they have to be sorted, and that takes time. But it pays off in the longer run.

Researcher 1: Excellent, well, let's quickly sum this up. Surely it is like you [nephrologist] said, when such a work has been done, there is no sense in keeping it to one's self. [. . .] And it will be nice to hear what kind of feedback you'll get on your referrals. [. . .]

GP: I could include an attachment, or an attachment to a referral I already sent.

Nephrologist: May I say something?

Researcher 1: Yes.

Nephrologist: Now before this work is completed, it may be that somebody kind of, not gets aggravated but wonders, if these care agreements begin to come in, before this practice has been officially fixed and its implementation announced.

Researcher 1: Right, so in this case . . .

Nephrologist: . . . So this is at an early stage. So I think that if we now send it, surely the physician who receives the referral is glad to get as much information as possible. But it may require a small explanation.

Researcher 1: Just so.

GP: Yes.

This lengthy excerpt can be used to demonstrate the utility of all five principles of activity theory in the analysis of emerging forms of distributed agency at work. First of all, the principle of object orientation guides us to ask: What is actually the object here? What are these people talking about and trying to accomplish? In the excerpt, the talk is focused on the use and development of tools. This is triggered by the initial question of Researcher 2: "What are we going to do with this agreement, what will be done with it now?" In effect, the tools seem to have become the object here. We have analyzed such object–tool shifts in other contexts (Engeström & Escalante, 1995; Hasu & Engeström, 2000; see also the care plan analyzed in Chapter 5 of this book) and found them to be very problematic. Often the tool actually replaces the original object and becomes a substitute object, creating a hermetic bubble of design for the sake of design. The object (the client, the patient, the illness) is excluded from the discourse. Is this what is happening in the preceding excerpt?

Early on in the excerpt, Researcher 2 specifies her initial question by bringing in the patient: "And now that O [the GP] refers R [the patient] to different places..." A little later, the GP brings in the patient with an identity situated in time and place: "Yes, that's how I started to make sense of the reality in which the lady had lived the years before returning to Finland and after it." And shortly after that, the GP takes up the object of patients with multiple simultaneous illnesses in a more general sense: "I mean, the first contact is heavy because there are so many things, and they have to be sorted, and that takes time. But it pays off in the longer run." These references to the object indicate that the object–tool shift in this case may not lead to the formation of a self-sufficient substitute object.

The second principle, *mediation by tools and signs*, asks us to look at the potentials of artifacts as means of eliciting or triggering voluntary action. As I mentioned earlier in this chapter, rudimentary prompts may be regarded as early forms of mediated collective intentionality. The discussion in the excerpt focuses on the creation and implementation of such a rudimentary prompt. Researcher 1 states that "There is no reason not to send it all with a small statement, telling that 'here is background information which may be helpful, and I am ready to discuss if needed,' something like this." The GP agrees and suggests that "I could include an attachment, or an attachment to a referral I already sent." Finally, the experienced nephrologist refines the idea: "But it may require a small explanation." This is an example of the design phase of mediated collective intentionality.

The third principle, *mutual constitution of actions and activity*, calls attention to the relationship between decision making and envisioning. The excerpt shows how activity-level envisioning began to approach and resemble action-level decision making. The participants were working on a future-oriented model: "this is at an early stage." Yet, they were also working out a here-and-now decision: "I could include an attachment." What was particularly future-oriented about this decision was that the participants agreed that not only would the new mediating artifacts (care agreement, care map, care calendar) be attached to the referrals of this patient, they would also be introduced by a short note explaining their purpose to the receiving specialist. This note was to have a standard text prepared by the researchers and signed by the respective managing physicians of the primary care and the Central University Hospital. Yet, this general note was to be prepared quickly so that this particular physician could use it in the referrals for this specific patient. In other words, the particular decision was simultaneously a general vision.

The fourth principle directs our analysis to *contradictions and deviations as source of change*. In the excerpt, the initial questioning of Researcher 2 revealed a contradiction between administrative efficiency and patient-oriented quality of care. This tension was crisply articulated by the GP: "How much would it then...? If I'm completely honest, having worked as a replacement for a specialist at one time, I sense that the less extra [paperwork] one got beyond one's own specialty the happier most colleagues were." The decisive push to resolve the dilemma in an expansive manner came from the nephrologist, who pointed out succinctly that the work done by the GP should not be wasted. This statement was a significant deviating action in that it came as if from the other side of the fence, from a leading hospital specialist whose position would normally suggest a very different script of reasoning.

The fifth principle, *historicity*, prompts us to ask what historical type of work and collaboration is being performed in the excerpt. The excerpt, and more generally all three examples from the laboratory sessions previously presented, represent an attempt to break out of the confines of medical care divided horizontally into strictly bounded functional specialties and vertically into separate levels of expertise. The conscious aim in those sessions was to achieve negotiated knotworking between practitioners and patients. It is not yet clear what it will take to make such knotworking sustainable, or indeed whether it will even be possible in the near future. These sessions may thus be regarded as spearheads, microcosms that anticipate possible future developments in health care.

Learning Agency in a Landscape of Knotworking and Social Production

The five principles of activity theory just sketched and used offer a framework for analyzing agency. These principles do not assume that the foundational agent is an individual. To the contrary, all five principles, most obviously the principle of mutual constitution of actions and activity, the principle of contradictions as source of change, and the principle of historicity call for a serious examination of the social constitution and institutional embeddedness of agency.

The fictional case of Hillerman's *The Sinister Pig* and the empirical material from our fieldwork in medical settings point to an emerging landscape of knotworking and social production in which agency and collective intentionality may be taking on interesting new qualities. Earlier I suggested that the nature of agency in network organizations may be condensed in the imperative "Connect and reciprocate." Now this no longer seems sufficient. First of all, in both the fictional and empirical examples I have discussed, the connecting and reciprocating are *focused on and circling around a complex object*. Secondly, the connecting and reciprocating are done in fields of multiple, often severely divided activity systems. Reaching beyond and across the dividing boundaries and gaps between activity systems needs to be acknowledged as a foundational feature of this type of agency – perhaps better characterized as *inter*agency. Tentatively, the imperative of this type of agency might be formulated as "Dwell in the object; connect and reciprocate across boundaries."[3]

Formations such as the agentic collaboration between actors in *The Sinister Pig* or the knotworking between practitioners and patients in our laboratory sessions in Helsinki perform a dual job: they solve very complex problems and contribute to the reshaping of the entire way of working in their given fields. They are very cost-efficient in that they do not require establishing new positions or new organizational centers. Indeed, these formations tend to reject such attempts. Rejection and deviation from standard procedures and scripted norms are foundational to the success of such formations. Their efficacy and value lie in their distributed agency, their collective intentionality.

In a world of work that seeks ways to organize collaboration beyond teams, the learning challenge is above all that of constructing and acquiring distributed agency. In Chapters 3, 4, and 8 of this book, I have repeatedly used and enriched the concepts of coordination, cooperation, and communication as a scheme that describes one dimension of the learning challenge involved in the formation and functioning of teams. Teams at their best are excellent in cooperative solving of problems. They run into trouble and find their limits when faced with objects that require questioning the division of labor, rules, and boundaries of the team and the wider organization – in short, reflective communication.

What might be the nature of agency, coordination, and learning in social production and amoeba-like wildfire activities? What are the basic patterns of movement in such a landscape? Table 9.1 sketches a first answer to these questions by presenting rough historical characterizations of dominant

---

[3] By *dwelling in the object* I mean a longitudinal dialogical relationship with the object that goes beyond focusing on or appropriating the object.

Table 9.1. *Framework for conceptualizing distributed agency: toward social production*

	Nature of object	Locus of agency	Dominant mode of interaction	Coordinating mechanism	Learning movement
Craft	Personal object	Individual actor	Coordination	Identification and subordination	Peripheral participation, gradual transition toward the center
Mass production	Problematic object	Team	Cooperation	Process management	Focal involvement, linear and vertical improvement
Social production	Runaway object	Knots in mycorrhizae	Reflective communication	Negotiation and peer review	Expansive swarming engagement, multi-directional pulsation

features of craft, mass production, and social production. Co-configuration as described by Victor and Boynton (1998) would appear to be a transitional form between mass production and social production.

It seems that reflective communication is one aspect of the distributed agency required in knotworking. But it is only the interactional aspect. I will now sketch a more complete framework for analysis and development of agency in and for a landscape of knotworking and social production. The framework is condensed in Table 9.1.

In the first column of Table 9.1, mainly the notion of a runaway object requires further elaboration at this point. The notion is related to the concept of a *runaway world*, developed by Giddens (1991, 2000). Claudio Ciborra (2002, p. 98) characterizes the phenomenon as follows:

> We experience control in the age of globalization as more limited than ever. We are creating new global phenomena (global warming and greenhouse effects, nuclear threats, global production processes, and so on) that we are able to master only in part. Although information infrastructures appear to be important instruments for governing global phenomena, they possess ambiguities which make their eventual outcome difficult to determine. Consequently, they may serve to curb our control capabilities just as much as they enhance them.

In Hillerman's fictional case presented in this chapter, the runaway object was trafficking in narcotics. In the empirical health care case, it was chronic illness. Runaway objects have the potential to escalate and expand up to a global scale of influence. They are objects that are poorly under anybody's control and have far-reaching, unexpected side effects. Actor-network theorists (Law, 1991) point out that such objects are often monsters: They seem to have a life of their own that threatens our security and safety in many ways. They are contested objects that generate opposition and controversy. They can also be powerfully emancipatory objects that open up radically new possibilities of development and well-being, as exemplified by the Linux operating system.

Contrary to mega-projects (Altshuler & Luberoff, 2003; Flyvbjerg, Bruzelius, & Rothengatter, 2003), most runaway objects do not start out as big and risky. More commonly, they begin as small problems or marginal innovations, which makes their runaway potential difficult to predict and utilize. They often remain dormant, invisible, or unseen for lengthy periods of time, until they break out in the form of acute crises or breakthroughs (e.g., Vickers, 2001).

In the second column of Table 9.1, the most demanding concept is *mycorrhizae*. I use it much in the same general sense in which Deleuze and Guattari (1987) used the concept of *rhizome*. They wanted to highlight the importance of horizontal and multidirectional connections in human lives, in contrast to the dominant vertical, treelike images of hierarchy. Originally a biological concept, rhizome refers to a horizontal underground stem, such as found in many ferns, where only the leaves may be visible. As such, I find the implications of rhizome somewhat limited.

I am more interested in the invisible organic texture underneath visible fungi. Such a formation is called mycorrhizae. It is a symbiotic association between a fungus and the roots or rhizoids of a plant. Fungi are not able to ingest their food, as animals do, nor can they manufacture their own food, as plants do. Instead, fungi feed by absorbing nutrients from their environment. They accomplish this by growing through and within the substrate on which they feed. This filamentous growth means that the fungus is in intimate contact with its surroundings; it has a very large surface area compared to its volume. Most plants rely on a symbiotic fungus to aid them in acquiring water and nutrients from the soil. The specialized roots that the plants grow and the fungus that inhabits them are together known as mycorrhizae, or *fungal roots*. The fungus, with its large surface area, is able to soak up water and nutrients over a large area and provide them to the plant. In return, the plant provides energy-rich sugars manufactured through photosynthesis.

The visible mushrooms are reproductive structures. Even these structures are sometimes quite large, but the invisible body of the fungus, mycorrhizae, can be truly amazing. When molecular techniques were used, one Michigan fungus (*Armillaria bulbosa*), which grew in tree roots and soil and had a body constructed of tubular filaments, was found to extend over an area of 37 acres and to weigh 110 tons, equivalent to the weight of a blue whale. An even larger fungal clone of *Armillaria ostoyae*, reported earlier in the state of Washington, covered over 1,500 acres. Each clone began with the germination of a single spore over 1,000 years ago. Although they probably have fragmented and are no longer continuous bodies, such organisms give us a reason to think about what constitutes an individual.

A mycorrhiza is difficult, if not impossible, to bound and close, yet it is not indefinite or elusive. It is very hard to kill but also vulnerable. It may lie dormant for lengthy periods of drought or cold and then generate vibrant visible mushrooms when the conditions are right. It is made up of heterogeneous participants working symbiotically, thriving on mutually beneficial and also exploitative partnerships with plants and other organisms.

As I see it, knotworking eventually requires a mycorrhiza-like formation as its medium or base. In Hillerman's case, the interconnections between the actors depicted in Figure 9.1 may be seen as a simple mycorrhiza-like formation. In the health care case, the laboratory sessions that brought together the patient and medical professionals from different clinics were an attempt to trigger the creation of a mycorrhiza. Such a formation typically does not have strictly defined criteria for membership, but its members can be identified by their activism. The 2,605 development team members and the 1,562 bug reporting team members of the Linux mycorrhizae mentioned by Lee and Cole (2003) were identified on the basis of their publicly available contributions to the development and perfection of the object, the Linux operating system. It is very likely that a mycorrhiza includes a large variety of members, ranging from grassroots activists, clients, or victims to certified professionals, researchers, entrepreneurs, and spokespersons.

A mycorrhiza is simultaneously a living, expanding process (or bundle of developing connections) *and* a relatively durable, stabilized structure; both a mental landscape or *mindscape* (Zerubavel, 1997) and a material infrastructure. In this, it resembles the *cognitive trails* of Cussins (1992) and the *flow architecture* described by Knorr-Cetina (2003, p. 8) as "a reflexive form of coordination that is flat (non-hiearchical) in character while at the same time being based on a comprehensive summary view of things – the reflected and projected global context and transaction system."

As we have seen in this book, the triangular model of an activity system is a functioning tool for the analysis of teams and organizations. But does it have any use when we step into the fluid world of mycorrhizae? The answer is that horizontal and invisible mycorrhizae do not eliminate visible, erect, bounded, and institutionalized activity systems. As I pointed out earlier, mycorrhizae depend on plant roots and generate mushrooms that are visible, vertical, and more or less durable. Knorr-Cetina (2003, p. 18) points out that the mycorrhiza-like formation of global financial markets is crucially dependent on institutionalized, stable *bridgehead centers*. In Hillerman's fictional case, the mycorrhiza was punctuated by the institutional activity systems of law enforcement agencies. In the health care case, the different practitioners who come together to form a temporary knot represent and return to their clinics. Without these "plants" and "mushrooms," the knotworking mycorrhizae will not take shape. If anything, careful analyses of the dynamics of the activity systems involved are more important than ever before.

The fourth column of Table 9.1 sketches the typical coordinating mechanisms in different types of production. In craft-based organizations, where each practitioner is focused on his or her own object or fragment of the object, practitioners are commonly held together by externally imposed or tradition-based identification and subordination. In industrial organizations, teams emerged as units for cooperative solving of problems. Their efforts are typically coordinated by various forms of explicit process management. However, teams run into trouble and find their limits when faced with objects that require constant questioning and reconfiguration of the division of labor, rules, and boundaries of the team and the wider organization – in short, negotiation across horizontal and vertical boundaries of the given process.

Negotiation is a central coordinating mechanism of the distributed agency required in knotworking within social production. Negotiation is required when the object of the activity is unstable, resists attempts at control and standardization, and requires rapid integration of expertise from various locations and traditions. Negotiation is more than an instrumental search for a singular, isolated compromise decision. It is basically a construction of a *negotiated order* (Strauss, 1978) in which the participants can pursue their intersecting activities. As Firth (1995, p. 7) put it, "in quite implicit ways, negotiation activity implicates the discourse process itself, revolving around such things as acceptability of categories used to describe objects or concepts, and the veridicality of facts, reasons or assessments." Putnam (1994, pp. 339–340) goes a step further and points out that successful negotiations tend to transform the dispute, not just reach an instrumental end:

> By transforming a dispute, I refer to the extent that a conflict has experienced fundamental changes as a result of the negotiation. Fundamental changes might entail transforming the way individuals conceive of the other person, their relationship, the conflict dilemma, or the social-political situation. . . . In the transformative approach, conflicts are no longer problems to be resolved; rather, they are opportunities to create a new social reality, a new negotiated order, a different definition of a relationship, or a transformed situation.

As noted previously by Lee and Cole, social production such as the Open Source software movement is dependent on constant, publicly accessible critical commentary and peer review. When peer review becomes reciprocal, open, and continuous, it coincides with Putnam's notion of transformative negotiation.

In the fifth column of Table 9.1, again all three layers need to be briefly explained. *Peripheral participation* refers to novices moving gradually toward a perceived center of an activity or community of practice (Lave & Wenger,

1991). *Focal involvement* involves intense closure around a shared problem object. *Expansive swarming engagement* refers to more multidirectional movement where the participants disperse to pursue their various trails and to expand the scope of the mycorrhizae, but also return and come together in various ways to contribute to the forging of the runaway object. The notion of swarming, or swarm intelligence, comes from the study of distributed collaboration patterns among social insects such as ants and bees (Bonabeau, Dorigo, & Theraulaz, 1999). Models from the insect worlds are simulated to build systems of artificial intelligence. Interestingly, mycorrhizae behave somewhat similarly to the social insects: When one of the filaments contacts a food supply, the entire fungal colony mobilizes and reallocates resources to exploit the new food. Unfortunately, popular applications of the notion of swarming in studies on organizations and innovations (e.g., Gloor, 2006) have thus far added little to the basic idea.

Expansive swarming is not just hectic active movement. It has multiple rhythms of improvisation and persistence that correspond to the dual dynamics of swift situational concerted action and pursuit of a repeatedly reconfigured long-term perspective in knotworking. Improvisation has attracted the attention of organizational researchers seeking models for swift trust and weakly scripted but well-focused collaborative problem solving in jazz and other forms of improvised collective performance. *Persistence* refers to patient dwelling on the object over long periods of time, alternating between intense action and more detached observation or even partial withdrawal. It includes pausing, backing up, regrouping, and finding detours or new openings in the face of obstacles. Interestingly, Whorf's (1956) classic description of *preparation* in Hopi culture displays some crucial features of persistence:

> A characteristic of Hopi behavior is the emphasis on preparation. This includes announcing and getting ready for events well beforehand, elaborate precautions to insure persistence of desired conditions, and stress on good will as the preparer of right results. (Whorf, 1956, p. 148)

> To the Hopi, for whom time is not motion but a "getting later" of everything that has ever been done, unvarying repetition is not wasted but accumulated. It is storing up an invisible change that holds over into later events. (Ibid., p. 151)

Moving horizontally across the last layer in Table 9.1, the agency called for in knotworking may be summarized as *negotiated communicative engagement with runaway objects in knots and mycorrhizae*. This is a fairly challenging, if not monstrous, string of words. Perhaps that is unavoidable.

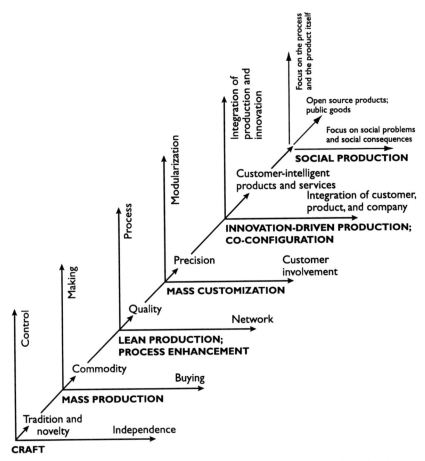

Figure 9.2. Historical types of production completed: toward social production.

In Chapter 8, I presented a figure that summarized the historical types of production and their internal tensions (Figure 8.5). I will now complete the figure by placing the emerging social production in it (Figure 9.2).

Social production is not limited to open-source software production, as evidenced by phenomena such as Wikipedia and the free science movement (Kelty, 2005). Although social production is still in its infancy, the inward-outward dimension used in Figure 8.5 may be tentatively applied to it. The inward orientation is exemplified by the Linux developers, whose main interest has been the creation and continuous improvement of a technically impressive shareable product. The outward orientation is exemplified by the community called *The Synaptic Leap* (http://thesynapticleap.org/?q=).

It is an open-source biomedical research community that describes its object as follows:

> Diseases found exclusively in tropical regions predominantly afflict poor people in developing countries. The typical profit-driven pharmaceutical economic model fails with these diseases because there is simply no money to be made. However, the very fact that there's no profit incentive to research these diseases makes them perfect candidates for open source style research; there's no profit incentive to keep secrets either. Our pilot research communities focusing on tropical diseases are: Malaria, schistosomiasis, tuberculosis.

It is too early to judge to what extent The Synaptic Leap will be able to produce new ways to combat tropical diseases. However, as Benkler (2006, p. 121) observes, its success is not dependent on medical researchers' benevolence only:

> The capital cost of effective economic action in the industrial economy shunted sharing to its economic peripheries (. . .). The emerging restructuring of capital investment in digital networks – in particular, the phenomenon of user-capitalized computation and communications capabilities – are at least partly reversing that effect.

When this technological and economic opportunity is combined with a powerful runaway object such as tropical diseases, something radically new may indeed emerge. However, as the metaphor of mycorrhizae reminds us, this is happening in a field of symbiotic forms. Most of the researchers involved in The Synaptic Leap will continue working in their traditional research institutions while contributing simultaneously to the open-source effort. This opens up an interesting landscape of learning to negotiate and balance multiple parallel loyalties, both mutually enriching and hostile to one another.

The concepts of the framework suggested in this chapter are far from completed and stabilized. They are first approximations meant to open up a field for further debate, theoretical work, and experimentation in activity fields with complex runaway objects, seeking to build collaboration in knotlike ways, beyond the models of stable, well-bounded institutions and teams.

References

Adler, P. S. (1993). Time-and-motion regained. *Harvard Business Review*, January–February, 97–108.

Adler, P. S., & Cole, R. E. (1993). Designed for learning: A tale of two auto plants. *Sloan Management Review*, *34*(3), 85–94.

Adler, P. S., & Cole, R. E. (1994). Rejoinder. *Sloan Management Review*, *35*(2), 45–49.

Adler, P. S., & Heckscher, C. (2006). Towards a collaborative community. In C. Heckscher & P. S. Adler (Eds.), *The firm as a collaborative community: Reconstructing trust in the knowledge economy* (pp. 11–105). Oxford: Oxford University Press.

Ahonen, H., Engeström, Y., & Virkkunen, J. (2000). Knowledge management – the second generation: Creating competencies within and between work communities in the Competence Laboratory. In Y. Malhotra (Ed.), *Knowledge management and virtual organizations* (pp. 282–305). Hershey, PA: Idea Group Publishing.

Alexander, J. C. (Ed.). (1987). *The micro-macro link*. Berkeley: University of California Press.

Alter, C., & Hage, J. (1993). *Organizations working together*. Newbury Park, CA: Sage.

Altshuler, A., & Luberoff, D. (2003). *Mega-projects: The changing politics of urban public investment*. Washington, DC: Brookings Institution.

Ancona, D. G. (1990). Outward bound: Strategies of survival in an organization. *Academy of Management Journal*, *33*, 334–365.

Ancona, D. G. (1991). *The changing role of teams in organizations: Strategies for survival*. Working Paper No. 37–91, the International Center for Research on the Management of Technology. Cambridge, MA: Sloan School of Management, Massachussets Institute of Technology.

Ancona, D., Bresman, H., & Kaeufer, K. (2002). The comparative advantage of X-teams. *Sloan Management Review*, *43*(3), 33–39.

Ancona, D. G., & Caldwell, D. F. (1992). Bridging the boundary: External activity and performance in organizational teams. *Administrative Science Quarterly*, *37*, 634–665.

Applebaum, E., & Batt, R. (1994). *The new American workplace*. Ithaca, NY: ILR Press.

Argyris, C. (1986). Skilled incompetence. *Harvard Business Review*, *64*(5), 74–80.

Argyris, C., & Schön, D. A. (1978). *Organizational learning: A theory of action perspective.* Reading, MA: Addison-Wesley.

Bakhtin, M. M. (1982). *The dialogic imagination: Four essays by M. M. Bakhtin.* Austin: University of Texas Press.

Bakhurst, D. (1991). *Consciousness and revolution in Soviet philosophy: From the Bolsheviks to Evald Ilyenkov.* Cambridge: Cambridge University Press.

Baldo, A. (1990). Vanishing viewers: Here's a paradox, as audiences shrink, ad prices rise; Capital Cities/ABC shows why. *Financial World,* August 7, 26.

Barker, J. R. (1993). Tightening the iron cage: Concertive control in self-managing teams. *Administrative Science Quarterly, 38,* 408–437.

Barker, R. S. (1999). *The discipline of teamwork: Participation and coercive control.* Thousand Oaks, CA: Sage.

Barnes, B. (2000). *Understanding agency: Social theory and responsible action.* London: Sage.

Bartunek, J. M., & Reid, R. D. (1992). The role of conflict in a second order change attempt. In D. M. Kolb & J. M. Bartunek (Eds.), *Hidden conflict in organizations: Uncovering behind-the-scenes disputes* (pp. 116–142). Newbury Park, CA: Sage.

Bateson, G. (1972). *Steps to an ecology of mind.* New York: Ballantine Books.

Becker, H. S. (1982). *Art worlds.* Berkeley: University of California Press.

Beloff, J. S., & Willet, M. (1968). Yale studies in family health care: III. The health care team. *Journal of the American Medical Association, 205,* 10.

Benkler, Y. (2006). *The wealth of networks: How social production transforms markets and freedom.* New Haven, CT: Yale University Press.

Berggren, C. (1994). NUMMI vs. Uddevalla. *Sloan Management Review, 35*(2), 37–45.

Beyerlein, M. M. (Ed.). (2000). *Work teams: Past, present, and future.* Dordrecht: Kluwer.

Beyerlein, M. M., Beyerlein, S. T., & Johnson, D. A. (Eds.). (2003). *Team-based organizing.* Amsterdam: JAI Press.

Beyerlein, M. M., Beyerlein, S. T., & Kennedy, F. A. (Eds.). (2005). *Collaborative capital: Creating intangible value.* Amsterdam: Elsevier.

Beyerlein, M. M., Freedman, S., McGee, C., & Moran, L. (2002). *Beyond teams: Building the collaborative organization.* San Francisco: Jossey-Bass/Pfeiffer.

Beyerlein, M. M., & Johnson, D. A. (Eds.). (1994). *Theories of self-managing work teams.* Greenwich, CT: JAI Press.

Beyerlein, M. M., Johnson, D. A., & Beyerlein, S. T. (Eds.). (1995). *Knowledge work in teams.* Greenwich, CT: JAI Press.

Beyerlein, M. M., Johnson, D. A., & Beyerlein, S. T. (Eds.). (2000a). *Product development teams.* Stamford, CT: JAI Press.

Beyerlein, M. M., Johnson, D. A., & Beyerlein, S. T. (Eds.). (2000b). *Team development.* Amsterdam: JAI Press.

Beyerlein, M. M., Johnson, D. A., & Beyerlein, S. T. (Eds.). (2000c). *Team performance.* Stamford, CT: JAI Press.

Beyerlein, M. M., Johnson, D. A., & Beyerlein, S. T. (Eds.). (2001). *Virtual teams.* Amsterdam: JAI Press.

Billig, M., Condor, S., Edwards, D., Gane, M., Middleton, D. & Radley, A. (1987). *Ideological dilemmas: A social psychology of everyday thinking.* London: Sage.

Bion, W. R. (1961). *Experiences in groups.* London: Tavistock.

Blackler, F. (1993). Knowledge and the theory of organizations: Organizations as activity systems and the reframing of management. *Journal of Management Studies, 30*, 863–884.

Blackler, F., Crump, N., & McDonald, S. (2000). Organizing processes in complex activity networks. *Organization, 7*, 277–300.

Blackler, F., McDonald, S., & Crump, N. (1999). Managing experts and competing through innovation: An activity theoretical analysis. *Organization, 6*, 5–31.

Bonabeau, E., Dorigo, M., & Theraulaz, G. (1999). *Swarm intelligence: From natural to artificial systems*. New York: Oxford University Press.

Borden, I. (2001). *Skateboarding, space and the city: Architecture, the body and performative critique*. New York: Berg.

Bowers, J. M., & Benford, S. D. (Eds.). (1991). *Studies in computer supported cooperative work: Theory, practice and design*. Amsterdam: North-Holland.

Bowker, G. C., & Star, S. L. (1999). *Sorting things out: Classification and its consequences*. Cambridge, MA: MIT Press.

Bratman, M. E. (1999). *Faces of intention: Selected essays on intention and agency*. Cambridge: Cambridge University Press.

Broadcasting (1991). One of TV's best kept secrets: How ABC, CBS, and NBC have taken the bite out of program costs. *Broadcasting*, December 9, 3.

Bruce, N. (1980). *Teamwork for preventive care*. Chichester, UK: Research Studies Press.

Bruner, J. S. (1966). *Toward a theory of instruction*. Cambridge, MA: Harvard University Press.

Buchwald, C. (1993). *Collaborative curriculum construction without a textbook*. Paper presented at the Fifth Conference on Ethnographic and Qualitative Research in Education, Amherst, MA, June 5.

Buchwald, C. (1995). *New work in old institutions: Collaborative curriculum work of a teacher team*. Unpublished dissertation, University of California, San Diego.

Button, G. (Ed.). (1993). *Technology in working order: Studies of work, interaction, and technology*. London: Routledge.

Chaiklin, S., & Lave, J. (Eds.). (1993). *Understanding practice: Perspectives on activity and context*. Cambridge: Cambridge University Press.

Chatwin, B. (1987). *The songlines*. London: Jonathan Cape.

Ciborra, C. (1993). *Teams, markets and systems: Business innovation and information technology*. Cambridge: Cambridge University Press.

Ciborra, C. (2000). A critical review of the literature on the management of corporate information infrastructure. In C. Ciborra (Ed.)., *From control to drift: The dynamics of corporate information infrastructures* (pp. 15–40). Oxford: Oxford University Press.

Ciborra, C. (2002). *The labyrinths of information: Challenging the wisdom of systems*. Oxford: Oxford University Press.

Clarke, A., & Fujimura, J. H. (Eds.). (1992). *The right tools for the job: At work in twentieth-century life sciences*. Princeton, NJ: Princeton University Press.

Cole, M., & Engeström, Y. (1993). A cultural-historical approach to distributed cognition. In G. Salomon (Ed.), *Distributed cognitions: Psychological and educational considerations* (pp. 1–46). Cambridge: Cambridge University Press.

Cole, R. E. (1993). The Leadership, Organization and Co-determination Programme and its evaluation: A comparative perspective. In F. Naschold, R. E.

Cole, B. Gustavsen, & H. van Beinum (Eds.), *Constructing the new industrial society* (pp. 123–132). Maastricht: van Gorcum.

Conley, J. M., & O'Barr, W. M. (1990). *Rules versus relationships: The ethnography of legal discourse.* Chicago: University of Chicago Press.

Coupland, N., Giles, H., & Wiemann, J. M. (Eds.). (1991). *Miscommunication and problematic talk.* London: Sage.

Cross, R., Baker, W., & Parker, A. (2003). What creates energy in organizations? *Sloan Management Review, 44*(4), 51–56.

Cuban, L. (1984). *How teachers taught: Constancy and change in American classrooms, 1890–1980.* New York: Longman.

Cussins, A. (1992). Content, embodiment and objectivity: The theory of cognitive trails. *Mind, 101,* 651–688.

Davydov, V. V. (1988). Problems of developmental teaching. *Soviet Education, 30*(8–10).

Davydov, V. V. (1990). *Types of generalization in instruction: Logical and psychological problems in the structuring of school curricula.* Reston, VA: National Council of Teachers of Mathematics.

Deleuze, G., & Guattari, F. (1977). *Anti-Oedipus: Capitalism and schizophrenia.* New York: Viking.

Deleuze, G., & Guattari, F. (1987). *A thousand plateaus: Capitalism and schizophrenia.* Minneapolis: University of Minnesota Press.

DiBona, C., Ockman, S., & Stone, M. (Eds.). (1999). *Open sources: Voices from the Open Source revolution.* Sebastopol, CA: O'Reilly.

Dixon, N. M. (1994). *The organizational learning cycle: How we can learn collectively.* London: McGraw-Hill.

Donellon, A. (1996). *Team talk: The power of language in team dynamics.* Boston: Harvard Business School Press.

Drew, P., & Heritage, J. (Eds.). (1992). *Talk at work: Interaction in institutional settings.* Cambridge: Cambridge University Press.

Dreyfus, H. L., & Dreyfus, S. E. (1986). *Mind over machine: The power of human intuition and expertise in the era of the computer.* Oxford: Basil Blackwell.

Ellegård, K. (1995). The creation of a new production system at the Volvo automobile assembly plant in Uddevalla. In Å. Sandberg (Ed.), *Enriching production: Perspectives on Volvo's Uddevalla plant as an alternative to lean production* (pp. 37–60). Aldershot: Avebury.

Emery, F. (1976/1993). The assembly line: Its logic and our future. In E. Trist & H. Murray (Eds.), *The social engagement of social science: A Tavistock anthology. Volume II: The socio-technical perspective* (pp. 202–213). Philadelphia: University of Pennsylvania Press.

Engeström, R. (1995). Voice as communicative action. *Mind, Culture, and Activity, 2,* 192–214.

Engeström, Y. (1987). *Learning by expanding: An activity-theoretical approach to developmental research.* Helsinki: Orienta-Konsultit.

Engeström, Y. (1990). *Learning, working and imagining: Twelve studies in activity theory.* Helsinki: Orienta-Konsultit.

Engeström, Y. (1991a). Activity theory and individual and social transformation. *Multidisciplinary Newsletter for Activity Theory, 7/9,* 6–17.

Engeström, Y. (1991b). Developmental work research: Reconstructing expertise through expansive learning. In M. I. Nurminen & G. R. S. Weir (Eds.), *Human jobs and computer interfaces* (pp. 265–290). Amsterdam: Elsevier Science.

Engeström, Y. (1991c). Non scolae sed vitae discimus: Toward overcoming the encapsulation of school learning. *Learning and Instruction, 1,* 243–259.

Engeström, Y. (1992). *Interactive expertise: Studies in distributed working intelligence.* Research Bulletin #83. University of Helsinki, Department of Education.

Engeström, Y. (1993). Developmental studies of work as a testbench of activity theory: The case of primary care medical practice. In S. Chaiklin & J. Lave (Eds.), *Understanding practice: Perspectives on activity and context* (pp. 64–103). Cambridge: Cambridge University Press.

Engeström, Y. (1994a). Teachers as collaborative thinkers: Activity-theoretical study of an innovative teacher team. In I. Carlgren, G. Handal, & S. Vaage (Eds.), *Teachers' minds and actions: Research on teachers' thinking and practice* (pp. 43–61). London: Falmer Press.

Engeström, Y. (1994b). The Working Health Center Project: Materializing zones of proximal development in a network of organizational innovation. In T. Kauppinen & M. Lahtonen (Eds.), *Action research in Finland* (pp. 233–272). Helsinki: Ministry of Labour.

Engeström, Y. (1994c). *Training for change: New approach to instruction and learning in working life.* Geneva: International Labour Organization.

Engeström, Y. (1995a). Innovative organizational learning in medical and legal settings. In L. M. W. Martin, K. Nelson, & E. Tobach (Eds.), *Sociocultural psychology: Theory and practice of doing and knowing* (pp. 326–356). Cambridge: Cambridge University Press.

Engeström, Y. (1995b). Objects, contradictions and collaboration in medical cognition: An activity-theoretical perspective. *Artificial Intelligence in Medicine, 7,* 395–412.

Engeström, Y. (1996a). Developmental work research as educational research: Looking ten years back and into the zone of proximal development. *Nordisk Pedagogik, 16,* 131–143.

Engeström, Y. (1996b). The tensions of judging: Handling cases of driving under the influence of alcohol in Finland and California. In Y. Engeström & D. Middleton (Eds.), *Cognition and communication at work* (pp. 199–232). Cambridge: Cambridge University Press.

Engeström, Y. (1999a). Communication, discourse and activity. *The Communication Review, 3*(1–2), 165–185.

Engeström, Y. (1999b). Expansive visibilization of work: An activity-theoretical perspective. *Computer Supported Cooperative Work, 8,* 63–93.

Engeström, Y. (2000a). Activity theory and the social construction of knowledge: A story of four umpires. *Organization, 7,* 301–310.

Engeström, Y. (2000b). Activity theory as a framework for analyzing and redesigning work. *Ergonomics, 43,* 960–974.

Engeström, Y. (Ed.). (2001). *Activity theory and social capital.* Technical Reports No. 5. Helsinki: Center for Activity Theory and Developmental Work Research, University of Helsinki.

Engeström, Y. (2005a). *Developmental work research: Expanding activity theory in practice.* Berlin: Lehmanns Media.

Engeström, Y. (2005b). Knotworking to create collaborative intentionality capital in fluid organizational fields. In M. M. Beyerlein, S. T. Beyerlein, & F. A. Kennedy (Eds.), *Collaborative capital: Creating intangible value* (pp. 307–336). Amsterdam: Elsevier.

Engeström, Y. (2007). Enriching the theory of expansive learning: Lessons from journeys toward co-configuration. *Mind, Culture, and Activity, 12,* 23–39.

Engeström, Y., & Blackler, F. (2005). On the life of the object. *Organization, 12,* 307–329.

Engeström, Y., Engeström, R., & Kärkkäinen, M. (1995). Polycontextuality and boundary crossing in expert cognition: Learning and problem solving in complex work activities. *Learning and Instruction, 5,* 319–336.

Engeström, Y., Engeström, R., & Kerosuo, H. (2003). The discursive construction of collaborative care. *Applied Linguistics, 24,* 286–315.

Engeström, Y., Engeström, R., & Vähäaho, T. (1999). When the center does not hold: The importance of knotworking. In S. Chaiklin, M. Hedegaard, & U. J. Jensen (Eds.), *Activity theory and social practice: Cultural-historical approaches* (pp. 345–374). Aarhus, Denmark: Aarhus University Press.

Engeström, Y., & Escalante, V. (1995). Mundane tool or object of affection? The rise and fall of the Postal Buddy. In B. Nardi (Ed.), *Consciousness in context: Activity theory and human-computer interaction.* Cambridge, MA: MIT Press.

Engeström, Y., Lompscher, J., & Rückriem, G. (Eds.). (2005). *Putting activity theory to work: Contributions from developmental work research.* Berlin: Lehmanns Media.

Engeström, Y., & Middleton, D. (Eds.). (1996). *Cognition and communication at work.* Cambridge: Cambridge University Press.

Engeström, Y., Miettinen, R., & Punamäki, R.-L. (Eds.). (1999), *Perspectives on activity theory.* Cambridge: Cambridge University Press.

Engeström, Y., Puonti, A., & Seppänen, L. (2003). Spatial and temporal expansion of the object as a challenge for reorganizing work. In D. Nicolini, S. Gherardi, & D. Yanow (Eds.), *Knowing in organizations: A practice-based approach* (pp. 151–186). Armonk, NY: M E. Sharpe.

Engeström, Y., Virkkunen, J., Helle, M., Pihlaja, J., & Poikela, R. (1996). Change Laboratory as a tool for transforming work. *Lifelong Learning in Europe, 1*(2), 10–17.

Ezzamel, M., & Willmott, H. (1998). Accounting for teamwork: A critical study of group-based systems of organizational control. *Administrative Science Quarterly, 43,* 358–396.

Fabrikant, G. (1987). Not ready for prime time? *The New York Times Magazine,* April 12, 30.

Falmagne, R. J. (1995). The abstract and the concrete. In L. M. W. Martin, K. Nelson, & E. Tobach (Eds.), *Sociocultural psychology: Theory and practice of doing and knowing* (pp. 205–228). Cambridge: Cambridge University Press.

Fichtner, B. (1984). Co-ordination, co-operation and communication in the formation of theoretical concepts in instruction. In M. Hedegaard, P. Hakkarainen, & Y. Engeström (Eds.), *Learning and teaching on a scientific basis: Methodological and epistemological aspects of the activity theory of learning and teaching* (pp. 207–227). Aarhus, Denmark: Aarhus Universitet, Psykologisk Institut.

Firth, A. (1995). Introduction and overview. In A. Firth (Ed.), *The discourse of negotiation: Studies of language in the workplace* (pp. 3–39). Oxford: Pergamon.

Flyvbjerg, B., Bruzelius, N., & Rothengatter, W. (2003). *Megaprojects and risk: An anatomy of ambition.* Cambridge: Cambridge University Press.

Fogel, A. (1993). *Developing through relationships: Origins of communication, self, and culture.* Chicago: University of Chicago Press.

Foot, K. (2001). Cultural-historical activity theory as practical theory: Illuminating the development of a conflict monitoring network. *Communication Theory, 11,* 56–83.

Francis, A., Turk, J., & Willman, P. (Eds.). (1983). *Power, efficiency and institutions: A critical appraisal of the 'markets and hierarchies' paradigm.* London: Heinemann.

Gagliardi, P. (Ed.). (1990). *Symbols and artifacts: Views of the corporate landscape.* Berlin: Walter de Gruyter.

Galegher, J., Kraut, R., & Egido, C. (Eds.). (1990). *Intellectual teamwork: Social and technological bases of cooperative work.* Hillsdale, NJ: Erlbaum.

Garratt, B. (1990). *Creating a learning organisation: A guide to leadership, learning and development.* Cambridge: Director Books.

Gatto, J. T. (1992). *Dumbing us down: The hidden curriculum of compulsory schooling.* Philadelphia: New Society.

Gell, A. (1998). *Art and agency: An anthropological theory.* Oxford: Clarendon Press.

Gersick, C. J. G. (1988). Time and transition in work teams: Toward a new model of group development. *Academy of Management Journal, 31,* 9–41.

Gersick, C. J. G. (1989). Marking time: Predictabe transitions in task groups. *Academy of Management Journal, 32,* 274–309.

Ghoshal, S., & Bruch, H. (2003). Going beyond motivation to the power of volition. *Sloan Management Review,* Spring, 51–57.

Gibbs, R. W., Jr. (2001). Intentions as emergent products of social interactions. In B. F. Malle, L. J. Moses, & D. A. Baldwin (Eds.), *Intentions and intentionality: Foundations of social cognition* (pp. 105–124). Cambridge: MIT Press.

Giddens, A. (1991). *Consequences of modernity.* Cambridge: Polity Press.

Giddens, A. (2000). *Runaway world: How globalization is reshaping our lives.* London: Brunner-Routledge.

Gilmore, J. H., & Pine, B. J., II. (1997). The four faces of mass customization. *Harvard Business Review, 1,* 101–110.

Ginnett, R. C. (1993). Crews as groups: Their formation and their leadership. In E. L. Wiener, B. G. Kanki, & R. L. Helmreich (Eds.), *Cockpit resource management* (pp. 71–98). San Diego, CA: Academic Press.

Gloor, P. A. (2006). *Swarm creativity: Competitive advantage through collaborative innovation networks.* Oxford: Oxford University Press.

Goffman, E. (1959). *The presentation of self in everyday life.* New York: Doubleday.

Goffman, E. (1974). *Frame analysis: An essay on the organization of experience.* Boston: Northeastern University Press.

Goodwin, C. (1994). Professional vision. *American Anthropologist, 96,* 606–633.

Goodwin, C. (1995). Seeing in depth: Space, technology and interaction on a scientific research vessel. *Social Studies of Science, 25,* 237–274.

Goodwin, M. H. (1990). *He-said-she-said: Talk as social organization among black children.* Bloomington: Indiana University Press.

Gordon, T., Holland, J., & Lahelma, E. (1999). *Making spaces: Citizenship and difference in schools.* Basingstoke, UK: Macmillan.

Greenbaum, J., & Kyng, M. (Eds.). (1991). *Design at work: Cooperative design of computer systems.* Hillsdale, NJ: Erlbaum.

Greenberg, S. (Ed.). (1991). *Computer-supported cooperative work and groupware.* London: Academic Press.

Grimshaw, A. D. (Ed.). (1990). *Conflict talk: Sociolinguistic investigations of arguments in conversations.* Cambridge: Cambridge University Press.

Gustavsen, B. (1992). *Dialogue and development.* Assen: Van Gorcum.

Gutierrez, K. D., Rymes, B., & Larson, J. (1995). Script, counterscript, and underlife in the classroom – Brown, James versus Brown v. Board of Education. *Harvard Educational Review, 65,* 445–471.

Guzzo, R. A., Salas, E., and associates. (1995). *Team effectiveness and decision making in organizations.* San Francisco: Jossey-Bass.

Haavisto, V. (2002). *Court work in transition: An activity-theoretical study of changing work practices in a Finnish district court.* Helsinki: Department of Education, University of Helsinki.

Habermas, J. (1984). *The theory of communicative action. Vol. 1: Reason and the rationalization of society.* London: Heinemann.

Hammer, M., & Champy, J. (1993). *Reengineering the corporation: A manifesto for business revolution.* New York: HarperBusiness.

Hart-Landsberg, S., & Reder, S. (1995). Teamwork and literacy: Teaching and learning at Hardy Industries. *Reading Research Quarterly, 30,* 1016–1047.

Hasu, M., & Engeström, Y. (2000). Measurement in action: An activity-theoretical perspective on producer–user interaction. *International Journal of Human-Computer Studies, 53,* 61–89.

Hatch, M. J., & Ehrlich, S. B. (1993). Spontaneous humor as an indicator of paradox and ambiguity in organizations. *Organization Studies, 14,* 505–526.

Heath, C., & Luff, P. (1996). Convergent activities: Line control and passenger information on the London Underground. In Y. Engeström & D. Middleton (Eds.), *Cognition and communication at work* (pp. 96–129). Cambridge: Cambridge University Press.

Heath, C., & Luff, P. (2000). *Technology in action.* Cambridge: Cambridge University Press.

Helman, C. G. (1985). Disease and pseudo-disease: A case history of pseudo-angina. In R. A. Hahn & A. D. Gaines (Eds.), *Physicians of Western medicine: Anthropological approaches to theory and practice* (pp. 293–331). Dordrecth: Reidel.

Henry, J. (1963). *Culture against man.* New York: Vintage Books.

Heydebrand, W., & Seron, C. (1990). *Rationalizing justice: The political economy of federal district courts.* Albany: State University of New York Press.

Hickey, D. T. (2003). Engaged participation versus marginal nonparticipation: A stridently sociocultural approach to achievement motivation. *The Elementary School Journal, 103,* 401–429.

Hillerman, T. (2001). *Seldom disappointed: A memoir.* New York: HarperCollins.

Hillerman, T. (2003). *The sinister pig.* New York: HarperCollins.

Høeg, P. (1994). *Borderliners.* New York: Farrar, Straus and Giroux.

Holland, D., & Reeves, J. R. (1996). Activity theory and the view from somewhere: Team perspectives on the intellectual work of programming. In B. A. Nardi (Ed.), *Context and consciousness: Activity theory and human–computer interaction* (pp. 257–282). Cambridge, MA: MIT Press.

Holt, G. R., & Morris, A. W. (1993). Activity theory and the analysis of organizations. *Human Organization, 52,* 97–109.

Holt, J. (1964). *How children fail.* New York: Pitman.

Horwitz, J. J. (1970). *Team practice and the specialist.* Springfield, IL: Charles C. Thomas.

Hoy, S. M., Robinson, M. C., & Armstrong, E. L. (Eds.). (1976). *History of public works in the United States, 1776–1976.* Chicago: American Public Works Association.

Hutchins, E. (1995). *Cognition in the wild.* Cambridge, MA: MIT Press.

Hutchins, E., & Klausen, T. (1996). Distributed cognition in an airline cockpit. In Y. Engeström & D. Middleton (Eds.), *Cognition and communication at work* (pp. 15–34). Cambridge: Cambridge University Press.

Il'enkov, E. V. (1982). *The dialectics of the abstract and the concrete in Marx's "Capital."* Moscow: Progress.

Ilyenkov, E. V. (1977). *Dialectical logic: Essays in its history and theory.* Moscow: Progress.

Kärkkäinen, M. (1999). *Teams as breakers of traditional work practices: A longitudinal study of planning and implementing curriculum units in elementary school teacher teams.* Research Bulletin 100. Helsinki: Department of Education, University of Helsinki.

Katzenbach, J. R., & Smith, D. K. (1993). *The wisdom of teams: Creating the high-performance organization.* Boston: Harvard Business School Press.

Keating, A. D. (1994). *Invisible networks: Exploring the history of local utilities and public works.* Malabar, FL: Krieger.

Keller, C. M., & Keller, J. D. (1996). *Cognition and tool use: The blacksmith at work.* Cambridge: Cambridge University Press.

Kelty, C. (2005). Free science. In J. Feller, B. Fitzgerald, S. A. Hissam, & K. R. Lakhani (Eds.), *Perspectives on free and open software* (pp. 415–430). Cambridge, MA: MIT Press.

Kenney, M., & Florida, R. L. (1993). *Beyond mass production: The Japanese system and its transfer to the U.S.* New York: Oxford University Press.

Kerosuo, H. (2006). *Boundaries in action: An activity-theoretical study of development, learning and change in health care for patients with multiple and chronic illnesses.* Helsinki: Department of Education, University of Helsinki.

Kerosuo, H., & Engeström, Y. (2003). Boundary crossing and learning in creation of new work practice. *Journal of Workplace Learning, 15,* 345–351.

Ketchum, L. D., & Trist, E. (1992). *All teams are not created equal: How employee empowerment really works.* Newbury Park, CA: Sage.

Klein, G. (1998). *Sources of power: How people make decisions.* Cambridge, MA: MIT Press.

Kleinman, A. (1980). *Patients and healers in the context of culture.* Berkeley: University of California Press.

Knorr-Cetina, K. (1997). Sociality with objects: Social relations in postsocial knowledge societies. *Theory, Culture & Society, 14*(4), 1–30.

Knorr-Cetina, K. (1999). *Epistemic cultures: How the sciences make knowledge.* Cambridge, MA: Harvard University Press.

Knorr-Cetina, K. (2001). Objectual practice. In T. R. Schatzki, K. Knorr-Cetina, & E. von Savigny (Eds.), *The practice turn in contemporary theory* (pp. 175–188). London: Routledge.

Knorr-Cetina, K. (2003). From pipes to scopes: The flow architecture of financial markets. *Distinktion, 7,* 7–23.

Knorr-Cetina, K., & Cicourel, A. (Eds.). (1981). *Advances in social theory and methodology: Toward an integration of micro- and macro-sociologies.* Boston: Routledge & Kegan Paul.

Kobus, D. K. (1983). The developing field of global education: A review of the literature. *Educational Research Quarterly, 8,* 21–28.

Kotha, S. (1995). Mass customization: Implementing the emerging paradigm for competitive advantage. *Strategic Management Journal, 16,* 21–42.

Lampel, J., & Mintzberg, H. (1996). Customizing customization. *Sloan Management Review, 38*(1), 21–30.

Lashof, J. C. (1968). The health care team in the Mile Square Area, Chicago. *Bulletin of the New York Academy of Medicine, 44,* 11.

Latour, B. (1987). *Science in action: How to follow scientists and engineers through society.* Cambridge, MA: Harvard University Press.

Latour, B. (1988). *The Pasteurization of France.* Cambridge, MA: Harvard University Press.

Latour, B. (1992). Where are the missing masses? The sociology of a few mundane artifacts. In W. Bijker & J. Law (Eds.), *Shaping technology/building society: Studying sociotechnical change* (pp. 225–259). Cambridge, MA: MIT Press.

Latour, B. (1993). *We have never been modern.* Cambridge, MA: Harvard University Press.

Latour, B. (1996). On interobjectivity. *Mind, Culture and Activity, 3,* 228–245.

Latour, B. (2004). *Politics of nature: How to bring the sciences into democracy.* Cambridge, MA: Harvard University Press.

Lave, J. (1988). *Cognition in practice: Mind, mathematics and culture in everyday life.* Cambridge, MA: Cambridge University Press.

Lave, J. (1993). The practice of learning. In S. Chaiklin & J. Lave (Eds.), *Understanding practice: Perspectives on activity and context* (pp. 3–32). Cambridge: Cambridge University Press.

Lave, J., & Wenger, E. (1991). *Situated learning: Legitimate peripheral participation.* Cambridge: Cambridge University Press.

Law, J. (Ed.). (1991). *A sociology of monsters: Essays on power, technology, and domination.* London: Routledge.

Leadbeater, C. (2000). *Living on thin air: The new economy.* London: Penguin Books.

Leakey, R. E., & Lewin, R. (1983). *People of the lake: Mankind and its beginnings.* New York: Avon Books.

Lee, G. K., & Cole, R. E. (2003). From a firm-based to a community-based model of knowledge creation: The case of the Linux kernel development. *Organization Science, 14,* 633–649.

Lektorsky, V. A. (1984). *Subject, object, cognition*. Moscow: Progress.

Leonard-Barton, D. (1995). *Wellsprings of knowledge: Building and sustaining the sources of innovation*. Boston: Harvard Business School Press.

Leont'ev, A. N. (1978). *Activity, consciousness, and personality*. Englewood Cliffs, NJ: Prentice-Hall.

Leont'ev, A. N. (1981). *Problems of the development of the mind*. Moscow: Progress.

Lesser, E. (Ed.). (2000). *Knowledge and social capital: Foundations and applications*. London: Butterworth-Heinemann.

Lewin, K. (1947). Group decision and social change. In T. M. Nedwcomb & E. L. Hartley (Eds.), *Readings in social psychology* (pp. 340–344). New York: Holt.

Lewin, K. (1951). *Field theory in social science: Selected theoretical papers*. New York: Harper & Row.

Lin, N., Cook. K. S., & Burt, R. S. (Eds.). (2001). *Social capital: Theory and research*. New York: Aldine de Gruyter.

Lipnack, J., & Stamps, J. (1997). *Virtual teams: Reaching across space, time, and organizations with technology*. New York: Wiley.

Litowitz, B. E. (1990). Just say no: Responsibility and resistance. *The Quarterly Newsletter of the Laboratory of Comparative Human Cognition, 12*, 135–141.

Luff, P., Hindmarsh, J., & Heath, C. (Eds.). (2000). *Workplace studies: Recovering work practice and informing system design*. Cambridge: Cambridge University Press.

Luria, A. R. (1978). *The making of mind: A personal account of Soviet psychology*. Cambridge, MA: Harvard University Press.

Lynch, M. (1984). "Turning up signs" in neurobehavioral diagnosis. *Symbolic Interaction, 7*, 67–86.

Malone, T. W. (2004). *The future of work: How the new order of business will shape your organization, your management style, and your life*. Boston: Harvard Business School Press.

Marx, K. (1973 [1939]). *Grundrisse: Foundations of the critique of political economy (rough draft)*. London: Penguin Books.

Mazzocco, D. W. (1994). *Networks of power: Corporate TV's threat to democracy*. Boston: South End Press.

Meggle, G. (Ed.). (2002). *Social facts and collective intentionality*. London: Fouque London.

Merry, S. E. (1990). *Getting justice and getting even: Legal consciousness among working-class Americans*. Chicago: University of Chicago Press.

Meyerson, D., Weick, K. E. & Kramer, R. M. (1996). Swift trust and temporary groups. In R. M. Kramer & T. R. Tyler (Eds.), *Trust in organizations: Frontiers of theory and research* (pp. 166–195). London: Sage.

Miller, E. J. (1975/1993). The Ahmedabad experiment revisited: Work organization in an Indian weaving shed, 1953–70. In E. Trist & H. Murray (Eds.), *The social engagement of social science: A Tavistock anthology. Volume II: The socio-technical perspective* (pp. 130–156). Philadelphia: University of Pennsylvania Press.

Moody, P. E. (1993). *Breakthrough partnering: Creating a collective enterprise advantage*. Essex Junction, VT: Oliver Wight.

Nardi, B. A. (Ed.).(1996). *Context and consciousness: Activity theory and human-computer interaction*. Cambridge: MIT Press.

Nardi, B. A., & Engeström, Y. (1999). A web on the wind: The structure of invisible work. *Computer Supported Cooperative Work, 8*, 1–8.

Nespor, J. (1997). *Tangled up in school: Politics, space, bodies, and signs in the educational process*. Mahwah, NJ: Erlbaum.

Nonaka, I., & Takeuchi, H. (1995). *The knowledge-creating company: How Japanese companies create the dynamics of innovation*. New York: Oxford University Press.

Norman, D. A. (1988). *The psychology of everyday things*. New York: Basic Books.

Norman, D. A. (1993). *Things that make us smart: Defending human attributes in the age of the machine*. Reading, MA: Addison-Wesley.

Nunes, T., Schliemann, A. D., & Carraher, D. W. (1993). *Street mathematics and school mathematics*. Cambridge: Cambridge University Press.

Obmascik, M. (2004). *The big year: A tale of man, nature, and fowl obsession*. New York: Free Press.

Ochs, E., Gonzales, P., & Jacoby, S. (1996). "When I come down, I'm in a domain state": Grammar and graphic representation in the interpretive activity of physicists. In E. Ochs, E. A. Schegloff, & S. Thompson (Eds.), *Interaction and grammar* (pp. 328–369). Cambridge: Cambridge University Press.

Orsburn, J. D., Moran, L., Musselwhite, E., & Zenger, J. H. (1990). *Self-directed work teams: The new American challenge*. Homewood, IL: Irwin.

Ouchi, W. G. (1984). *The M-form society*. Reading, MA: Addison-Wesley.

Paris, C. L. (1993). *Teacher agency and curriculum making in classrooms*. New York: Teachers College Press.

Parker, A. W. (1972). *The team approach to primary health care*. Berkeley: University of California, Berkeley, University Extension.

Parker, M., & Slaughter, J. (1988). *Choosing sides: Unions and the team concept*. Boston: Labor Notes.

Perrow, C. (1984). *Normal accidents: Living with high-risk technologies*. New York: Basic Books.

Perrow, C. (1986). *Complex organizations: A critical essay* (3rd ed). New York: Random House.

Pickering, A. (1995). *The mangle of practice: Time, agency, and science*. Chicago: University of Chicago Press.

Pine, B. J., II (1993). *Mass customization: The new frontier in business competition*. Boston: Harvard Business School Press.

Powell, W. W. (1990). Neither market nor hierarchy: Network forms of organization. In B. M. Staw & L. L. Cummings (Eds.), *Research in organizational behavior* (Vol. 12, pp. 295–336). Greenwich, CT: JAI Press.

Powell, W. W., Koput, K. W., & Smith-Doerr, L. (1996). Interorganizational collaboration and the locus of innovation: Networks of learning in biotechnology. *Administrative Science Quarterly, 41*, 116–145.

Prahalad, C. K., & Ramaswamy, V. (2004). *The future of competition: Co-creating unique value with customers*. Boston: Harvard Business School Press.

Puonti, A. (2004). *Learning to work together: Collaboration between authorities in economic-crime investigation*. Vantaa, Finland: National Bureau of Investigation.

Putnam, L. (1985). Contradictions and pradoxes in organizations. In L. Thayer (Ed.), *Organization – communication: Emerging perspectives* (Vol. 1, pp. 151–167). Norwood, NJ: Ablex.

Putnam, L. (1994). Challenging the assumptions of traditional approaches to negotiation. *Negotiation Journal, 10,* 337–346.

Raeithel, A. (1983). *Tätigkeit, Arbeit und Praxis.* Frankfurt am Main: Campus.

Rafael, V. L. (2003). The cell phone and the crowd: Messianic politics in the contemporary Philippines. *Public Culture, 15,* 399–425.

Rasmussen, J., Brehmer, B., & Leplat, J. (Eds.). (1991). *Distributed decision making: Cognitive models for cooperative work.* New York: Wiley.

Reason, J. (1990). *Human error.* Cambridge: Cambridge University Press.

Rentsch, J. R., & Hall, R. J. (1994). Members of great teams think alike: A model of team effectiveness and schema similarity among team members. In M. M. Beyerlein & D. A. Johnson (Eds.), *Advances in interdisciplinary studies of work teams. Vol. 1. Theories of self-managing teams* (pp. 223–261). Greenwich: JAI Press.

Resnick, L. B., Levine, J. M., & Teasley, S. D. (Eds.). (1991). *Perspectives on socially shared cognition.* Washington, DC: American Psychological Association.

Rheingold, H. (2002). *Smart mobs: The next social revolution.* Cambridge, MA: Perseus.

Rice, A. (1958). *Productivity and social organisation: The Ahmedabad experiment.* London: Tavistock.

Rittenberg, W. (1985). Mary; Patient as emergent symbol on a pediatrics ward: The objectification of meaning in social process. In R. A. Hahn & A. D. Gaines (Eds.), *Physicians of western medicine: Anthropological approaches to theory and practice* (pp. 141–153). Dordrecht: Reidel.

Rogalski, J. (1994). Analysing distributed cooperation in dynamic environment management: The "distributed crew" in automated cockpits. In R. Oppermann, S. Bagnara, & D. Benyon (Eds.), *Human–computer interaction: From individuals to groups in work, leisure, and everyday life* (pp. 187–199). Sankt Augustin, Germany: GMD.

Rorabaugh, W. J. (1986). *The craft apprentice: From Franklin to the machine age in America.* Oxford: Oxford University Press.

Rumsey, A., & Weiner, J. F. (Eds.). (2001). *Emplaced myth: Space, narrative, and knowledge in Aboriginal Australia and Papua New Guinea.* Honolulu: University of Hawaii Press.

Salili, F., Chiu, C., & Hong, Y. (Eds.). (2001). *Student motivation: The culture and context of learning.* New York: Kluwer Academic.

Salomon, G. (Ed.). (1993). *Distributed cognitions: Psychological and educational considerations.* Cambridge: Cambridge University Press.

Sandberg, Å. (1995). The Uddevalla experience in perspective. In Å. Sandberg (Ed.), *Enriching production: Perspectives on Volvo's Uddevalla plant as an alternative to lean production* (pp. 1–35). Aldershot, UK: Avebury.

Sarason, S. (1990). *The predictable failure of educational reform: Can we change course before it's too late?* San Francisco: Jossey-Bass.

Saxe, G. (1991). *Culture and cognitive development: Studies in mathematical understanding.* Hillsdale, NJ: Erlbaum.

Schank, R., & Abelson, R. (1977). *Scripts, plans, goals, and understanding.* Hillsdale, NJ: Erlbaum.

Schatzki, T. R. (2002). *The site of the social: A philosophical account of the constitution of social life and change.* University Park: Pennsylvania State University Press.

Schmidt, K., & Bannon, L. (1992). Taking CSCW seriously: Supporting articulation work. *Computer Supported Cooperative Work, 1*, 7–40.

Schrage, M. (1990). *Shared minds: The new technologies of collaboration.* New York: Random House.

Schrage, M. (1995). *No more teams: Mastering the dynamics of creative collaboration.* New York: Doubleday.

Scott, W. R., Ruef, M., Mendel, P. J., & Caronna, C. A. (2000). *Institutional change and healthcare organizations: From professional dominance to managed care.* Chicago: University of Chicago Press.

Scribner, S. (1985). Vygotsky's uses of history. In J. V. Wertsch (Ed.), *Culture, communication, and cognition: Vygotskian perspectives* (pp. 119–145). Cambridge: Cambridge University Press.

Searle, J. R. (1990). Collective intentions and actions. In P. R. Cohen, J. Morgan, & M. E. Pollack (Eds.), *Intentions in communication* (pp. 401–415). Cambridge, MA: MIT Press.

Senge, P. M. (1990). *The fifth discipline: The art and practice of the learning organization.* New York: Doubleday.

Seppänen, L. (2004). *Learning challenges in organic vegetable farming: An activity-theoretical study of on-farm practices.* Mikkeli: University of Helsinki, Institute of Rural Research and Training.

Seron, C. (1990). The impact of court organization on litigation. *Law and Society Review, 24*, 451–465.

Sewell, G. (1998). The discipline of teams: The control of team-based industrial work through electronic and peer surveillance. *Administrative Science Quarterly, 43*, 397–428.

Shortell, S. M., Gillies, R. R., Anderson, D. A., Erickson, K. M., & Mitchell, J. B. (2000). *Remaking health care in America: The evolution of organized delivery systems* (2nd ed.). San Francisco: Jossey-Bass.

Shweder, R. A. (1991). *Thinking through cultures: Expeditions in cultural psychology.* Cambridge, MA: Harvard University Press.

Simon, H. A. (1973). The structure of ill-structured problems. *Artificial Intelligence, 4*, 181–201.

Smith, B. C. (1996). *On the origin of objects.* Cambridge, MA: MIT Press.

Snyder, B. R. (1971). *The hidden curriculum.* New York: Knopf.

Spekman, R. E., Isabella, L. A., & MacAvoy, T. C. (2000). *Alliance competence: Maximizing the value of your partnerships.* New York: Wiley.

Spence, J. (1988). *Up close and personal: The inside story of network television sports.* New York: Atheneum.

Star, S. L. (1991). The sociology of the invisible: The primacy of work in the writings of Anselm Strauss. In D. Maines (Ed.), *Social organization and social process: Essays in honor of Anselm L. Strauss* (pp. 265–283). Hawthorne, NY: Aldine de Gruyter.

Star, S. L. (1996). Working together: Symbolic interactionism, activity theory and distributed artificial intelligence. In Y. Engeström & D. Middleton (Eds.), *Cognition and communication at work* (pp. 296–318). Cambridge: Cambridge University Press.

Starkey, K., Barnatt, C., & Tempest, S. (2000). Beyond networks and hierarchies: Latent organizations in the U.K. television industry. *Organization Science, 11*, 299–305.

Strauss, A. L. (1978). *Negotiations: Varieties, contexts, processes, and social order.* San Francisco: Jossey-Bass.

Strauss, A. L., Fagerhaugh, S., Suczek, B., & Wiener, C. (1985). *Social organization of medical work.* Chicago: University of Chicago Press.

Suchman, L. (1987). *Plans and situated actions: The problem of human–machine communication.* Cambridge: Cambridge University Press.

Suchman, L. (2006). *Human–machine reconfigurations: Plans and situated action* (2nd ed.). Cambridge: Cambridge University Press.

Swezey, R. W., & Salas, E. (1992). *Teams: Their training and performance.* Norwood, NJ: Ablex.

Tapscott, D. (1996). *The digital economy: Promise and peril in the age of networked intelligence.* New York: McGraw-Hill.

Tarr, J., & Dupuy, G. (Eds.). (1988). *Technology and the rise of the networked city in Europe and America.* Philadelphia: Temple University Press.

Taylor, J. R. (1995). Shifting from a heteronomous to an autonomous worldview of organizational communication: Communication theory on the cusp. *Communication Theory, 5,* 1–35.

Teasley, S., Covi, L., Krishnan, M. S., & Olson, J. S. (2000). How does radical collocation help a team succeed? In *Proceedings of the ACM 2000 Conference on Computer Supported Cooperative Work* (pp. 339–346). New York: ACM.

Tharp, R. G., & Gallimore, R. (1988). *Rousing minds to life: Teaching, learning, and schooling in social context.* Cambridge: Cambridge University Press.

Tichy, N. M. (1977). *Organization design for primary care: The case of the Dr. Martin Luther King, Jr. Health Center.* New York: Praeger.

Tjosvold, D. (1995). Cooperation theory, constructive controversy, and effectiveness: Learning from crisis. In R. A. Guzzo, E. Salas, and associates (Eds.), *Team effectiveness and decision making in organizations* (pp. 79–112). San Francisco: Jossey-Bass.

Tjosvold, D., & Tjosvold, M. M. (1994). Cooperation, competition, and constructive controversy: Knowledge to empower self-managing work teams. In M. M. Beyerlein & D. A. Johnson (Eds.), *Advances in interdisciplinary studies of work teams, Vol. 1: Theories of self-managing teams* (pp. 119–144). Greenwich, CT: JAI Press.

Toiviainen, H. (2003). *Learning across levels: Challenges of collaboration in a small-firm network.* Helsinki: Department of Education, University of Helsinki.

Trist, E. (1993). Introduction. In E. Trist & H. Murray (Eds.), *The social engagement of social science: A Tavistock anthology. Volume II: The socio-technical perspective* (pp. 36–60). Philadelphia: University of Pennsylvania Press.

Trist, E., & Bamforth, K. (1951/1993). The stress of isolated dependence: The filling shift in the semi-mechanized longwall three-shift mining cycle. In E. Trist & H. Murray (Eds.), *The social engagement of social science: A Tavistock anthology. Volume II: The socio-technical perspective* (pp. 64–83). Philadelphia: University of Pennsylvania Press.

Trist, E., & Murray, H. (Eds.). (1993). *The social engagement of social science: A Tavistock anthology. Volume II: The socio-technical perspective.* Philadelphia: University of Pennsylvania Press.

Tubbs, S. (1994). The historical roots of self-managing work teams in the twentieth century: An annotated bibliography. In M. M. Beyerlein & D. A. Johnson (Eds.), *Theories of self-managing work teams* (pp. 39–102). Greenwich, CT: JAI Press.

Tuckman, B. W. (1965). Developmental sequence in small groups. *Psychological Bulletin, 63*, 384–399.

Tuomela, R. (2002). *The philosophy of social practices: A collective acceptance view.* Cambridge: Cambridge University Press.

Tuomi-Gröhn, T., & Engeström, Y. (Eds.). (2003). *Between school and work: New perspectives on transfer and boundary-crossing.* Amsterdam: Pergamon.

Tye, B. B., & Tye, K. A. (1992). *Global education: A study of school change.* Albany: State University of New York Press.

Tye, K. A. (Ed.). (1990). *Global education: From thought to action. 1991 yearbook of the Association for Supervision and Curriculum Development.* Alexandria, VA: ASCD.

van Ejnatten, F. (Ed.). (1993). *The paradigm that changed the work place.* Assen: Van Gorcum.

Vedeler, D. (1991). Infant intentionality as object directedness: An alternative to representationalism. *Journal for the Theory of Social Behaviour, 21*, 431–448.

Vickers, M. H. (2001). *Work and unseen chronic illness: Silent voices.* London: Routledge.

Victor, B., & Boynton, A. C. (1998). *Invented here: Maximizing your organization's internal growth and profitability.* Boston: Harvard Business School Press.

Virkkunen, J. (1991). Toward transforming structures of communication in work: The case of Finnish labor protection inspectors. *The Quarterly Newsletter of the Laboratory of Comparative Human Cognition, 13*, 97–107.

Virkkunen, J., & Ahonen, H. (2004). Transforming learning and knowledge creation on the shop floor. *International Journal of Human Resources Development and Management, 4*, 57–72.

Volet, S., & Järvelä, S. (Eds.). (2001). *Motivation in learning contexts: Theoretical and methodological implications.* Amsterdam: Pergamon.

Volosinov, V. N. (1971). Reported speech. In L. Matejka & K. Pomorska (Eds.), *Readings in Russian poetics: Formalist and structuralist views* (pp. 149–175). Cambridge, MA: MIT Press.

von Bertalanffy, L. (1950). An outline of general system theory. *British Journal for the Philosophy of Science, 1*, 139–164.

von Hippel, E. (1988). *Sources of innovation.* New York: Oxford University Press.

von Hippel, E. (2005). *Democratizing innovation.* Cambridge, MA: MIT Press.

von Hippel, E., & Tyre, M. J. (1995). How learning by doing is done: Problem identification in novel process equipment. *Research Policy, 24*, 1–12.

Vygotsky, L. S. (1978). *Mind in society: The development of higher psychological processes.* Cambridge, MA: Harvard University Press.

Vygotsky, L. S. (1997). *The collected works of L. S. Vygotsky. Vol. 4: The history of higher mental functions.* New York: Plenum.

Vygotsky, L. S. (1999). *The collected works of L. S. Vygotsky. Vol. 6: Scientific legacy.* New York: Kluwer/Plenum.

Wagner, A. (1987). 'Knots' in teachers' thinking. In J. Calderhead (Ed.), *Exploring teachers' thinking* (pp. 161–178). London: Cassell.

Walker, A. G. (1986). The verbatim record: The myth and the reality. In S. Fischer & A. D. Todd (Eds.), *Discourse and institutional authority: Medicine, education, and law* (pp. 205–222). Norwood, NJ: Ablex.

Wallace, P. (2004). *The Internet in the workplace: How new technology is transforming work*. Cambridge: Cambridge University Press.

Wartofsky, M. (1979). *Models: Representation and scientific understanding*. Dordrecht: Reidel.

Weber, S. (2004). *The success of open source*. Cambridge, MA: Harvard University Press.

Weick, K. E. (1979). *The social psychology of organizing*. Reading, MA: Addison-Wesley.

Weick, K. E. (1993). The collapse of sensemaking in organizations: The Mann Gulch disaster. *Administrative Science Quarterly, 38*, 628–652.

Weick, K. E., & Roberts. K. H. (1993). Collective mind in organizations: Heedful interrelating on flight decks. *Administrative Science Quarterly, 38*, 357–381.

Wertsch, J. V. (Ed.). (1981). *The concept of activity in Soviet psychology*. Armonk, NY: M. E. Sharpe.

Wertsch, J. V. (1991) *Voices of the mind: A sociocultural approach to mediated action*. Cambridge, MA: Harvard University Press.

West, C. (1984). *Routine complications: Troubles with talk between doctors and patients*. Bloomington: Indiana University Press.

Whalen, J., Zimmerman, D. H., & Whalen, M. R. (1988). When words fail: A single case analysis. *Social Problems, 35*, 335–362.

Whorf, B. L. (1956). *Language, thought, and reality: Selected writings of Benjamin Lee Whorf*. Cambridge, MA: MIT Press.

Williams, H. (1989). *Beyond control: ABC and the fate of the networks*. New York: Atheneum.

Williamson, O. E. (1975). *Markets and hierarchies: Analysis and antitrust implications*. New York: Free Press.

Wilms, W., Hardcastle, A., & Zell, D. (1994), Cultural transformation at NUMMI. *Sloan Management Review, 36*, 99–113.

Womack, J. P., Jones, D. T., & Roos, D. (1990). *The machine that changed the world: The story of lean production*. New York: Harper.

Yeatts, D. E., & Hyten, C. (1998). *High-performing self-managed work teams: A comparison of theory to practice*. Thousand Oaks, CA: Sage.

Zerubavel, E. (1997). *Social mindscapes: An invitation to cognitive sociology*. Cambridge, MA: Harvard University Press.

Zuboff, S. (1988). *In the age of the smart machine: The future of work and power*. New York: Basic Books.

Author Index

Subject Index

The Learning in Doing series was founded in 1987 by Roy Pea and John Seely Brown.

CPSIA information can be obtained at www.ICGtesting.com
Printed in the USA
BVOW022211290212

284143BV00002B/1/P